Leveraging Latency

DISRUPTIVE TECHNOLOGY AND INTERNATIONAL SECURITY

Series editors

BENJAMIN JENSEN
Marine Corps University and Center for Strategic and International Studies

JACQUELYN SCHNEIDER
Hoover Institution, Stanford University

BRANDON VALERIANO
Marine Corps University

Leveraging Latency

How the Weak Compel the Strong with Nuclear Technology

TRISTAN A. VOLPE

OXFORD
UNIVERSITY PRESS

Oxford University Press is a department of the University of Oxford. It furthers
the University's objective of excellence in research, scholarship, and education
by publishing worldwide. Oxford is a registered trade mark of Oxford University
Press in the UK and certain other countries.

Published in the United States of America by Oxford University Press
198 Madison Avenue, New York, NY 10016, United States of America.

Library of Congress Cataloging-in-Publication Data
Names: Volpe, Tristan A., author.
Title: Leveraging latency : how the weak compel the strong with nuclear technology /
Tristan A. Volpe.
Description: New York, NY : Oxford University Press, [2023] |
Series: Disruptive technology and international security series |
Includes bibliographical references and index.
Identifiers: LCCN 2022040749 (print) | LCCN 2022040750 (ebook) |
ISBN 9780197669532 (hardback) | ISBN 9780197669556 (epub)
Subjects: LCSH: Nuclear nonproliferation—Political aspects. |
Nuclear weapons. | Nuclear arms control. | International relations.
Classification: LCC JZ5675 .V65 2023 (print) | LCC JZ5675 (ebook) |
DDC 327.1/747—dc23/eng/20221021
LC record available at https://lccn.loc.gov/2022040749
LC ebook record available at https://lccn.loc.gov/2022040750

DOI: 10.1093/oso/9780197669532.001.0001

1 3 5 7 9 8 6 4 2

Printed by Sheridan Books, Inc., United States of America

Contents

Acknowledgments

The inspiration for this book emerged during a discussion with friends on a muggy night in Washington, DC, over the summer of 2011. Iran's nuclear program was ramping up enrichment activities at the time. I had just returned from a short course on the nuclear fuel cycle at Brookhaven National Laboratory. Grant Schneider deserves credit for suggesting that the Iranians may have already acquired some degree of coercive leverage with their enrichment capabilities. I spent the next decade investigating this basic idea across four institutions.

I enjoyed several formative years at the George Washington University and the Institute for Security and Conflict Studies (ISCS) at the Elliott School of International Affairs. From 2011 to 2013, I began my dissertation research under the superb mentorship of Charles Glaser, Alex Downes, and George Quester. They created an excellent environment for me to refine early ideas about compellence with nuclear latency. The incredible pool of faculty and graduate student talent at ISCS also provided critical feedback on my research, notably Austin Carson, Rose Kelanic, Inwook Kim, Sameer Lalwani, Julia Macdonald, Harris Mylonas, Elizabeth Saunders, Josh Shifrinson, and Caitlin Talmadge.

In 2013, I took up residence at Lawrence Livermore National Laboratory (LLNL) to finish the dissertation under the supervision of George Anzelon. I learned how to think about the technical aspects of foreign nuclear programs from George, who is a true national treasure. The Center for Global Security Research provided a stellar home under the leadership of Mona Dreicer, Bruce Goodwin, and Brad Roberts. Jonathan Pearl, Ben Bahney, and Zach Davis offered comments and much-needed support on the dissertation. Robert Gromell and Charlie Mahaffey also let me observe nuclear diplomacy in action from a desk at the State Department's Office of Regional Affairs in the Bureau of International Security and Nonproliferation during the final stage of the LLNL fellowship.

I had the great fortune to arrive at the Carnegie Endowment for International Peace's Nuclear Policy Program (NPP) as a Stanton Nuclear Security Fellow in 2015. James Acton, Toby Dalton, and George Perkovich established the perfect intellectual home for me to convert a dissertation into several more polished journal articles (I thank Taylor and Francis for the permission to reuse some of this previously published content in the book). They taught me the role that academic research can play in gaining traction over fast-moving foreign policy issues. A grant from the John D. and Catherine T. MacArthur Foundation enabled me to spend 2016–2017 at NPP continuing to explore the policy implications of my research. Bert Thompson was a great research assistant. Collaborations with Wyatt Hoffman and Ulrich Kühn proved to be most fruitful. I am grateful to Ulrich for sharing his mastery of German politics and history. In addition, Tim Mauer, Mark Hibbs, Togzhan Kassenova, Eli Levite, Tong Zhao, Karim Sadjadpour, Frederic Wehrey, and Neil Narang (University of California, Santa Barbara) provided valuable feedback on various stages of my research at Carnegie.

I finished the book at the Naval Postgraduate School as a faculty member. My colleagues in the Defense Analysis Department created a welcoming perch in Monterey. John Arquilla, Bradley Strawser, Doug Boer, and Michael Freeman served as great mentors. Brian Rose and Kelsey Hartigan managed the US Special Operations Command work portfolio so I could focus on the book. My research benefited from working with the brilliant Nicholas Miller at Dartmouth on several coauthored articles during this time. Charles Glaser graciously returned to chair a book workshop for me in October 2019, where I received exceptional comments from Scott Sagan, Vipin Narang, Matthew Fuhrmann, Reid Pauly, and Jeffrey Knopf. Jim Stokes provided financial support for the workshop and my research from the Countering Weapons of Mass Destruction Systems Office in the Office of the Assistant Secretary of Defense for Nuclear, Chemical, and Biological Defense Programs. I presented a heavily revised manuscript in September 2020 at the virtual "Before the Bomb" workshop co-organized with Eric Brewer, Toby Dalton, and Jane Vaynman; feedback from participants and especially Rebecca Gibbons and Richard Nephew helped me complete the project. Jackie Schneider, Brandon Valeriano, and Benjamin Jensen helped me match the manuscript with the Disruptive Technology and International Security Series; Angela Chnapko provided excellent editorial guidance at Oxford University Press.

The book also benefited from feedback at several other events over the years, notably the Nuclear Studies Research Initiative retreat in 2015, and workshops organized by the Project on Strategic Stability Evaluation, the Center for New American Security, and the Project on Nuclear Issues at the Center for Strategic and International Studies. Numerous others have read and commented on various versions of this manuscript over the years: Todd Sechser, Frank Gavin, Mark Bell, Nicholas Miller, James Graham Wilson, John Warden, Erik Gartzke, Matthew Kroenig, Alex Montgomery, Andrew Coe, Robert Adcock, Daniel Jacobs, Jeff Kaplow, Rachel Stein, Mira Rapp-Hooper, Adam Stulberg, Brian Radzinsky, Michael Joseph, Adam Mount, and Timothy McDonnell. The MacArthur Foundation funded the final stages of my work on the book [G-1802-152803]; special thanks to Theo Kalionzes for supporting my research over the years.

Finally, I could not finish this book without strong support from friends and family. Jane Vaynman provided constant encouragement and guidance as I toiled away before and after Covid-19 arrived. Daniel Gruver, Brandon Keefe, Michael Brown, Michael Brieman, David Slunngaard, and my brother Travis kept me grounded. I owe everything to my wife Manar, who has been my lodestar from the start and an incredible mother to our children Rami and Nadim. I am grateful to my mother Constance and late father Alan for cultivating my love of science and technology. I dedicate this book to the memory of my father—he would have been excited to read it.

Abbreviations

ACDA	Arms Control and Disarmament Agency
AEOI	Atomic Energy Organization of Iran
CIA	Central Intelligence Agency
DNSA	Digital National Security Archive
DPRK	Democratic People's Republic of Korea
EDC	European Defense Community
ENR	enrichment and/or reprocessing
EU	European Union
EURATOM	European Atomic Energy Community
FRG	Federal Republic of Germany
FRUS	Foreign Relations of the United States
HEU	highly enriched uranium
IAEA	International Atomic Energy Agency
IRGC	Islamic Revolutionary Guard Corps
JCPOA	Joint Comprehensive Plan of Action
JCS	Joint Chiefs of Staff
JPOA	Joint Plan of Action
LTBT	Limited Test Ban Treaty
MEK	Mujahedin-e-Khalq
MLF	Multilateral Force
MRBM	medium range ballistic missile
NATO	North Atlantic Treaty Organization
NIE	National Intelligence Estimate
NPG	Nuclear Planning Group
NPT	Nuclear Nonproliferation Treaty
NSAM	National Security Action Memoranda
NSC	National Security Council
NSG	Nuclear Suppliers Group
NSSM	National Security Study Memorandum
ROK	Republic of Korea
TRR	Tehran Research Reactor
UN	United Nations
UNSC	United Nations Security Council

1

Introduction

This book is about how the weak coerce the strong in world politics. Nations sometimes threaten to acquire atomic weapons as an instrument of black-mail or coercion. I investigate when nuclear latency—the technical capacity to build the bomb—enables states to compel concessions from great powers.

Compellence with nuclear latency is an enduring feature of the global landscape. In the past, select allies and partners used their nuclear programs to put pressure on patrons for security commitments or military assistance. During the halcyon era of atomic energy in the 1960s, for example, Australia, Italy, Japan, and West Germany all attempted to gain diplomatic leverage over the United States by sowing suspicion about their civil nuclear investments. In the early 1970s, South Korea tried to build up its bomb-making capacity to stem American retrenchment. Some US officials even believed Pakistan considered using its military nuclear program as a "bargaining chip" to elicit greater support from Washington in the late 1970s.[1] More recently, Saudi Arabia promised to match Iran's nuclear capabilities in 2015 before demanding a formal defense treaty and advanced weapons from the United States.

Other nations leveraged latency against great power adversaries. Amid the crisis over Berlin in the early Cold War, officials in Bonn exploited Soviet and American fears of West German proliferation to underwrite diplomatic demands from both superpowers. In the early 1990s, North Korea pioneered the playbook for wringing material benefits out of the United States with more explicit proliferation ultimatums. The North Koreans dusted off this strategy again in the 2000s after US officials exposed their covert quest for the bomb. In 2003, Libya traded away its blown uranium enrichment program for sanctions relief from the West. The revelation of secret nuclear facilities also led Iran toward diplomacy in 2003 to ward off preventive military action. According to a member of Iran's nuclear negotiation team at the time (Mousavian 2012: 99–100), Iranian leaders leveraged latency to "obtain maximum concessions from [the West] in return for cooperation"—an approach Tehran continued to pursue over the next fifteen years.

Leveraging Latency. Tristan A. Volpe, Oxford University Press. © Oxford University Press 2023.
DOI: 10.1093/oso/9780197669532.003.0001

Yet this strategy yielded mixed results. As I document in the book, some allies and adversaries successfully used their nuclear programs to compel concessions from great powers such as the United States. For many other countries, however, the gambit failed to elicit any advantages and generated blowback from powerful sheriffs of the nonproliferation regime. When does compellence with nuclear latency work?

The conventional wisdom is that leveraging latency is most effective when states are close to the bomb. This intuitive idea enjoys a long intellectual lineage. At the dawn of the nuclear age, the Acheson-Lilienthal (1946) report envisioned a world where the distribution of atomic bomb-making materials would compel countries to forgo actual weapons (Ford 2011: 131–34). The subsequent spread of latent capabilities around the globe led the Central Intelligence Agency to portend in 1975 that "future nuclear politics will almost certainly include states which will exploit their threshold positions, as much or more than their actual capabilities."[2] Indeed, Henry Kissinger (2012) warned decades later that once Iran achieved "a military nuclear program at the very edge of going operational," other countries in the region would "be driven to reorient their political alignment toward Tehran." In a similar vein, Michael Green and Katsuhisa Furukawa (2008: 364) found that Japan's massive nuclear energy enterprise provided Tokyo with a "bomb in the basement" it used "to signal or increase its leverage with both Washington and Beijing." Once a country can build the bomb quickly, it may be in a strong position to dial up coercive pressure on great powers.

Contrary to this prevalent belief, I find that more nuclear latency does not always translate into greater bargaining advantages. In a merger of coercion theory with nuclear proliferation scholarship, this book presents a new framework for explaining how states leverage latency as an effective coercive instrument. Compellence creates a sharp trade-off between making proliferation threats *and* nonproliferation assurances credible. I identify a menu of bargaining tactics states can employ to get off the horns of this dilemma. However, states need just enough latency to make these tactics effective. At low levels, proliferation threats are not credible. Marching to the cusp of the bomb solves this problem. But it also becomes increasingly costly and difficult for state leaders to offer assurances as they face growing barriers to nuclear reversal. I uncover a Goldilocks zone where it is easiest to make both threats and assurances credible. Compellence with nuclear latency is most likely to work when states are in this fissile material sweet spot.

The rest of the introduction sets up my framework and previews the book's main findings in six parts. The first makes explicit my assumptions about compellence with nuclear latency. The second part scopes out the main actors—great power sheriffs and potential proliferators who pursue this strategy for different reasons. The third part surveys the historical track record of latent nuclear compellence outcomes over time. The fourth part summarizes my argument about the sweet spot for bargaining with nuclear latency. The fifth part reviews the research approach guiding the empirical chapters. The final part summarizes the book's contributions and lays out a road map for the study.

Illuminating the Strategy

Compellence is a form of coercion for persuading an actor to undertake an action it prefers not to execute.[3] The strategy involves three main features. First, one state (the challenger) issues demands for another state (the target) to change the status quo in some way.[4] Second, the challenger inflicts, or threatens to inflict, punishment until the target complies with these demands. Challengers use a wide range of tools to underwrite compellent threats. As Robert Art and Kelly Greenhill (2018b: 78) underscore, the key is to impose "some cost or pain to the target, or explicit threats thereof, with the implied threat of increasing the cost or pain if the target does not concede." Third, the challenger promises to end the coercive process once the target yields. This assurance is crucial to making compellence work, as it guides the target down an offramp where it can avoid punishment by complying with the challenger's demands.

Strategies of compellence are successful when challengers wrest concessions or other behavioral changes from targets. I follow Robert Art (1980: 8) in defining success as "how closely and quickly the target conforms to one's stipulated wishes." Even when the target yields, however, challengers must factor in the costs they pay to achieve this outcome. The process of mobilizing military forces to underwrite compellent demands, for example, can generate operational costs and blowback. If these "enforcement costs" exceed the benefits reaped from coercion, Lawrence Freedman (1998: 30) notes, then the challenger achieves a Pyrrhic victory. Compellence is most successful when the aspirant puts enough pressure on the target to concede while incurring minimal enforcement costs.

What is nuclear latency and how can it underwrite compellence strategies? Scholars have long referred to potential or "latent" power as the resources available for a state to build up its military forces.[5] Nuclear latency is a special type of potential power—it refers to a nation's capability to build atomic weapons (Fuhrmann and Tkach 2015). Scott Sagan (2011: 230) defines the concept as "a measure of how quickly a state could develop a nuclear weapon from its current state of technological development if it chose to do so." In particular, nuclear latency is based on the capacity to make the fissile material—highly enriched uranium or plutonium—that fuels the explosive core of an atomic weapon. Without this critical ingredient, a country cannot make the bomb. Latent nuclear capability, therefore, reflects the concrete assets a nation has on hand to enrich uranium and reprocessing plutonium.

Countries leverage latency by putting pressure on others to forestall an adverse shift in the balance of power. Nuclear latency enables a potential proliferator to become the coercive challenger by moving, or threatening to move, closer to the bomb until the target concedes. This process creates a power transition where the target worries its capabilities are in decline relative to the rising challenger. But an opportunity emerges to manipulate the target's fear of the future. Atomic weapons are great equalizers among nations. If the challenger builds even a small nuclear force, it undercuts the target's military capabilities and freedom of action on the world stage (Horowitz 2010: 106). Proliferation also increases the risk of deliberate or accidental nuclear attack against the target (Sagan 2002). Instead of realizing this dark future, the challenger offers to forgo atomic weapons in exchange for concessions. The target may consider complying with the challenger's demands to avoid living under the nuclear sword of Damocles. "In this fashion," Christopher Ford (2011: 145) concludes, "potential future nuclear weapons are exploited in order to reap current security benefits."

Scoping Out the Actors

This book focuses on the interaction between two types of actors: great power sheriffs of the nonproliferation regime and nuclear aspirants who leverage latency against them. The existing literature identifies the incentives for great powers—notably the United States and the Soviet Union—to prevent the spread of atomic weapons to adversaries and allies alike (Coe and Vaynman 2015; Lanoszka 2018b; Miller 2018). I draw on this scholarship to explain why great power opposition to proliferation makes them the prime targets for compellence with nuclear latency. Recent research on nuclear proliferation also unpacks variation in how states develop latent capabilities. In an extension of this work, I show that nuclear aspirants face different opportunities to leverage latency depending on their proliferation strategy and relationship with the great power—allies hedging in plain sight are not in the same position as adversaries caught hiding nuclear facilities.

The Targets

Who are the primary targets of compellence with nuclear latency? Not all nations are equally susceptible to this strategy. I assume challengers only go after states with robust nonproliferation interests—one cannot exploit the fear of the future if the target stops worrying about the bomb. This scope condition matters because proliferation need not cast a dark shadow over international affairs. Some nations may expect war to be less likely when adversaries shield themselves from existential threats with atomic arsenals (Waltz 2002).[6] Selective proliferation to allies or partners can also seem useful in some situations, such as strengthening external balancing coalitions or undermining powerful rivals (Coe and Vaynman 2015; Kroenig 2009). Challengers need to target nations who see considerable downsides from nuclear proliferation.

Great powers are ideal targets for two reasons. First, they face strong incentives to oppose proliferation. As the most dominant states in the system, great powers enjoy the ability to project military force and shape outcomes across the globe.[7] Yet atomic weapons neutralize many of these advantages, making it harder for great powers to do what they want with less capable states (Gavin 2015: 23). Weaker adversaries can employ atomic weapons to deter great powers from attacking them, thereby opening up space to pursue more aggressive foreign policies (Bell 2019). Nuclear-armed allies become difficult to control, as they depend less on their patrons for security (Gavin 2015: 22). The spread of atomic weapons leaves great powers worse off with less military capability and political influence. As a result, proliferation is a sensitive pressure point where great powers are vulnerable to threats from latent nuclear challengers.

Second, opposition to the bomb leads great powers to act as sheriffs who police the nuclear ambitions of potential proliferators.[8] The stark power advantage enables sheriffs to wield three main nonproliferation tools: (1) international institutions to monitor nuclear programs and manage the spread of sensitive technology; (2) coercive diplomacy to coax nuclear aspirants away from weapons aspirations; and (3) preventive military strikes to stop proliferators from acquiring the bomb (Brewer 2021; Gibbons 2022; Miller 2018).[9] Sheriffs are susceptible to latent nuclear compellence because they prefer to engage in coercive diplomacy before resorting to military operations. This point seems to cut against the grain of power transition theory, since marching toward the bomb creates preventive motivations for war.[10] Indeed, great powers possess the military and intelligence capabilities to use force against weaker proliferators. But bargaining with nuclear aspirants can offer a lower-cost option to achieve nonproliferation goals.[11]

In essence, great power sheriffs are the prime targets because they oppose proliferation yet often favor coercive diplomacy over preventive war.[12] They therefore create the market for proliferators to trade away their weapons ambitions.

The Challengers

Who leverages latency against great powers? Nuclear aspirants are likely to be selective about adopting this compellence strategy. Fissile material production technology is expensive to develop and can foment insecurity.[13] States often launch nuclear projects to achieve core national interests, such as making themselves more prosperous with atomic energy or secure with nuclear weapons (Sagan 2011). As a result, it makes little sense to accumulate latency for the sole purpose of wresting concessions from great powers.[14] Over the long life span of a nuclear program, however, some states may face incentives to turn this investment into a coercive instrument. Drawing upon research about how states march toward the bomb, I identify two general situations where compellence with nuclear latency may be attractive.

First, some countries opt for compellence while building nuclear infrastructure in plain sight. Hedgers develop latent capabilities for ostensibly peaceful purposes. But they can sow doubt about their future weapons intentions to put pressure on great powers. These nuclear aspirants avoid telltale signs of military weaponization. Instead, they often appear to be hedging their nuclear bets against potential security risks, such as the rise of an adversary or ally abandonment. Hedging can either be a deliberate strategy choice to acquire—but not yet solve—all the technical pieces of the nuclear jigsaw puzzle, as Ariel Levite (2003: 69) and Vipin Narang (2016: 117–20) find. Or it may just be the inadvertent byproduct of developing dual-use nuclear technology with the potential to fulfill both civilian and military ends, according to Itty Abraham (2006) and Matthew Fuhrmann (2012).[15]

Both types of hedgers may find latent nuclear compellence to be attractive. Keeping nuclear programs out in the open for great powers to watch dampens the risk of preventive war (Bas and Coe 2016). The duality of nuclear technology helps hedgers protect themselves under a veil of plausible deniability about civilian applications (see also Hiim 2022). At the same time, the intrinsic capacity of these nuclear programs to produce weapons often leads sheriffs to worry about future proliferation aspirations. Hedgers can prey upon this uncertainty to intimidate sheriffs with implicit proliferation threats: "You know we have a nice peaceful nuclear program here. It would be shame if someone happened to weaponize it." Alternatively, they can adopt a subtler coercive approach via transactional diplomacy: "You seem worried about our nuclear program. We can ease your concerns. But do us a favor, though." Hedgers offer to allay fears about possible weapons intentions in exchange for concessions from great powers.

Second, other states leverage latency under duress after they are caught in secret pursuit of nuclear weapons. The goal of hiding nuclear activities, Narang (2016: 121) explains, "is to present the fait accompli of a nuclear weapons capability before it is discovered or to achieve at least sufficient progress to deter prevention." But this subterfuge often sparks an international crisis upon discovery. When a hider is caught before the bomb, "Diplomatic or military mobilization against it may be more likely because of the perceived illegitimacy of hiding a nuclear capability," Narang (2016: 121) argues. Under mounting pressure from sheriffs, an exposed hider faces incentives to transform its nuclear program from a liability into a means of leverage. Compellence offers these states one way to manage the consequences from exposure while extracting concessions from sheriffs.[16]

The rub is that bargaining with nuclear latency is always a second-best outcome for hiders who originally wanted the bomb. Exposure marks an inflection point in the evolution of the nuclear program where survival becomes the paramount goal. This shift away from weapons acquisition matters because it shapes the purpose of compellence. Hiders now want to protect themselves and their nuclear assets from punishment while trying to get the best deal possible with sheriffs. Their compellent demands tend to focus on ending economic sanctions imposed over the hidden nuclear program and making nonproliferation promises conditional on material rewards. Some leaders may use diplomacy as a ruse to buy time, holding out hope that they can resume the quest for the bomb later after the crisis subsides. The outcome of negotiations can shape whether they go back to the pursuit of weapons or abandon the quest altogether.

The transition from hiding to leveraging latency also does not happen overnight. It tends to be a messy multiyear process whereby leaders muddle through various responses—notably deception and resistance—before opting for compellence. In contrast to hedgers, hiders must reconfigure the technical parameters of the nuclear enterprise to support the new survival strategy. Some of the investments made for pursuing actual weapons no longer make sense when it comes to leveraging latency in a more calibrated manner. Domestic politics can further complicate the process as elite actors vie to retain influence over nuclear technology projects. In the time period after nuclear exposure, compellence may not be the immediate first choice for many hiders. But it can be a viable fallback strategy once other options fail.

Beyond these pathways to compellence, the broader political relationship between challengers and sheriffs shapes distinct uses of the strategy. Allies and adversaries often want to extract different political, economic, and military concessions from great powers (Ford 2011: 145; Levite 2019: 26–27). For an ally protégé, the capacity to "exit" the alliance with an independent nuclear force may provide a useful means to shore up security commitments or wrest other foreign policy concessions from the great power patron (Castillo and Downes 2020; Lanoszka 2015: 138). Leveraging latency can be a strategy for the protégé to resolve divergent interests within an otherwise advantageous alliance system.[17] By contrast, adversaries tend to face more existential threats to their survival from great powers, especially if they are caught hiding nuclear programs. Negotiations help them ward off conflict, alleviate economic sanctions, or protect the underlying nuclear infrastructure.

In sum, hiders and hedgers sometimes find compellence with latency to be an alluring strategy as they develop nuclear programs, albeit for different reasons. Allies and adversaries also leverage latency in distinct strategic contexts to compel different types of concessions from great powers. All challengers pursue the same basic logic of compellence as they attempt to make threats and assurances credible. But when does this form of compellence work?

Surveying Compellence Outcomes

Table 1.1 identifies the countries that have pursued compellence with nuclear latency against nonproliferation sheriffs throughout the nuclear age. For a country to be included, it needs to do more than just threaten to build atomic weapons. Explicit or implicit proliferation threats must be linked to clear demands for the sheriff to change the status quo. This extension of Todd Sechser's (2011) criteria for coding militarized compellence cases helps to identify specific episodes when nuclear aspirants leveraged latency in this manner. In line with the metrics from Art (1980), the success or failure of each outcome denotes whether the sheriff conformed to the compellent demands.

An initial examination highlights three waves of compellence with nuclear latency. During the first wave (1956–1974), some US allies attempted to gain concessions from Washington and Moscow as the superpowers

Table 1.1 Patterns of Latent Nuclear Compellence, 1956–2015

Country (compellence years)	Sheriff	Outcome
France (1956–1957)	US	Failure
Japan (1957–1960)	US	Failure
West Germany (1961–1963)	US; USSR	Failure
West Germany (1963–1966)	US; USSR	Partial success
Japan (1964–1970)	US	Success
West Germany (1966–1969)	US; USSR	Success
Italy (1967–1969)	US	Success
Australia (1968)	US	Failure
South Korea (1974–1975)	US	Failure
Pakistan (1978–1979)	US	Failure
South Africa (1977–1978)	US	Failure
Romania (1985)	USSR	Failure
North Korea (1991–1994)	US	Success
Libya (2003)	US; UK	Success
Iran (2003–2005)	US; EU3	Partial success
North Korea (2002–2008)	US	Failure
Iran (2009–2010)	US	Failure
Iran (2013–2015)	US	Success
Saudi Arabia (2015)	US	Failure

established the nonproliferation regime. Most of these states were hedgers who exploited the dual-use nature of their civilian nuclear programs as bargaining chips. Indeed, many US allies were able to accumulate nuclear latency in plain sight without breaking any rules. Concerns about American abandonment in the early Cold War largely drove these allies to develop nuclear hedge postures, which some leaders then found useful to leverage as a means of compellence.[18] In the second wave (1974–1991), leveraging latency appears to have become less attractive, as only four allies or partners pursued this strategy against either the United States or Soviet Union. This dip in compellence was the byproduct of several larger factors, notably the solidification of alliance relationships and especially the codification of supply-side controls under the Nuclear Suppliers Group in 1974, which drove the next generation of proliferators to pursue hiding instead of hedging strategies.[19] Compellence made a comeback during the third wave (1991–2015). But it was adopted almost exclusively by US adversaries caught with clandestine nuclear programs. This shift from ally hedgers to adversarial hiders reflects a broader change in the type of countries that developed the capacity to build the bomb over time (Lissner 2017; Miller 2018: 5). Whereas the early atomic age was rife with superpower allies building nuclear programs, only a handful of US adversaries pursued the bomb after the Cold War.

The checkered track record makes clear that there is no apparent relationship between country type and the ultimate outcome of compellence.[20] Allies and adversaries have both proven to be successful at using nuclear latency to wrest concessions from great powers. Even more puzzling, some of the countries that failed at this strategy possessed the technical capacity to build the bomb on short notice. Marching to the cusp of the bomb does not necessarily guarantee success at the negotiation table. This raises fundamental questions about how compellence with nuclear latency works and when it is most likely to be effective.

The Argument in Brief

I argue that compellence is most likely to succeed when challengers possess a modest amount of nuclear latency. My theory identifies a trade-off between threatening proliferation and promising nuclear restraint. Challengers need enough latency to make their proliferation threats credible, but not so much that it becomes difficult to offer nonproliferation assurances. I find that the boundaries of this Goldilocks zone align with the capacity to produce the fissile material at the heart of an atomic weapon. More bomb-making capacity does not always provide states with greater bargaining power. This book's core claim is that challengers can wrest concessions from great powers once they enter the fissile material sweet spot. As a result, the mere capacity to enrich uranium or reprocess plutonium can be a disruptive instrument of compellence in world politics.

Compellence presents challengers with a dilemma between making threats and assurances credible. On the one hand, they must convey their resolve to build the bomb unless compliance is forthcoming. On the other hand, however, challengers need to commit themselves to nuclear restraint once the sheriff concedes. Nuclear latency makes it difficult to resolve this credibility problem. The benefits at stake are often lower than the high costs of proliferation. Challengers therefore face incentives to misrepresent their nuclear aspirations. Sheriffs also harbor suspicions about nonproliferation promises. Challengers must go to great lengths to resolve this dilemma with actions that tie hands, sink costs, run risks, or impose pressure. I use these coercive mechanisms to derive a menu of tactics for bargaining with nuclear latency. This typology specifies how a challenger can manipulate its nuclear program to convey information and calibrate pressure on the international stage. In addition, it also brings the domestic politics of nuclear latency into focus. Some tactics enable state leaders to constrain their nuclear choices by handing over control to other elites or cultivating support among the mass public.

Challengers can employ these bargaining tactics at any stage of nuclear development. However, a sharp trade-off emerges along the latency continuum between threatening proliferation and promising nuclear restraint. When a challenger's nuclear program is in its infancy, this low level of latency may not be enough for the tactics to be effective. Great powers tend to brush off proliferation threats as infeasible. Marching to the cusp of the bomb certainly makes proliferation threats more credible. But assurance tactics become harder to employ at higher levels of latency for three reasons: (1) challengers face mounting domestic costs to altering the course of the nuclear program as it matures; (2) challengers often cede control to elite stakeholders within the country as they bring large nuclear projects online, and (3) the costs associated with cutting a deal can start to outweigh the potential benefits. More latency may not be better when it comes to compellence.

Variation in nuclear latency shapes the severity of the threat-assurance trade-off. The tension between the competing requirements of compellence should be most acute at low and high levels of latency. But I uncover a sweet spot in the middle where challengers possess just enough bomb-making capacity to make threats and assurances credible. Once a nuclear program enters this Goldilocks zone, it becomes harder for great powers to inhibit proliferation with unilateral tools. Each step forward puts pressure on the great power to cut a diplomatic deal before it is too late. At this modest level of latency, however, challengers should still find it relatively easy to underwrite nonproliferation assurances. Domestic politics is also less likely to distort the incentives leaders face when it comes to limiting the nuclear program.

Where are the boundaries of this sweet spot along the latency continuum? A challenger's level of latent capability reflects the amount of time it would take to turn uranium into weapons-usable material at enrichment or reprocessing (ENR) plants. At the low end, a nuclear program lacks the capacity to produce fissile material. Given the scale and complexity of ENR plants, it may take many years and perhaps even decades for the nuclear program to master the requisite technologies. At the high end, the challenger can produce enough fissile material for atomic weapons on short notice. Nuclear programs attain this high level of latency when they harvest enough highly enriched uranium or plutonium to fuel the core of an atomic bomb— what analysts refer to as a "significant quantity" of fissile material (Hymans 2010).[21] But countries need not sit on a stockpile of weapons-usable material to acquire an advanced latent capability. On the uranium route, for example, a fuel enrichment plant can acquire enough low-enriched uranium to be capable of producing a bomb's worth of material on short order. At this final stage of latency, the nuclear program may only be weeks or months away from the bomb.

A nuclear program falls in the sweet spot between low and high levels of latency when it is on the cusp of producing enough fissile material for an atomic weapon. But it must still take additional steps to enrich uranium or reprocess plutonium at weapons-usable scale. Nuclear aspirants enter this zone when they acquire all the pieces needed to traverse down either the enrichment or reprocessing pathway. States leave the sweet spot by launching fissile material production campaigns at large ENR facilities. Technical signposts include clear efforts to master ENR technology at pilot plants with construction underway on larger facilities capable of producing significant quantities of fissile material. These metrics set the foundation to select cases that exhibit variation in latency over time.

The Goldilocks principle of bargaining with nuclear latency outperforms three alternative explanations. First, some scholars believe that nuclear latency is unlikely to ever provide bargaining advantages in world politics. I find little logical or empirical support for this skepticism. Second, many others claim that compellence with nuclear latency is more likely to be successful when the challenger can build atomic weapons on short notice. These maximalists offer a stronger counterargument. But I show that they tend to ignore the assurance side of the compellence equation, which leads them to overlook the problems challengers face with leveraging advanced nuclear programs. Third, pessimists suspect it is difficult and costly for challengers to make compellence work along the entire latency continuum. This position most closely aligns with my argument. However, I demonstrate that states should be in a better position to leverage latency in the fissile material sweet spot.

Empirical Approach

This book employs a comparative research design to study four countries that leveraged latency against great powers: Japan, West Germany, North Korea, and Iran. I select these countries because each exhibits variation in latency across discrete compellence episodes over time. This allows me to assess multiple cases within a single country. In addition, the countries reflect an even mix of both types of challengers: ally hedgers and adversarial hiders. The case study approach offers three advantages for assessing the empirical validity of my theory (George and Bennett 2005).

First, it is optimal for identifying why different countries decided to leverage latency. The case studies examine the economic and security factors that drove the four countries to develop their respective nuclear programs. Much of this information can only be pieced together from the documentary record on the nuclear capabilities and intentions of each country at the time. I find that Japan and West Germany acquired latency as a byproduct of civilian-led investments in the nuclear fuel cycle during the 1960s. Despite the peaceful nature of these nuclear programs, leaders in Tokyo and Bonn quietly leveraged latency by making implicit threats in private discussions with American and Soviet officials. By contrast, North Korea and Iran only came to the bargaining table after they were caught hiding nuclear facilities. North Korean and Iranian officials also tended to make much more explicit proliferation threats. This historical context helps to account for the distinct ways in which ally hedgers and adversarial hiders pursued compellence with nuclear latency.

Second, a qualitative approach is useful for tracing out the relationship between nuclear latency and compellence outcomes. By breaking down each country into several subcases with different levels of latency, I employ a most-similar method to control for other factors (Gerring 2004). This enables me to assess how variation in nuclear latency shaped the severity of the threat-assurance trade-off. My main finding is that all four challengers were most successful when they could make threats and assurances credible in the fissile material sweet spot. By contrast, Japan and West Germany struggled to play the nuclear card at lower levels of latency. North Korea and Iran were effective at putting pressure on the United States at higher levels of latency. But leaders in Pyongyang and Tehran appeared to face greater barriers to reversing course as they approached the nuclear weapons threshold.

Third, the case studies are useful for probing whether the boundaries of the sweet spot remained constant across space and time. My study reveals that the capacity to produce fissile material has long constituted the middle zone in the latency continuum. More important, the threat-assurance trade-off appears to be mild for states in the fissile material sweet spot. This result is surprising given the pace of technological progress over the last seven decades. Innovations along the nuclear fuel cycle have arguably made it easier for nations to develop enrichment or reprocessing capabilities. For instance, Scott Kemp (2012) claims that uranium gas centrifuges eroded the technical barriers to proliferation because the devices were simple enough for most nations to manufacture and operate. Yet the boundaries of the sweet spot for compellence with nuclear latency do not appear to shift in response to this technological flux. Countries have consistently been able to wrest concessions from great powers well before they cross the nuclear weapons threshold.

Contributions

My study of compellence with nuclear latency makes several contributions to international relations scholarship and nonproliferation policy.

For scholars of proliferation, the theory and empirical results shed light on the choices states make before the bomb. Much of the recent research in this area examines how great power sheriffs wield coercive instruments to inhibit proliferation (Gavin 2012a; Gibbons 2022; Lanoszka 2018; Mehta 2020; Miller 2018). But my work points out that there is another side to this story. Nuclear aspirants are seldom content to sit idly by as sheriffs ramp up pressure. They face incentives to leverage latency. An ally hedger can exploit a patron's fear of the bomb by dropping nuclear hints and cutting implicit quid pro quo deals. An adversarial hider may want to reset the chessboard in the aftermath of exposure. In both situations, the great power becomes the target of compellence with nuclear latency. By bringing this strategy into focus, the book joins an ongoing effort to better understand how states develop and utilize nuclear technology.[22]

My research also addresses a debate about the political consequences of nuclear latency. Scholars offer conflicting claims about whether the capacity to build the bomb gives states additional bargaining power.[23] According to skeptics, nuclear latency cannot be wielded as a means of compellence at all. It is only useful for acquiring atomic weapons. By contrast, maximalists contend that states can reap bargaining advantages from latency, but they must be on the cusp of the bomb. My framework resolves this debate by specifying when states are most and least likely to gain bargaining advantages from nuclear latency. I account for both the costs and benefits states incur along the latency continuum. This assessment suggests that skeptics and maximalists are both wrong. States only need modest amounts of latency to wrest concessions from great powers.

Beyond the nuclear realm, the book advances the study of coercion in world politics. The threat-assurance trade-off is a generalizable mechanism for explaining how potential power shapes the viability of compellence. Scholars have long claimed that states can gain coercive leverage by threatening to build military force. In his study of military power, for instance, Klaus Knorr (1956: 56) argued that states can "make their foreign policies more effective . . . by demonstrating the ease with which potential strength can be converted into additional strength-in-being." But this literature tends to focus on the process of making compellent threats credible, such as mobilizing armament factories or cueing public support (Schultz 2001; Slantchev 2005; Lupton 2020).[24] My study suggests that the development of large technology projects can further enhance threat credibility by creating domestic barriers to demobilization. However, state leaders may then find it difficult to offer credible assurances. The severity of this trade-off can help to account for the surprising failure of coercive demands at high levels of latent power.

In addition, my assessment of compellence contributes to research on asymmetrical relationships between strong and weak states. As Paul Musgrave (2019) notes, much of this work challenges the classic notion espoused by the Athenians that the strong do what they can in world politics. Recent research in this vein helps us understand why strong states such as the United States often fail to coerce weaker states (Sechser 2010; Haun 2015; Chamberlain 2016). A related strand of scholarship argues that the weak need not always suffer what they must (Arreguín-Toft 2005; Greenhill 2010; Womack 2016). In line with this research program, my work shows how weaker states can overcome structural disadvantages to influence the behavior of great powers. By threatening to equalize one element in the power asymmetry, the weak can compel concessions from the strong.

Finally, the book offers three policy implications. First, my research indicates that the United States and possibly China will be the primary targets of compellence with nuclear latency going forward. The viability of this strategy for weaker states depends on the degree to which Washington maintains its long-standing opposition to proliferation. China's rise to great power status also makes it a potential target. But Beijing will need to adopt stronger nonproliferation preferences in the years ahead. Second, in terms of calibrating nonproliferation policy, my framework suggests that the United States should consider "buying out" the fissile material ambitions of states before they enter the sweet spot. Nuclear deals become much harder and costlier for Washington to conclude at higher levels of latency, as exemplified by recent experiences with North Korea and Iran. Third, the book has broader implications for efforts to regulate dual-use technologies. Many modern technologies are dual use in nature because they have both civilian and military applications. States invest in these technologies to reap economic and security dividends. My work indicates that they may also find it useful to leverage such investments as a bargaining chip. The final chapter of the book unpacks these implications in greater detail.

Road Map

The rest of the book is organized as follows. In Chapter 2, I present my theory of compellence with nuclear latency. This framework weaves coercion theory together with research on nuclear proliferation. I identify the threat-assurance trade-off, create a typology of latent nuclear bargaining tactics, and derive a set of hypotheses. The chapter then compares my core claim about the sweet spot against alternative arguments, especially the notion that more latency is better when it comes to compellence. I also develop criteria for measuring the boundaries of the sweet spot. The final part of the chapter crafts a research design strategy and selects four countries from the universe of cases to evaluate the theory.

Chapters 3 and 4 focus on ally hedgers who leveraged latency against the United States in the early atomic age. In Chapter 3, I study several attempts by Japan to shore up defense commitments and wrest back territorial control of Western Pacific islands from the United States from 1957 to 1970. Despite the peaceful nature of Japan's nuclear energy program, Japanese leaders put pressure on Washington by making implicit proliferation threats and entangling nonproliferation promises with the fate of Okinawa and the alliance. Japan's nuclear program lacked the capacity to produce fissile material during the first episode (1957–1960). But it quickly moved into the sweet spot by the start of the second episode (1964–1970). Japan therefore provides two subcases to assess how variation in latency shaped its bargaining leverage over time.

Continuing with this theme, Chapter 4 examines how West Germany bargained with nuclear latency amid the initial peak of the Cold War. The prospect of Bonn building the bomb hung over Washington and Moscow throughout most of the 1960s. Much like Japan, West German leaders exploited the fear of proliferation on multiple occasions as a diplomatic lever. In the first episode (1961–1963), Bonn tried to strengthen West Germany's position within the North Atlantic Treaty Organization (NATO) while forcing concessions from the Soviets over reunification. Given the low level of latency at the time, the West Germans should have struggled to make their proliferation threats credible. In the second episode (1963–1966), Bonn launched another campaign to secure German participation in NATO nuclear sharing arrangements. West Germany's atomic energy program moved into the fissile material sweet spot during this era. According to my theory, Bonn should have been able to surmount the threat-assurance trade-off at this level of latency and wrangle concessions from Washington. The Federal Republic remained in the sweet spot for the third episode (1966–1969), when Bonn pushed back against the superpower fait accompli over the Treaty on the Non-Proliferation of Nuclear Weapons (NPT), demanding core changes to the treaty and additional assurances from the Americans. If the book's theory is correct, West German leaders should have had just enough nuclear latency on hand to extract concessions from the superpowers at this stage. Indeed, Bonn leveraged latency to shape foundational pillars of the NPT and the US nuclear umbrella.

Chapters 5 and 6 shift the focus to adversarial hiders who fell back on compellence in the wake of nuclear exposure. In Chapter 5, I assess North Korea's track record of leveraging latency against the United States. Washington launched the initial diplomatic effort to curb Pyongyang's plutonium program in the early 1990s. But North Korea soon figured out how to blackmail the United States with explicit nuclear mobilization and brinksmanship tactics. In addition, North Korea increased its level of latency across two compellence episodes. Pyongyang benefited from being in the fissile material sweet spot during the first nuclear crisis (1991–1994). North Korea then marched up the latency continuum throughout the second nuclear crisis (2002–2008), even going so far as to test a nuclear weapon. This controlled comparison between medium and high levels of latency helps me to assess the Goldilocks hypotheses against alternative explanations.

Chapter 6 examines Iran's multiple attempts to leverage latency after the discovery of its covert nuclear program. The growth in latency across three subcases (2003–2006, 2009–2010, 2013–2015) presents a hard test of my theory. Specifically, the success of diplomacy at an ultra-high level of latency in 2015 seems to undercut my claim about the sweet spot for compellence. Despite inching close to the weapons threshold, Iran traded away some nuclear assets and made nonproliferation assurances in exchange for concessions. However, the chapter reveals that Iranian leaders still faced a severe threat-assurance trade-off after the nuclear program left the fissile material sweet spot in 2006.

Chapter 7 summarizes the book's results and considers its implications for scholars and policy practitioners. I focus on the surprising result that the fissile material sweet spot remained remarkably stable over the last seven decades. Enrichment and reprocessing capabilities have arguably become easier for states to acquire from a purely technical standpoint. Recent advances in industrial production technology—notably additive manufacturing—promise to further erode the barriers to acquisition. But I demonstrate that these innovations have not fundamentally reshaped the bargaining tactics states employ to send signals and make commitments with their nuclear programs. This augurs well for the future of nonproliferation policy. But Washington and possibly Beijing must be ready to "buy out" the fissile material aspirations of nuclear aspirants, especially allies and partners who are increasingly interested in hedging with nuclear latency.

2

A Theory of Compellence with Nuclear Latency

In the past, nations threatened to acquire nuclear weapons as an instrument of coercive leverage. Some used nuclear latency to put pressure on ally patrons for greater security commitments or military assistance. Others attempted to wrest sanctions relief and other concessions from adversaries by issuing more explicit proliferation ultimatums. But the strategy generated a range of outcomes. At times, allies and adversaries alike succeeded at compelling concessions from great power sheriffs such as the United States. In other situations, leveraging latency failed to elicit any changes in the status quo. When does compellence with nuclear latency work?

This chapter develops a framework to explain how states use nuclear latency as an effective bargaining instrument in world politics.[1] The core finding is that states need just enough bomb-making potential to make both proliferation threats and promises of nuclear restraint credible. I present this theory in five main parts. The first part explores the dilemma challengers face between making proliferation threats and nonproliferation assurances credible. The second part presents hypotheses about when this strategy is likely to succeed or fail. I uncover a sweet spot amount of latency where compellence should be most likely to work because challengers can underwrite both threats and assurances. The third part compares these claims to alternative explanations. The fourth part grounds the boundaries of the sweet spot in actual nuclear technology. The final part of the chapter formulates a research strategy and selects cases to evaluate the theory.

The Threat-Assurance Trade-off

How do states use latent nuclear capabilities to wrest concessions from great power sheriffs?[2] I develop the logic of compellence with nuclear latency in three sections. The first identifies the main problem with using

Leveraging Latency. Tristan A. Volpe, Oxford University Press. © Oxford University Press 2023.
DOI: 10.1093/oso/9780197669532.003.0002

nuclear latency as an instrument of coercion: challengers confront a trade-off between making threats and assurances credible. This dilemma haunts strategies of compellence in general. I show that it is especially vexing for latent nuclear challengers who must demonstrate determination to build the bomb, while also committing themselves to nuclear restraint once the sheriff complies. The second section reviews the general ways challengers can manage this dilemma. The third section generates a specific typology of latent nuclear bargaining tactics from these mechanisms. The typology sheds light on the tension challengers face between underwriting proliferation threats and nonproliferation assurances.

The Problem

Challengers often confront a dilemma between making compellent threats and assurances credible. On the one hand, they must convey their resolve to harm the great power sheriff unless compliance is forthcoming. The sheriff estimates threat credibility in terms of the challenger's capability and intent to inflict punishment. But therein lies the taproot of the problem with making coercive threats credible. Challengers face incentives to misrepresent their resolve for harming the sheriff. Deception is especially alluring when it would be costly for the challenger to carry out the threatened punishment (Ellsberg 1968: 21). In military crisis bargaining, for example, the challenger can overstate its capacity and appetite for waging war to gain leverage. "If a state might get a better deal in a negotiated settlement by exaggerating its willingness to use force," James Fearon (1992: 140) argues, "it can have an incentive to do so." Compellence puts pressure on challengers to distinguish themselves from irresolute actors who lack the mettle to follow through with the threat.

On the other hand, however, the challenger must offer an assurance to exercise restraint once the sheriff complies with its demands. Compellence "involves *initiating* an action," Thomas Schelling (1966: 72) notes, "that can cease, or become harmless, only if the opponent responds." Assurances play a critical role, he argues, because this "action has to be one that can be stopped or reversed when the enemy complies, or else there is no inducement" (1966: 76). Yet making such promises credible is no easy task (Pauly 2019). The underlying issue is that the challenger's incentives to uphold its assurance may change over time. The sheriff anticipates this temptation and comes to doubt that the challenger will live up to the promise (Morrow 1999: 96). Compellence deepens this commitment problem because challengers often retain some capacity for punishment in world politics (Sechser 2010). To allay fears about the future, the challenger needs to make an assurance that is relatively immune to changing conditions down the road.

Compellence with nuclear latency pulls challengers onto the horns of this threat-assurance dilemma. They must convey resolve to build the bomb, while ultimately giving up this nuclear quest once the sheriff concedes. The challenger needs to be capable of building atomic weapons for its proliferation threat to carry any weight. Moving up the latency continuum enables the challenger to signal its intent to follow through with the threat unless the sheriff yields. Yet each step toward the bomb must be offset with an assurance to exercise nuclear restraint. Otherwise, there is no reason for the sheriff to concede. Threatening proliferation could just trigger punitive sanctions and preventive motivations for war.

Nonproliferation promises are therefore essential for compellence work. The goal is to convince the sheriff that complying with the challenger's demands will stop the bomb-building process. The challenger must convey it plans to abstain from atomic weapons once the sheriff complies. In addition, the nonproliferation pledge must guard against future temptations for the challenger to resume its nuclear quest or dust off the coercive playbook down the road.

Challengers tend to struggle with making proliferation threats and nonproliferation assurances credible for three reasons. First, the benefits at stake in coercive diplomacy may be lower than the high costs of proliferation. Challengers want to extract valuable concessions. But the general problem with compellence, Todd Sechser and Matthew Fuhrmann (2017: 50) argue, is that these "disputes often involve bargaining over issues that the coercer has already learned to live without—suggesting that it could continue to do so." The small stakes can undermine the credibility of compellent threats with large consequences, such as building the bomb. Fuhrmann (2019: 300) drives home this point in his research on latent nuclear deterrence, emphasizing that "it is not credible to build or use nuclear weapons in retaliation for minor transgressions." This makes it difficult for challengers to brandish their willingness to incur the costs of going nuclear for minimal rewards.

Second, challengers face incentives to misrepresent their nuclear aspirations. Proliferation strategy can shed some light on the challenger's goals. But intent is still hard for the sheriff to divine with high confidence because it is a form of private information. This creates room for the challenger to manipulate information and come across as driven to build the bomb if and only if the sheriff resists (Jervis 1970). In addition, the tendency for great powers to exhaust diplomatic options before using military force creates a moral hazard situation (Arrow 1963). With the prospect of severe punishment held at bay, states with little proclivity for nuclear weapons may pursue otherwise risky behavior: pretending to march toward the bomb to extract concessions. Great powers anticipate this temptation, which leads them to suspect that some challengers are exaggerating their weapons ambitions. As a result, challengers must separate themselves from less resolved types who are bluffing with nuclear latency.

Third, sheriffs harbor suspicions about nonproliferation assurances. For some challengers, the process of compellence itself may be subterfuge to sell the great power a bad nuclear deal. For example, negotiations could just be a ruse to buy time and ward off more serious punishment. Such challengers may offer a false promise of nuclear restraint, only to sprint toward the bomb later. Sheriffs push challengers for strong pledges of nuclear restraint to better distinguish these wolves from the sheep. Other challengers want to trade away their nuclear ambitions in exchange for concessions. But the incentives these states face to abstain from the bomb can change over time. This commitment problem is difficult to resolve because challengers end up retaining some bomb-making potential, even after they give up major nuclear facilities. Challengers must often go to great lengths to commit themselves to nuclear restraint.

The Solution

Although the threat-assurance dilemma haunts compellence with nuclear latency, it is possible for challengers to resolve this tension. The extensive scholarship on international crisis bargaining demonstrates that states can make threats and assurances credible by tying hands, sinking costs, running risks, and imposing pressure.[3] I review these four mechanisms to specify how challengers convey information, create commitments, and ratchet up punishment during coercive diplomacy.

The first mechanism operates by tying the challenger's hands to a coercive commitment. These actions increase the costs the challenger will pay if it fails to follow through with the threat or uphold its promise of restraint (Fearon

1997: 70; Slantchev 2005: 533). In addition, the challenger can also boost the benefits it stands to receive from carrying out the threat or assurance. The mechanism helps commit the challenger to a course of action, lest it suffer consequences or forgo rewards. Some international actions tie hands in this manner, such as treaty obligations with punitive provisions or preparations to achieve victory in war. However, many scholars contend that domestic audiences play a more prominent role in shaping the cost-benefit calculus of leaders who pursue compellence on the world stage (Fearon 1994; Schultz 2001; Weeks 2014). We therefore need to examine whether groups exist within the state that can hold leaders accountable for making compellent threats and assurances.[4]

The second mechanism involves sinking costs into the issue at stake. By incurring up-front expenses to make threats or assurances, the challenger signals its resolve to the target. These ex ante costs are paid at the outset regardless of the outcome (Fearon 1997). In militarized coercion, for instance, the challenger brandishes its mettle by taking resource intensive steps to arm and mobilize forces. This process helps challengers separate themselves from irresolute actors who do not value the issue enough to incur high up-front costs.[5] Pure sunk-cost actions are difficult to find in world politics, however. Military mobilization does more than just incur financial costs. It also prepares the challenger to succeed on the battlefield, thereby boosting the benefits of war and tying one's hand to the compellent threat.[6] In practice, the tactics for sinking costs can bleed into other signaling mechanisms.

The third mechanism relies on running risks of mutual disaster with the target. Some threats are not believable in normal circumstances, especially when following through involves serious consequences for the challenger. Nuclear arsenals often create this credibility-of-use issue in coercive diplomacy. Following through on the threat to strike a target with atomic weapons would create huge costs for the challenger, such as triggering retaliation or international condemnation (Sechser and Fuhrmann 2013). Brinkmanship tactics can make such incredible threats more believable, Thomas Schelling (1966: 91) argues, by "setting afoot an activity that may get out of hand, initiating a process that carries some risk of unintended disaster." The challenger exploits the danger that it may inadvertently drag the target over the brink of war, thereby putting pressure on both sides to resolve the dispute.[7]

The fourth mechanism involves putting pressure on the target until it provides concessions. According to Daniel Altman (2018: 68), challengers can "impose pressure by unilaterally enacting a new state of affairs that inflicts costs until and unless a concession is forthcoming." For example, covert interventions to seize territory can impose costs without provoking further escalation (or evoking brinksmanship), as Austin Carson (2018) demonstrates. In contrast to traditional coercive tactics, pressure mechanisms need not rely on "signaling resolve in order to establish the credibility of threats," Altman (2018: 66) explains. Instead, the challenger needs to maintain the new status quo until concessions are forthcoming from the target. Plausible deniability can play a key role by making it less risky and costly for the challenger to sustain the operation. By separating themselves from especially provocative actions, challengers can also revert to the status quo ante without losing face.

In sum, each mechanism explains how actions undertaken by challengers shape the process of coercive diplomacy. The next section translates these general principles into specific tactics for bargaining with nuclear latency.

The Tactics

The coercive mechanisms set the foundation to generate a typology of latent nuclear bargaining tactics. The typology details the menu of actions available for challengers to surmount the threat-assurance dilemma. Under the tactics of *mobilization*, *protection*, and *intervention*, the challenger is a unitary actor who manipulates different features of its nuclear program to convey information and calibrate pressure on the international stage. By contrast, *elite empowerment* and *public activation* take place within the challenger at the level of domestic politics. State leaders can constrain their nuclear choices by handing over control to other elites or cultivating support among the mass public. A deep dive into each tactic uncovers the points of tension between making proliferation threats and nonproliferation assurances credible.

Mobilization

Under the classic tactic of mobilization, the challenger increases its latent capabilities to demonstrate resolve and apply pressure on the sheriff. Ariel Levite (2019) underscores that mobilizing latency is useful when challengers want to fire a preverbal "shot across the bow" in coercive diplomacy. Ramping up production at fuel enrichment plants, Levite (2019: 26–27) suggests, can "make it credibly look like a state is both determined to pursue and capable of pursuing nuclear weapons if left to its own devices." In general, nuclear programs help challengers send sunk-cost signals because they are expensive endeavors to undertake. As Michael Horowitz (2010: 103) aptly sums up, "Acquiring nuclear weapons is an intensive financial process." An irresolute actor is unlikely to make such an investment in the first place. The high cost of mobilizing latency screens out opportunistic bluffers. Moving up the latency continuum does more than just convey information about nuclear intentions, of course. It also puts the challenger in a better position to build the bomb. Mobilization therefore helps commit the challenger to follow through with its compellent threat by boosting the benefits of proliferation.

Challengers also mobilize nuclear latency to ratchet up pressure on sheriffs. Moving closer to the bomb or achieving technical milestones creates a worrisome situation for great powers. The dual-use nature of nuclear technology enables challengers to maintain plausible deniability over their weapons intentions as they mobilize latency. Since nuclear programs are useful for both civilian and military purposes, challengers can dial up latency under the guise of attaining peaceful atomic energy goals.[8] This duality dampens the risks of blowback and preventive war, which helps challengers maintain the pressure campaign until the great power concedes. In addition, plausible deniability holds the door open for challengers to come back into compliance with their nonproliferation obligations (Pauly 2021).

When it comes to making nonproliferation assurances credible, challengers can reverse the mobilization process by decreasing nuclear latency. Giving up the technical capacity to produce atomic weapons on short notice sends a costly signal of the challenger's intent to cooperate with the sheriff once compliance is forthcoming. A more determined proliferator using coercive diplomacy as a ruse would be unwilling to incur such delays or burn valuable latency investments. Demobilization tactics are often an essential step to walk back the proliferation threat.

Protection

Protection tactics focus on making the nuclear program less vulnerable to attack and foreign interference. Challengers can employ a range of measures to protect atomic assets, from hiding and hardening nuclear infrastructure to developing indigenous supply chains. These efforts enhance the credibility of proliferation threats in two distinct ways.

First, protection signals the challenger's resolve to build the bomb because it is an expensive method for developing nuclear latency. Building secret nuclear facilities in underground bunkers is more costly and labor intensive than traditional aboveground construction. Protection also tends to slow down the pace of technical progress. Such efforts often force nuclear aspirants to sacrifice speed for stealth.[9] The upshot is that these choices reveal a strong proclivity for the bomb if the state ends up pursuing latent nuclear compellence.

Second, challengers who hide nuclear facilities set the stage for brinkmanship. Recent research demonstrates that attempting to mask a nuclear program can increase the risk of preventive war (Bas and Coe 2016; Debs and Monteiro 2014). When the challenger is caught covering up its atomic activities or infrastructure, the great power comes to doubt whether the full extent of the nuclear program is known and observable. This uncertainty creates incentives for the great power to stop the challenger with military force before it builds the bomb in secret. But the challenger can turn this risk into an opportunity for brinkmanship (Benson and Wen 2011). By offering to pull back the veil of ambiguity over its nuclear enterprise for the right price, the challenger presents the sheriff with one last chance to avoid preventive war.

Protection tactics illuminate a countervailing set of actions for challengers to underwrite nonproliferation commitments. By making the nuclear program more vulnerable to attack and dependent on foreign suppliers, the challenger gives up its latent capability as a "hostage" that the sheriff can "execute" if promises are broken down the road.[10] Nuclear programs built in plain sight under international trade agreements stand to suffer high costs if the challenger decides to build the bomb (Miller 2017; Gibbons 2020). All else being equal, the more that the challenger exposes the nuclear program to international surveillance and stringent penalties for military activities, the stronger its commitment to forgo the bomb.

Intervention

Intervention utilizes the presence of outside actors to shape the calculus of building nuclear weapons. Just as Odysseus employed his crew to bind him to the mast against the Sirens, so, too, can other states and international actors help the challenger tie its hands to coercive commitments. Interveners come in a variety of forms, from ally patrons to neutral brokers and international organizations. The key feature of this tactic is that intervention promises to change either the benefits or consequences of nuclear proliferation for the challenger.

The potential for other actors to intervene on *behalf* of the challenger can make its proliferation threats more credible. If the challenger is under the protection of an ally patron, then it may be able to march toward the bomb without incurring high costs or fearing preventive attack (Debs and Monteiro 2016; Narang 2022). By lowering the expected costs of building atomic weapons, this type of intervener helps the challenger make credible threats. Neutral actors sometimes provide inadvertent protection to challengers as well. The International Atomic Energy Agency (IAEA), for example, monitors atomic energy programs to guard against military uses of nuclear technology. So long as the challenger keeps its nuclear program in full compliance with the agency, the great power sheriff may struggle to bring the case before the United Nations Security Council, thereby undermining multilateral efforts to levy sanctions or coordinate military action.

On the assurance side of the coin, an actor who promises to intervene *against* the challenger can help underwrite commitments to nuclear restraint. This type of third-party nuclear "guarantor" is especially useful when the challenger cannot resolve the commitment problem intrinsic to nuclear latency on its own. As Heins Goemans (2000: 32) argues in the context of war termination, the looming presence of an intervener can make agreements self-enforcing because all sides "anticipate intervention and its consequences." In the nuclear realm, the ideal guarantor has strong nonproliferation interests and can punish the challenger if it reneges on the nonproliferation promise down the road.

Elite Empowerment

Elite empowerment turns inward to use the domestic politics of building nuclear programs as a commitment device. This tactic reflects the relationship between two groups within the challenger itself: (1) state leaders who make policy decisions; and (2) elite actors in charge of running the nuclear program. The latter group consists of "bureaucratic, military, and legislative elites," Elizabeth Saunders (2019: 164) notes, "as well as scientists and technicians involved in nuclear projects." Leaders empower these elites by providing them with greater material resources and political autonomy. This type of state support generates two main benefits when it comes to making credible threats.

First, leaders who empower nuclear elites put themselves in a prime position to mobilize latency during coercive diplomacy. Nuclear programs are large and intricate scientific endeavors. Some projects struggle to make technical progress and end up stuck at lower stages of latency. Recent research finds that leaders can avoid this fate if they set nuclear elites up for success. According to Jacques Hymans (2012: 25), the optimal development strategy is for leaders to provide the nuclear establishment with "ample resources," and then "leave the professionals alone" to do science without political interference. Similarly, Malfrid Braut-Hegghammer (2016: 9) demonstrates that leaders need strong bureaucratic institutions to "plan and coordinate complex projects such as nuclear weapons programs." Delegating control and power to elites is therefore key to effective mobilization of nuclear latency.

Second, elite empowerment helps commit the state to move forward with the nuclear program. Leaders can bind themselves to the mast by giving elites more control over the trajectory of nuclear projects. Saunders (2019: 167) finds that nuclear policies are most likely to "stick" when leaders cultivate a broad base of elite stakeholders and embed the nuclear program within a powerful bureaucratic organization. Toby Dalton (2019: 250) also underscores the key role of "nuclear policy influencers," notably scientists, military officers, and politicians, in supporting state decisions about nuclear latency. As these elites gain power and authority within the state, they can impose costs on leaders who attempt to change the course of the nuclear enterprise.

But the coercive threat benefits of elite empowerment can turn into liabilities for making nonproliferation assurances. The main problem with delegating control over nuclear projects is that leaders then face costly domestic barriers to reversing course. Powerful nuclear elites operating within independent bureaucracies are more able to act "as a drag on a leader's ability to implement a policy change," Saunders (2019: 175) points out. From a unitary actor perspective, it may be optimal for the challenger to roll back its nuclear program after ratcheting up pressure on the sheriff. Elite empowerment distorts this logic because it presents leaders with more difficult and costly assurance options. The upshot is that leaders who do pay these high costs—for example, by wresting back institutional control to shutter facilities or intervening in the research portfolio—signal their intention to forgo the bomb.

Public Activation

Within the broader political arena at home, leaders can also use the public as a means for making nuclear commitments more credible. In a twist on the concept of domestic audience costs, this tactic involves leaders taking deliberate steps to activate support for the nuclear program among the public at large. A range of options exist for leaders to cultivate public support for atomic energy programs, from imbuing these projects with scientific prestige to promising greater economic dividends and energy security. Even overt steps forward with nuclear weapons programs can be sold to the public on nationalist or existential security grounds.

Public activation helps make proliferation threats more credible because it increases the domestic costs of nuclear reversal. By announcing clear commitments to attain nuclear goals in front of these audiences, leaders constrain themselves from backing down at the bargaining table. This tactic for tying one's hands is available to both democratic and autocratic leaders, albeit to varying degrees. As Susan Hyde and Elizabeth Saunders (2020: 3) explain, regime type sets "a default level of domestic audience constraint that is generally higher in democracies, but leaders maintain some agency within these institutions and can deliberately increase their exposure to or insulation from this constraint." Public opposition groups should be better able to constrain democratic leaders from giving up nuclear assets.[11] Autocratic regimes can generate similar constraints by using nuclear programs to enhance the legitimacy of their rule among public supporters.

Much like elite empowerment, priming the public to support nuclear projects can distort the menu of assurance options. Leaders may not be able to trade away nuclear assets without suffering serious consequences. Indeed, this is precisely how the tactic enhances coercive threat credibility. It therefore behooves leaders to explore how to save face and offset these domestic costs while giving up major elements of the nuclear program. Leaders may be able to exploit the dual-use nature of the technology to roll back only the most sensitive elements of the program without losing face. Or public opposition to nuclear energy projects on economic or safety grounds can provide leaders with an offramp to divest from latency. Alternatively, Jane Vaynman (2014) and Rupal Mehta (2020) demonstrate that leadership change—via elections or coups—can open a window of opportunity for nuclear rollback. When new leaders come into power who are not beholden to their predecessor's commitments, they may be able to offer strong nonproliferation assurances at the bargaining table.

As Table 2.1 summarizes, the typology classifies the full range of different actions challengers can undertake to surmount the threat-assurance dilemma. These tactics should be available to challengers at any stage of nuclear

Table 2.1 Latent Nuclear Bargaining Tactics

	Threats	Assurances
Mobilization	*Increase latency* Fire "shot across the bow" Ratchet up pressure	*Decrease latency* Signal intent to cooperate Relieve pressure
Protection	*Harden and hide infrastructure* Signal proclivity for the bomb Invoke brinkmanship risks	*Soften and expose infrastructure* Give up program as a "hostage" Accept vulnerability
Intervention	*On behalf of the challenger* Lowers proliferation costs Wards off punitive consequences	*Against the challenger* Raises costs of cheating Third-party "guarantor" of the deal
Elite empowerment	*Leaders delegate control to elites* Nuclear stakeholders gain greater autonomy and power Commit state to move forward	*Leaders wrest back control* Domestic barriers to reversal Powerful elites constrain national policy options
Public activation	*Leaders cue public to support nuclear goals* Clear constraint on giving up nuclear assets or backing down	*Leaders face consequences from nuclear rollback* Explore options to save face or offset domestic costs

development. But how much latency do challengers need to make these tactics most effective at underwriting threats and assurances?

The Goldilocks Principle

Challengers face trade-offs along the latency continuum between threatening to acquire atomic weapons and promising restraint. At low levels, they might not have enough capabilities on hand for the tactics to be effective. Moving up the latency continuum can help solve this threat credibility problem. However, the bargaining typology illustrates that some assurance tactics become harder to employ as the nuclear program matures. Points of friction begin to emerge—especially within the domestic arena—that can constrain challengers from dialing proliferation threats up and back down in a seamless fashion. The challenger's level of latency thereby shapes the severity of the threat-assurance dilemma.[12] This insight sets the foundation to deduce three hypotheses about when compellence is likely to succeed or fail as the challenger develops latent capabilities.

Too Little

At low levels of latency, compellence is most likely to fail. The crux of the issue is that challengers with emerging nuclear programs lack the capacity to make proliferation threats credible.

> *Hypothesis 1—Too Little (H1)*: At a low level of nuclear latency, compellence is most likely to fail because the challenger's threat to build atomic weapons is not credible.

In particular, the tactics for bargaining with nuclear latency tend to be ineffective at this stage for three reasons.

First, the challenger is too far away from the bomb to mobilize or protect its nascent nuclear assets. Spinning up a nuclear program may be a good way to fire a shot across the bow, as Levite (2019: 26–27) points out. But great powers are in the best position to prevent the challenger from firing the next warning shot or ultimately acquiring nuclear weapons. Scholars find that counterproliferation efforts are most effective at early stages of technical development, when nuclear programs are most vulnerable to technology denial, sabotage, and diplomatic pressure (Kreps and Fuhrmann 2011; Miller 2014b; Koch 2019). The challenger must also weather a long road to the bomb, leaving ample time for great powers to ratchet up the costs of proliferation. Rather than make concessions, great powers may find it easier and cheaper to stop the challenger with other nonproliferation levers.

Second, the challenger's latency investment may not be costly enough to convey its determination to build the bomb. Horowitz (2010: 99) reminds us that "the enormous level of financial intensity necessary to acquire nuclear weapons has always functioned as a significant constraint." The high proliferation costs make it difficult for the challenger to signal resolve with initial nuclear investments. In the absence of more extensive infrastructure, proliferation threats ring hollow—the challenger could just be inaugurating the nuclear program as a ploy for leverage. Instead of fulfilling compellent demands, the sheriff may just wait and see if the challenger is serious about pouring scarce national resources into its nuclear enterprise.

Third, state leaders face weak commitments from domestic groups to stay the course as the nuclear program is starting up. Some leaders end up "stuck" at low levels of latency because they retain direct control over nuclear programs, as research from Hymans (2012) and Braut-Hegghammer

(2016) demonstrates. Saunders (2019: 167) argues that these leaders often refuse to delegate authority "for fear of coups, ouster, or domestic-political costs." Without adequate political autonomy and material resources, the nuclear program tends to flounder at an early development stage. Other leaders empower elites and cue public support for nuclear endeavors from the outset. However, these domestic groups are not yet able to impose costs on leaders for changing course when the nuclear program is still in its infancy. Elite stakeholders need time and successful technological breakthroughs to gain power and institutionalize the nuclear enterprise. Public audiences seldom observe small nuclear research and development projects, especially when these efforts are kept secret. Domestic groups are less able to constrain leaders at lower levels of latency, which erodes the credibility of these central bargaining tactics.

Too Much

By contrast, proliferation threats are more credible at higher levels of latency. When the challenger is a mere "screwdriver turn away" from building atomic weapons, the burden may fall on the great power sheriff to cut a deal. Moving toward the cusp of the bomb makes the tactics for threatening proliferation more effective. The challenger is in a prime position to ratchet up pressure and signal resolve by mobilizing operational nuclear facilities. But more latency does not always translate into greater bargaining leverage. The dilemma between making both threats and promises credible becomes severe as challengers approach the weapons threshold.

> *Hypothesis 2—Too Much (H2)*: At a high level of nuclear latency, compellence is likely to fail or yield Pyrrhic victories as assurances become increasingly costly and difficult to make credible.

The problem is that nonproliferation assurances grow increasingly difficult and costly to make credible for three reasons.

First, leaders often cede control to elite stakeholders as they bring large nuclear projects online. Elite empowerment is not only helpful in getting nuclear programs off the ground, but also essential in developing infrastructure along the nuclear fuel cycle at later stages. These complex projects require firm commitments from state leaders to sustain capital-intensive construction over long time periods. William Walker (1999) finds that nuclear programs become embedded in a web of legal, financial, industrial, and political commitments as they develop major technology. "The snag," Walker (2000: 846) underscores, "is that the formation of commitments contains within it the seeds of intentional and unintentional entrapment in inferior options." Entrapment plays a key role in undermining compellence because it narrows the menu of bargaining tactics available to leaders. When contractual obligations or political promises entrap leaders into keeping nuclear facilities online, they may be unable to dampen proliferation threats at the negotiation table.

Second, leaders face mounting domestic costs to altering the course of the nuclear program as it matures. The issue is that nuclear technology exhibits what economists such as Brian Arthur (1994) refer to as "path dependency": each step forward produces benefits that increase the returns of staying on that pathway. As such positive feedback effects accumulate, Paul Pierson (2004: 18) explains, "they generate a powerful cycle of self-reinforcing activity," making it more difficult to reverse course over time.

Path dependency explains why marching toward the bomb creates internal barriers to making nonproliferation assurances. Even if leaders want to roll back latency, nuclear programs generate increasing returns to elite stakeholders. The scientific complex becomes entrenched in the political system and seeks to retain budget outlays. Politicians accrue power from managing these operations and may veto any attempts to curtail nuclear projects (Hymans 2011; Acton 2015b). Military officers or the energy industry push for tangible returns on the long-term investment.[13] Coalitions form strong incentives to pressure the leadership to stay the course, or at a minimum, not trade away the nuclear infrastructure. The domestic political costs of giving up or even restraining the nuclear program rise the more it matures into a valuable operational complex.

Third, the tactics for underwriting nonproliferation assurances can become so costly that compellence yields net negative benefits for the challenger—a Pyrrhic victory of sorts. Challengers must go to greater lengths to offer convincing assurances as they reach higher levels of latency. Demobilization is key to signaling benign intentions at this stage. Rollback is expensive and complex. The process can also introduce security risks for the challenger beyond the four corners of the nuclear deal. Mature nuclear programs require intrusive transparency measures to verify compliance and guard against reconstitution. But these transparency measures can sometimes reveal too much information about state secrets beyond boundaries of the nuclear program. If making a nonproliferation commitment credible could expose conventional military vulnerabilities or other critical information, then challengers will be reluctant to sign on to such a deal (Abbott 1993; Coe and Vaynman 2020).

In addition, challengers incur opportunity costs in the form of lost economic or military benefits as they divest from operational nuclear facilities. By accruing these significant costs and risks, challengers can distinguish themselves from cheaters seeking to build nuclear weapons in the future. The downside is that the coercive benefits may no longer outweigh the high assurance costs, which is problematic given the propensity for challengers to bargain over relatively low-stake issues. This hypothesis helps to explain why it becomes harder for states to play a delay game with compellence at higher levels of latency. As path dependency and entrapment effects kick in, assurances grow more costly for leaders to put on the table. Concessions can no longer be extracted for modest nonproliferation promises, thereby making it difficult to practice effective deception.

Just Enough

Challengers struggle with the threat-assurance dilemma at low and high levels of latency. In the early phases of development, nuclear programs lack the capacity to underwrite proliferation threats. At more advanced stages, challengers end up with too much latency to offer nonproliferation assurances. But there may be a sweet spot in between these extremes on the latency continuum—a Goldilocks zone where it is easier and cheaper to resolve the credibility dilemma.

> *Hypothesis 3—Just Enough (H3)*: In the latent nuclear sweet spot, compellence is most likely to be successful because the challenger can surmount the threat-assurance dilemma.

Compellence should be most likely to work in this zone because challengers have just enough latency to make both threats and assurances credible.

The sweet spot creates several advantages for challengers when it comes to threatening proliferation. Even at modest stages of latency, nuclear programs provide challengers with sufficient capabilities to begin clearly marching toward the bomb. Each step forward puts greater pressure on sheriffs to cut a deal before the challenger further mobilizes its budding nuclear enterprise. Moreover, it becomes harder for great powers to stop this proliferation process with military force. In order to make it into the sweet spot, nuclear programs must develop a cadre of scientists and engineers who are capable of running complex technology projects. This degree of technical knowledge and organization capacity enables such programs to reconstitute physical assets in the aftermath of an attack—sabotage or limited airstrikes might just delay progress or drive nuclear activities underground. Complying with the challenger's demands may be the best way for the great power to inhibit proliferation.

The conditions should also be favorable in the sweet spot for making promises of nuclear restraint. The operational costs and security risks of cutting a deal tend to be manageable for challengers. Since the nuclear program is not on the cusp of the bomb, basic verification measures or minimal rollback efforts can lend enough credence to nonproliferation assurances at this stage. In addition, domestic politics is less likely to distort the incentives leaders face around binding themselves to the atomic abstinence mast. Given the path dependency of nuclear technology, entrapment effects and reversal costs should be less severe before the program becomes fully operational. At the middle stages of technical development, leaders may still be able to reconfigure or even trade away the nuclear program without suffering serious consequences from elite stakeholders or the mass public. Challengers therefore enjoy greater latitude to offer nonproliferation assurances in exchange for concessions as they move into the latent nuclear sweet spot.

While the credibility dilemma points toward this Goldilocks zone, it does not stipulate a priori how much latency is enough for effective coercion. There should be a range of possible values in between having no bomb-making potential at all and teetering on the brink of weapons acquisition. The penultimate part of this chapter turns to the historical record to ground the boundaries of the sweet spot in actual nuclear programs over time. But the Goldilocks principle also cuts against the grain of existing explanations about when compellence strategies work. In the next section, I compare my theoretical claims to three distinct schools of thought and identify easy cases for these counterarguments. The comparison helps me devise a robust research design for probing the plausibility of my theory relative to these alternative accounts.

Alternative Explanations

Despite decades of scholarship on proliferation, there are still few complete explanations about when nuclear latency provides states with coercive benefits. This makes it difficult to stack my theory up against direct competitors.[14] However, it is possible to extract alternative explanations from research about the political effects of nuclear latency, the more general literature on nuclear strategy, and country specific studies of latent nuclear powers. Drawing on this literature, I compare my theoretical claims to three distinct schools of thought: (1) skeptics who reject the notion that nuclear latency provides any coercive utility; (2) maximalists who believe that more latency translates into greater bargaining leverage; as well as (3) pessimists who suspect it is more difficult for challengers to make compellence work along the entire latency continuum.

Skeptics

Some scholars contend that states cannot leverage latency. According to these skeptics, bomb-making potential is unsuitable for threatening costs or imposing pain on stronger nations. They claim that challengers must brandish the military means for inflicting violence in world politics to underwrite coercive threats. Scholars in this camp often view nuclear weapons as the ultimate tools for compelling targets to yield in the face of immense destruction (Beardsley and Asal 2009; Kroenig 2013). By extension, nuclear latency is not a tool of punishment at all—it is only useful for fueling atomic arsenal production. Even an advanced nuclear program or so-called "virtual arsenal," Kenneth Waltz (1997: 155) argues, is still "one step removed" from an operational coercive tool. In a similar vein, Kyle Beardsley and Victor Asal (2013: 266) find that nuclear "weapons programs do not in themselves give states additional bargaining power, but they carry a strong potential for greater bargaining power in the future," after one builds the bomb.

Alternative Hypothesis 1—Skepticism (A1): Compellence with nuclear latency is unlikely to ever work because atomic weapons are the ultimate instruments of blackmail in world politics.

If skeptics are correct, then states should derive no compellent advantages from nuclear programs until they cross the weapons threshold. This logic of coercive skepticism establishes a useful null hypothesis for my study: nuclear latency may not provide states with a tool of compellence at all. I look for country cases that appear to favor this claim to subject my theory to the hardest possible test. Skeptics often point to Iran's nuclear odyssey as a clear confirmation of their logic. Matthew Kroenig (2014: 51) provides an apt example in his study of US nonproliferation policy toward Iran:

> Iran's most important strategic goals are to deter foreign attack and to become the most dominant state in the Middle East. Actual nuclear weapons help Iran achieve both of these goals. A bunch of nuclear facilities does not help them accomplish either.

Kroenig (2014: 51) argues that it is therefore "ridiculous" to suggest that Iran can accomplish its objectives "by stopping a screw-driver's turn away from the bomb." Despite being more sanguine about a nuclear-armed Iran, Kenneth Waltz also doubted whether leaders in Tehran would derive any coercive benefits from nuclear latency. "The problem is that [an Iranian] breakout capability might not work as intended," Waltz (2012: 2–3) claimed, because "Israel would be less intimidated by a virtual nuclear weapon than it would be by an actual one." Since skeptics use Iran to demonstrate the plausibility of their argument, it should be an easy case for accepting their null hypothesis.

Maximalists

In contrast to the skeptics, many other scholars and policymakers believe that states can leverage latency to compel concessions in world politics. But the conventional wisdom is that compellence should be most effective when challengers reach high levels of nuclear latency. This prominent school of thought advances an intuitive idea: states gain coercive advantages from wielding the maximum amount of bomb-making potential at their disposal. Contrary to the Goldilocks principle, maximalists argue that more latency translates into greater bargaining power against sheriffs.

Alternative Hypothesis 2—Maximalism (A2): Compellence with nuclear latency is most likely to be successful when the challenger can build atomic weapons on short notice.

Several pathbreaking studies develop the maximalist position. The first comes from Mitchell Reiss's (1988: xix) investigation of nuclear forbearance, which explores in part how some "countries have attempted to manipulate the threat to acquire nuclear arms in order to better achieve their policy goals." Reiss (1988: xviii) proposes an intuitive relationship between proliferation threat credibility and coercive success: "The more credible the threat to go nuclear . . . the greater the benefit to be won in return for assurances that nuclear weapons are rejected." Although a wide range of actions can help states to augment their "nuclear credibility," Reiss (1988: xix) underscores that the level of "technological sophistication" plays a major role.

In his classic study of hedging with nuclear latency, Ariel Levite (2003: 72) finds that the "greatest appeal" of nuclear hedging "is the 'latent' or 'virtual' deterrence posture it generates . . . and the leverage it provides in reinforcing a state's coercive diplomacy strategy, particularly against the United States." Although Levite (2003: 69) does not develop an explanation of when this strategy works, he suggests that it rests on maintaining "a viable option for the relatively rapid acquisition of nuclear weapons, based on an indigenous technical capacity to produce them within a relatively short time frame." In the context of military coercion, William Spaniel (2019: 15) presents statistical evidence showing that "states with high levels of nuclear proficiency are . . . more likely to induce their opponents to back down than states with low levels."[15] Once challengers acquire the capability to build atomic weapons quickly, maximalists claim, they should be most able to wrest concessions from sheriffs.

Vipin Narang also illuminates how the maximalist logic underpins the nuclear posture choices of some states who stop short of fielding operational weapons. The goal of a "catalytic nuclear posture," Narang (2014: 16) explains, "is to compel a third party to intervene on the state's behalf." Under this posture, states straddle the thin line between latency and operational nuclear weapons, Narang (2014: 15) finds, by "threatening to break out known nuclear weapons capabilities or previously ambiguous or nonoperational nuclear capabilities and escalate a conflict if assistance is not forthcoming." The paradigmatic example, South Africa, was hardly a latent nuclear power, as it sat on a small number of atomic weapons. But the specific metrics used to identify catalytic nuclear postures leaves open the possibility that states could rely on ultra-high levels of latency in lieu of actual weapons. At a minimum, Narang (2014: 22) argues, states must maintain "the ability to assemble a handful of nuclear weapons" during a crisis. In the face of the threat to acquire and possibly use nuclear weapons, the United States or another great power patron may intervene on the state's behalf to deescalate the crisis. If catalytic nuclear postures are effective, then the Goldilocks principle may not be applicable to this unique form of compellence.

Scholars often invoke the maximalist argument to explain the political effects of nuclear latency in two distinct countries with advanced nuclear enterprises—Iran and Japan. In alignment with the coercive foundation of my theory, Thomas Juneau (2015: 176, 201) finds that "a latent nuclear capability . . . allowed Iran to blackmail the international community and to manipulate the fear its program induces to force them to offer concessions." Juneau (2015: 195) goes on to argue that more latency is better for Iran's compellence strategy: "As Iran makes further [nuclear] progress, its bargaining leverage increases: the further it progresses, the greater is its asking price to forgo some of its gains." Iran is therefore a critical case to compare the plausibility of claims from skeptics and maximalists against the Goldilocks principle of bargaining with nuclear latency.

Japan is held up as an example of how an ally can reap security dividends from peaceful investments in nuclear latency. Mark Fitzpatrick (2016: 114) views Japan's reprocessing and enrichment capabilities as "a means of diplomatic leverage to ensure continued American presence in East Asia and a way to keep options alive for the future should circumstances dramatically change." James Schoff and Richard Samuels (2013) find that key Japanese strategists espoused maximalist arguments in the past. They highlight a whitepaper from Takuya Kubo, the director of the Defense Bureau of the Japan Defense Agency, who suggested in 1971 that "[Japan should] establish a structure to *develop considerable nuclear armament capability* at any time . . . [so] the United States will get worried about unstable international relations due to nuclear proliferation and will desire to maintain the U.S.-Japan security regime including extended deterrence."[16] If we observe cases where Japan gains bargaining leverage over the United States as its nuclear program matures, this would undermine confidence in my theoretical claims.

Pessimists

The final counterargument is that compellence with nuclear latency is harder to make work than my logic suggests. Some scholars are more pessimistic about whether challengers can resolve several of the problems with leveraging latency, notably the low-stakes issue and blowback from threatening proliferation.

Matthew Fuhrmann concurs that it is possible for states to use bomb-making potential for political leverage on the world stage. In recent research about latent nuclear deterrence, however, he argues that states often struggle to make compellent threats credible unless they face a severe security situation—such as invasion or other forms of military aggression—where the stakes are high. "Compellence based on nuclear latency may be more difficult than deterrence, since the stakes involved are smaller for the latent nuclear power," Fuhrmann (2019: 301) concludes.[17] For Fuhrmann, the level of latency and its impact on the bargaining tactics does matter, but less than the geopolitical environment states face. Since the logic supporting his position is sound, I need to select cases where the stakes appear to be relatively low.[18] If my theoretical claims hold up in these instances, then the low stakes of coercion may be less of a problem for states who make it into the sweet spot.

Alternative Hypothesis 3—Pessimism (A3): Compellence with nuclear latency is unlikely to work at all levels of bomb-making capability unless the benefits at stake outweigh the costs of proliferation.

The second strand of pessimism comes from empirical assessments of latent nuclear coercion. In his study of the deterrent effects of various nuclear strategy choices, Vipin Narang (2014: 249) finds that catalytic postures tend to generate high costs and risks for latent nuclear powers: "For these states, pursuing nuclear weapons writes a security check that their catalytic deterrents cannot cash. In fact, the catalytic posture seems to backfire by creating incentives for preventive military action without an attendant ability to deter conflict." The corollary implication is that threatening to bring the bomb out of the basement is unlikely to compel security assistance from great power patrons. Rupal Mehta and Rachel Whitlark (2017: 517) offer additional statistical evidence supporting the conclusion that "latency offers few benefits and produces a number of costs," such as blowback from sheriffs in the form of economic sanctions. However, the study combines multiple coercive logics—notably deterrence and compellence—to examine the correlation between nuclear latency and various international outcomes, from militarized disputes to economic sanctions and foreign aid. Nuclear latency is also treated as a binary independent variable, so it is difficult to unpack how different levels of latency might shape international outcomes. Most important, the notion that challengers face consequences from leveraging latency does not necessarily invalidate my theory. The key is whether states in the sweet spot can manage these costs and risks.

The Fissile Material Sweet Spot

Where do countries fall along the continuum of nuclear latency? When does one have too little, too much, or just enough bomb-making potential for compellence? What technical signposts demarcate the Goldilocks zone from lower and higher thresholds in latent nuclear capability? In this part of the chapter, I offer objective criteria for measuring nuclear latency across all nations who pursued compellence strategies over time. Specifically, I show that fissile material production capacity offers a clear way to assess levels of nuclear latency. This metric enables me to draw boundaries between major thresholds in nuclear latency and then update the universe of cases.

Measuring Latent Nuclear Power

Analysts have used various metrics to gauge latent nuclear capabilities throughout the atomic age, from broad technological factors such as industrial production capacity to more narrow proficiency in manufacturing nuclear explosive devices.[19] Over the last fifteen years, however, scholars coalesced around a standard definition of nuclear latency as the capacity to produce enough fissile material—highly enriched uranium or plutonium—for an atomic weapon.[20] A country's level of latent capability therefore reflects the amount of time it would take to turn uranium into weapons-usable material at enrichment or reprocessing (ENR) plants. I provide a brief primer on fissile material production to identify critical technologies and activities.

The enrichment pathway on the "front end" of the nuclear fuel cycle begins with mining uranium from the ground. In this natural form, uranium has an isotopic composition of U-238 (99.3%) and U-235 (0.7%). Although a few reactors use natural uranium, U-238 cannot sustain the rate of fission needed to fuel modern reactors or atomic weapons. However, the much rarer U-235 fissions at the higher rate required for fast chain reactions. Enrichment refers to the process of separating out the minute amount of U-235 from natural uranium. A range of enrichment options exist, from the gaseous diffusion and electromagnetic methods developed by the Manhattan Project to the more modern centrifuge techniques (Wood, Glaser, and Kemp 2008). Enrichment technologies are also integral to the "front end" of the civilian nuclear fuel cycle. The fuel rods for most nuclear power reactors require uranium to be enriched to 3%–5% U-235. This means that an aspiring proliferator can use the same plant to keep enriching uranium until it contains enough fissile U-235 for a bomb. Indeed, a simple "gun-type" atomic weapon slams together masses of highly enriched uranium to ignite a supercritical nuclear chain reaction.[21]

The reprocessing method extracts another fissile material—plutonium—from irradiated uranium along the "back end" of the fuel cycle. Plutonium is not found in nature. The element is formed when uranium-238 sustains fission. This process happens in reactors fueled with uranium, although some are optimized to produce more plutonium than others. The rods of irradiated fuel then undergo processing to separate out the plutonium from the other elements. In the PUREX process, for instance, the rods are chopped up and dissolved in a bath of nitric acid. The constituent elements and isotopes within the radioactive slurry are separated out before being turned back into metallic form (Irish and Reas 1957). Spent fuel reprocessing provides one way for atomic energy programs to manage the toxic waste produced by nuclear power plants. Plutonium can also be fed back into the fuel cycle to power fast and breeder reactors (Program on Science and Global Security 2015). Unfortunately, the fissile nature of plutonium-239 makes it an ideal material for nuclear weapons. In a basic "implosion-type" weapon, high explosives compress a subcritical sphere of plutonium into a denser, supercritical mass that triggers the explosive reaction.[22]

Table 2.2 uses this technical overview to specify three successive levels of latency based on variation in fissile material capacity: low, medium, and high.

At the low end of the scale, a country's nuclear program lacks the capacity to produce fissile material and cannot acquire this critical capability in the near future—either through indigenous development or importing technology from abroad.[23] Given the scale and complexity of ENR plants, it is likely to take many years and perhaps even decades for the nuclear program

Table 2.2 Identifying Levels of Nuclear Latency

	Level of latency		
	Low	Medium	High
Fissile material capacity	Nuclear program cannot produce fissile material and is unlikely to acquire this capability in the near future	Nuclear program is on the cusp of producing fissile material but lacks larger production capability	Nuclear program can produce significant quantities of fissile material and turn it into a weapon quickly
Technical signposts	Foundation of nuclear research institutes and laboratories; construction of research and power reactors; limited uranium fuel stock	Experimental and pilot ENR plants with plans for industrial scale-up; operational reactors; growing uranium or spent fuel stock	Fully operational fuel enrichment or reprocessing plants; large material stockpile may be weapons-usable
Development timeline	More than five years	From one to five years	Less than one year

to master the requisite technologies. Great power sheriffs do not face a looming threat of proliferation at this stage because the nuclear program must still surmount numerous hurdles in nuclear fuel cycle development. Observable indicators range from countries with no nuclear infrastructure at all to more advanced programs that remain far away from mastering ENR technology.

The sweet spot for leveraging latency lies just beyond this initial stage in the middle of the capability continuum. Nuclear programs with medium levels of latency are on the cusp of being able to produce enough fissile material for atomic weapons. But they must still take additional steps to enrich uranium or reprocess plutonium at weapons-usable scale. Nuclear aspirants enter this zone when they acquire all the pieces needed to traverse down either the enrichment or reprocessing pathway. Scientists and engineers develop the skill set necessary to solve these technological puzzles. Some of this work could involve development of experimental facilities, such as hot cells for handling small quantities of plutonium. But the mere acquisition of hot cells alone would not push the nuclear program into the sweet spot—there would also need to be some larger plutonium-reprocessing capability close to coming online (along with a source of spent fuel). Similarly, on the uranium route, scientists often gain valuable experience from operating limited uranium gas centrifuge cascades. To move into the sweet spot, however, the enrichment program would need to use this knowledge to make tangible progress on building larger fuel enrichment plants. States leave the sweet spot by launching fissile material production campaigns at large ENR facilities. Technical signposts include clear efforts to master ENR technology at pilot plants with construction underway on larger facilities capable of producing significant quantities of fissile material.

At a high level of latency, nuclear programs can produce fissile material for atomic weapons on short notice. The clearest boundary separating this upper zone from the sweet spot is for a country to harvest enough highly enriched uranium (HEU) or plutonium to fuel the core of an atomic bomb—what analysts refer to as a "significant quantity" of fissile material. The IAEA (2002: 23) defines significant quantity values as 8 kilograms of plutonium and 25 kilograms of HEU (U-235 ≥ 20%). This metric is often unambiguous for the plutonium route, as industrial-scale reprocessing plants tend to produce more than a significant quantity of plutonium in a single campaign. But countries need not sit on a stockpile of weapons-usable material to acquire an advanced latent capability. This qualification is especially important for the uranium route because nuclear programs can also acquire enough nuclear material and enrichment capacity to be capable of producing a bomb's worth of material on short order. According to the IAEA (2002: 23), for example, a fuel enrichment plant that produced around 75 kilograms of low-enriched uranium (U-235 < 20%) would accumulate a significant quantity of indirect use fissile material, putting it in a prime position to rapidly enrich this LEU into enough weapons-grade HEU for a bomb. The indicators for this level of latency include either the production of significant quantities of HEU or plutonium at large ENR plants or the capacity to do so quickly. At this final stage of latency, the nuclear program may only be weeks or months away from the bomb.

Updating the Universe of Cases

With these conceptual containers in place, I specify how much latency each challenger in the universe of cases attempted to leverage. A recent study from Matthew Fuhrmann and Benjamin Tkach (2015: 446) provides a useful source for systematically measuring variation in nuclear latency because it identifies "all ENR facilities built in the world by thirty-two countries from

1939 to 2012." While this data set provides a strong empirical foundation, it only offers a binary measure of latency in terms of ENR plant development. Countries along the entire fissile material production continuum are all pooled together under the same general level of latent capability, regardless of whether they operated massive enrichment plants or just small plutonium laboratories. However, Fuhrmann and Tkach (2015: 446–47) recognize that "there is significant variation in the bomb-making capabilities of latent nuclear powers." In a series of appendices, they present the raw qualitative information used to identify ENR plants, including the scale and relative sophistication of fissile material assets in each host country. Table 2.3 uses this data as the basis to paint a more fine-grained picture of variation in latent nuclear capabilities among countries in the compellence case universe.

Four cases are added where the country lacked the ENR facilities necessary to be included in the Fuhrmann and Tkach data set, but still attempted to leverage latency. The final universe of cases in Table 2.3 contains nineteen total episodes with variation along the entire latency scale: six cases at low; seven cases at medium, the sweet spot; and six cases at high. This case universe exhibits full variation in terms of latent capabilities and compellence outcomes.

Managing Selection Issues

Nuclear aspirants are not chosen at random from a larger population of states. The subset of challengers who pursue compellence with nuclear latency is even more distinct. This nonrandom sample of cases raises two concerns about selection bias.

The first issue is whether countries who leverage latency enjoy attributes that make them better or worse at compellence for reasons beyond their respective nuclear programs. Many scholars contend that a state's material power, regime type, and security situation shape coercive outcomes. If challengers tend to be wealthy democracies in severe security environments, for example, then these characteristics may enhance the credibility of proliferation threats. Perhaps other nuclear aspirants avoid compellence because they lack the broader coercive attributes that would help them at the bargaining table. This selection effect would bias my results. If only a certain type of state attempts compellence, then the level of latency may not be doing much work in shaping coercive outcomes.

I address this problem by comparing the characteristics of states who leveraged latency to those that did not in the larger nuclear aspirant pool.

Table 2.3 Variation in Latency and Compellence Outcomes, 1956–2015

Country	Episode	Latency	Indicators	Outcome
France	1956–1957	High	Plutonium production and stockpile	Failure
Japan	1957–1960	Low	No ENR, but growing nuclear infrastructure	Failure
West Germany	1961–1963	Low	No ENR, but large nuclear energy complex	Failure
West Germany	1963–1966	Medium	Laboratory-scale ENR	Partial success
Japan	1964–1970	Medium	Laboratory ENR with industrial scale-up	Success
West Germany	1966–1969	Medium	ENR with large industrial scale-up	Success
Italy	1967–1969	Medium	Laboratory ENR capability	Success
Australia	1968	Low	No ENR capability	Failure
South Korea	1974–1975	Low	No ENR capability	Failure
Pakistan	1978–1979	High	Operational enrichment; HEU stockpile	Failure
South Africa	1977–1978	High	Industrial-scale enrichment; HEU stockpile	Failure
Romania	1985	Low	Plutonium hot cells; no other ENR capability	Failure
North Korea	1991–1994	Medium	Plutonium production capacity	Success
Libya	2003	Medium	Limited enrichment; no LEU stockpile	Success
Iran	2003–2005	Medium	Laboratory enrichment; no LEU stockpile	Partial success
North Korea	2002–2008	High	Full ENR; plutonium stockpile; weapons test	Failure
Iran	2009–2010	High	Enrichment plants; modest LEU stockpile	Failure
Iran	2013–2015	High	Enrichment plants; large LEU stockpile	Success
Saudi Arabia	2015	Low	No ENR; limited nuclear infrastructure	Failure

The overall universe of potential challengers includes all countries who developed some level of nuclear latency, even laboratory-scale hot cells or enrichment experiments.[24] Table 2.4 compares challengers to nonchallengers along several empirical dimensions: power as reflected by the Composite Index of National Capability (CINC) score, with values closer to 1

Table 2.4 State Characteristics of Challengers versus Nonchallengers

Country (challenger)	Compellence episode	Power (CINC)	Regime type (Polity)	Facing threat?
Australia	1968	0.003	10.0	No
France	1956–1957	0.033	8.0	Yes
Iran	2003–2005	0.013	−3.3	Yes
Iran	2009–2010	0.014	−7.0	Yes
Iran	2013–2015	0.015	−7.0	Yes
Italy	1967–1969	0.021	10.0	Yes
Japan	1957–1960	0.034	10.0	No
Japan	1964–1970	0.047	10.0	No
Libya	2003	0.002	−7.0	Yes
North Korea	1991–1994	0.013	−9.3	Yes
North Korea	2002–2008	0.013	−10.0	Yes
Pakistan	1978–1979	0.010	−7.0	Yes
Romania	1985	0.008	−8.0	No
Saudi Arabia	2015	0.017	−10.0	Yes
South Africa	1977–1978	0.007	4.0	No
South Korea	1974–1975	0.010	−8.0	Yes
West Germany	1961–1963	0.040	10.0	Yes
West Germany	1963–1966	0.039	10.0	Yes
West Germany	1966–1969	0.036	10.0	Yes

Country (nonchallenger)	ENR plant operation	Power (CINC)	Regime type (Polity)	Facing threat?
Algeria	1992–2012	0.004	−1.4	No
Argentina	1983–1989	0.006	7.9	No
Belgium	1966–1974	0.007	9.6	Yes
Brazil	1979–2012	0.025	5.9	No
Canada	1944–1976	0.013	10.0	No
Canada	1990–1993	0.012	10.0	No
China	1960–1964	0.109	−8.0	No
Czechia	1977–1998	0.007	−0.2	Yes/No
Egypt	1982–2012	0.009	−5.2	Yes/No
India	1964–1973	0.052	7.1	No
Iraq	1983–1991	0.010	−9.0	Yes
The Netherlands	1973–2012	0.006	10.0	Yes/No
Norway	1961–1968	0.001	10.0	Yes
South Korea	1979–1982	0.014	−6.5	Yes
South Korea	1997–2012	0.023	7.9	No
Sweden	1954–1972	0.004	10.0	Yes
Taiwan	1976–1978	0.006	−7.0	Yes
UK	1952	0.049	10.0	Yes
Yugoslavia	1954–1978	0.006	−7.0	Yes

representing a greater systemic share of material capabilities; as well as regime type as captured by the Polity Score, ranging from "autocracies" (−10) to "democracies" (+10).[25] I take the average of the CINC and Polity scores across every year of each discrete compellence episode for the challengers; or the period of ENR plant operation for the nonchallengers. I also conduct an informal assessment of the security environment by considering whether each state faced a conventionally superior proximate offensive threat.[26]

The summary of state characteristics in Table 2.4 shows that challengers exhibit variation similar to that of nonchallengers across all three variables. Regime type reflects an even split in both sample pools—autocracies and democracies are equally likely to select or avoid compellence with nuclear latency. National material capabilities also seem to vary for challengers and nonchallengers. However, most challengers have between 1% and 5% of global material capabilities when they select compellence; only four episodes involve challengers with less than a 1% share. But nonchallengers exhibit another even split, with nine possessing more than 1% and ten possessing less than 1% of material capabilities in the international system. Finally, many challengers and nonchallengers face severe security threats, but some do not. Taken together, these results indicate that challengers are roughly the same as nonchallengers across three state characteristics that shape coercive outcomes.

The second selection issue concerns whether states at lower or higher latency stages are systematically different in ways that could bias the results. States with low levels of latency may be more likely to receive preemptive concessions from sheriffs without making observable compellent demands. Because such demands are a defining feature of compellence, these states never make it into the case universe. Low amounts of latency could therefore be generating noncoercive benefits for these states as sheriffs induce them away from the bomb. Perhaps less latency is more when it comes to soliciting rewards from great powers. Unfortunately, this question is difficult to adjudicate, as scholars of nuclear latency offer mixed and contradictory empirical results. From a theoretical perspective, however, this trend would be compatible with my argument. Sheriffs face incentives to "buy out" the fissile material aspirations of states with fledging nuclear programs before they attain more bargaining leverage in the sweet spot. These inducements are likely to be less valuable compared to what the state might extract by making explicit compellent demands. As I discuss in the final chapter, it makes sense for the United States and other sheriffs to proactively "buy out" many nuclear aspirants at lower levels of latency, especially allies and partners. This could also be one reason why compellence with nuclear latency is so rare. Some states may be more likely to receive offers they cannot refuse as they start pursuing enrichment or reprocessing technology.

This issue extends to states who attain higher levels of latency. Compellence may be prone to fail because sheriffs had no interest in providing concessions to these states at earlier nuclear development stages. Adversaries could be especially likely to end up in this position, as sheriffs may be more comfortable with "buying out" nuclear ambitions of allies and partners. This driver of bargaining failure would overpower the threat-assurance trade-off. But my research design can manage this potential source of bias by selecting a mix of adversaries and allies that exhibit within-case variation in nuclear latency over time. In the book's conclusion, I look back over the empirical results, and consider the degree to which sheriffs let countries progress to high levels of latency instead of making concessions to them.

Research Design and Case Selection

This book employs a comparative research design to achieve three modest empirical goals (George and Bennett 2005: 75). The first is a plausibility probe to demonstrate that the mechanisms at the core of my theory—notably the threat-assurance trade-off and the bargaining tactics—shape compellence outcomes. A key evidentiary problem here is equifinality, as other factors undoubtedly influence dynamics between nuclear aspirants and great powers. I manage this issue by attempting to falsify the mechanisms with hard cases where nuclear latency should have had little to no effect relative to more pronounced factors, such as the political relationship or balance of power. If the evidence suggests that the mechanisms still exert an observable influence, then these results would partially validate my theoretical framework.

The second goal is to conduct a limited correlational test of the relationship between nuclear latency and compellence outcomes. Given the small number of episodes, a most-similar approach to comparative case selection is employed to control for other variables and isolate how variation in latent nuclear capabilities shapes bargaining dynamics. Specifically, I test the hypotheses from my theory against alternative arguments by selecting countries that move along the latency continuum while attempting to wrest concessions from sheriffs. If the Goldilocks principle is correct, then the success rate of compellence should resemble a bell curve over the latent capability scale—failure at low levels; success in the middle sweet spot; and then back to failure and ruinous Pyrrhic victories at high levels. Fortunately, the universe of cases contains multiple countries who marched up the latency scale across discreet compellence episodes.

The third goal is to confirm where the boundaries of the sweet spot lie in actual nuclear programs. I use the case studies in a heuristic manner to see if fissile material production capacity remains the core pillar of latent nuclear power amid eras of technological and political flux. To gain analytic leverage over this issue, I employ a least-similar method to select a diverse mix of countries over time. This enables me to determine whether the technical signposts around the sweet spot remain constant despite variation among all other attributes (e.g., nuclear aspirant's proliferation strategy, regime type, or political relationship with the sheriff) and structural conditions (e.g., the evolution of the nonproliferation regime or systemic shifts in polarity).

I select four countries with multiple subcases to advance these research goals (Gerring 2004). Japan used its nuclear energy program as a bargaining chip in negotiations with the United States (1957–1960; 1964–1970). Two features of this case make it attractive for evaluating my theory. First, Japan was an ally hedger marching up the latency continuum for peaceful purposes at the time. Japanese leaders also faced formidable barriers to threatening proliferation from elite stakeholders and public constituents who opposed nuclear weapons. This makes Japan a useful case for examining how an ally with strong motives to forgo the bomb can still leverage latency by making implicit threats and entangling nonproliferation promises with other issues. Second, Japan provides an ideal longitudinal study of the relationship between latency and compellence outcomes. The Japanese nuclear program remained at a low level of latency during the first episode (1957–1960). But then it rapidly developed the capacity to produce fissile material over the next decade. Japan glided into the sweet spot with a medium level of latency for the second episode (1964–1970). As a result, these twin cases provide a useful comparison for tracing out how variation in latency shaped the effectiveness of Japan's bargaining tactics over time.

West Germany provides another controlled comparison, as the prospect of Bonn building the bomb hung over Washington and Moscow during the 1960s. At the time, West Germany used its civil nuclear program to hedge against American abandonment and Soviet revanchism. But West German leaders also leveraged latency against both the United States and Soviet Union over several distinct issues throughout the decade (1961–1963; 1963–1966; 1963–1969). These three episodes provide several analytic benefits. First, Bonn exploited the fear of the German bomb to put pressure on both Washington *and* Moscow. The stakes of this gambit were quite high. West German leaders had to carefully apply pressure in private discussions to avoid escalating tensions between the United States and Soviet Union. Second, West Germany exhibits variation in nuclear latency across the three episodes. At a low level of latency (1961–1963), Bonn attempted to shore up US security commitments and resolve several issues with Moscow. In the second episode (1966–1969), West Germany focused on securing German participation in North Atlantic Treaty Organization nuclear sharing arrangements at a medium level of latency. The Federal Republic remained in the sweet spot for the third episode (1966–1969), when Bonn pushed back against the superpower fait accompli over the Treaty on the Non-Proliferation of Nuclear Weapons, demanding core changes to the treaty and additional assurances from the Americans. These latter episodes enable me to investigate how modest amounts of latency influenced West Germany's bargaining leverage over distinct diplomatic issues, while holding most other factors constant.

Decades later, North Korea pursued compellence with nuclear latency against the United States on several occasions (1991–1994; 2002–2008). Three features of the North Korean case make it useful for evaluating the Goldilocks principle. First, North Korea was pursuing a mixed proliferation strategy when the end of the Cold War drove Pyongyang to fall back on compellence with nuclear latency. The Soviet Union sheltered the North Koreans as they developed an indigenous plutonium production capability at the Yongbyon nuclear research complex. Pyongyang also hid the most sensitive aspects of this nuclear program from international inspectors. Second, the implosion of the Soviet Union pulled North Korea into confrontation with the United States over the budding weapons-production capability at Yongbyon. Although Washington launched the initial diplomatic salvo, Pyongyang quickly figured out how to blackmail the United States with the threat of proliferation. The explicit nature of North Korea's mobilization and brinkmanship campaigns should make it easy to determine how these bargaining tactics shaped the threat-assurance dilemma. Third, and most important, the level of latency in North Korea dramatically increased across two discrete compellence episodes. Pyongyang was in the fissile material sweet spot during the first nuclear crisis (1991 1994). During the second nuclear crisis (2002–2008), however, North Korea acquired a high level of latency and marched across the weaponization threshold. This variation in nuclear latency enables me to test the core Goldilocks hypotheses against alternative accounts.

Finally, Iran leveraged latency multiple times after the exposure of its covert nuclear program (2003–2006; 2009–2010; 2013–2015). I select this case for two reasons. First, Iran hid its nuclear program for years before the exposure of large sensitive facilities led it to adopt a safer hedge posture. Unlike North Korea, however, strategic decision-making in Tehran was not entirely opaque to the outside world. This makes Iran a useful case for investigating the internal deliberations around nuclear policy that occurred in the aftermath of exposure and later as the country adopted a compellence strategy. Second, Iran's march up the latency continuum makes it one of the hardest tests possible for the Goldilocks principle. Tehran should have been able to cut a deal given the modest amount of enrichment capability it possessed upon exposure in 2002. Moreover, the steady increase in fissile material capacity after 2006 should have created costly barriers to making credible nonproliferation assurances. Yet the apparent success of diplomacy in 2015 with the well-known Iran nuclear deal seems to cut against the grain of the Goldilocks hypotheses. I delve into this case in an attempt to falsify my theory.

What type of evidence would confirm my theory across all four cases? I organize each chapter to first check my assumptions about why states leverage latency against great powers. I assume countries do not develop nuclear programs just to gain bargaining chips, so there should be indicators of other economic and security factors at play. In general, I expect to find evidence that hedgers pursue a more implicit form of compellence after developing nuclear programs in plain sight. By contrast, hiders should only resort to a more explicit compellence strategy in the wake of nuclear exposure.

The focus of each chapter then shifts to tracing out how variation in nuclear latency shapes the threat-assurance dilemma and discrete bargaining outcomes. Evidence of proliferation threats lacking credibility at low levels of latency would partially support my theory. Indications of challengers being readily able to make threats and assurances credible in the fissile material sweet spot would help confirm the Goldilocks principle. But the critical body of evidence concerns the trade-off between credible threats and assurances at high levels of latency. If the case studies show that marching to the cusp of the bomb makes it relatively more costly and difficult for challengers to promise nuclear restraint, such evidence would lend strong support for my theory relative to the maximalist position.

3

Japan

In 1956, Japan launched its nuclear energy program with assistance from the United States under the Atoms for Peace initiative. The allure of energy independence and economic prosperity drove Tokyo to make foundational investments in nuclear technology during the 1950s and 1960s. Japan wanted to wean itself from foreign sources of energy by mastering the nuclear fuel cycle, especially the capacity to reprocess plutonium from spent reactor fuel. Advanced reactors were also being developed that promised to produce more plutonium than they consumed. Japanese political leaders and industrial stakeholders jumped at this opportunity to create a stable supply of fuel for commercial nuclear power plants. Japan began to build an extensive civil nuclear enterprise in plain sight, embedding it within a restrictive web of bilateral supplier contracts.

Despite developing the nuclear program for peaceful purposes, Japanese leaders leveraged latency against the United States on several occasions. Table 3.1 summarizes each case I analyze in this chapter along with the outcomes expected by the theory. In the first episode (1957–1960), Tokyo wanted to shore up US defense commitments and wrest back control of Western Pacific islands from Washington—the small Bonin archipelago and the larger Ryukyu chain of islands, including Okinawa. The first episode occurred soon after the genesis of Japan's nuclear program. At a low level of latency, leaders in Tokyo suggested that Japan might reconsider its nuclear options in 1957. These remarks coincided with contentious negotiations over the Western Pacific islands and the American alliance architecture more broadly. But the diplomatic effort ended in failure. US officials roundly rejected requests from Japanese leaders to return the islands and alter the security pact.

However, the second attempt to elicit these concessions proved to be far more successful (1964–1970). The Japanese nuclear energy program developed the capacity to produce fissile material during this period. Washington worried that Tokyo would keep its nuclear options open indefinitely, perhaps even setting the foundation to build the bomb later. Japanese leaders took advantage of these concerns. Prime Minister Satō Eisaku led a quiet

Leveraging Latency. Tristan A. Volpe, Oxford University Press. © Oxford University Press 2023.
DOI: 10.1093/oso/9780197669532.003.0003

Table 3.1 Compellence Cases by Japan

Episode (dates)	Latency	Target	Demands	Expected outcome
Security pact crisis (1957–1960)	Low	United States (ally)	Japanese leaders requested major changes to the existing US security treaty with Japan. They also demanded that the United States relinquish administrative rights over the Ryukyu and Bonin Islands.	Failure
Satō's Okinawa gambit (1964–1970)	Medium	United States (ally)	Japan again issued demands for stronger security commitments and the reversion of the Western Pacific islands. Specifically, Prime Minister Satō requested an explicit extended nuclear deterrent commitment from Washington and the return of Okinawa without US nuclear weapons.	Success

campaign that relied on subtle bargaining tactics, such as hinting at future weapons aspirations and then delaying accession to the Treaty on the Non-Proliferation of Nuclear Weapons (NPT). In tandem, Tokyo sent clear signals that it would forgo the bomb once Washington strengthened security guarantees and returned the Western Pacific islands. The United States ultimately met these demands, extending the US nuclear umbrella and reverting the Bonin and Ryukyu Islands to Japan.

The compellence cases are important to study for two reasons. First, Japan provides a useful longitudinal study of the relationship between latency and compellence outcomes. The Japanese nuclear energy program was at a low level of latency during the first episode (1957–1960), but soon moved into the sweet spot for the second episode (1964–1970). Although the United States grew more opposed to ally proliferation during the 1960s, many of the core issues at stake in the alliance negotiations remained the same. This allows me to examine how variation in latency shaped the effectiveness of Japan's bargaining tactics over time. Second, Japan demonstrates how an ally can leverage an ostensibly peaceful nuclear energy enterprise to wrest concessions from its great power patron. Many scholars, notably Vipin Narang (2016: 128) and Ariel Levite (2003: 71), consider Japan to be the most "salient" or "quintessential" example of a nuclear hedger.[1] This chapter finds that hedging can present leaders with a prime opportunity to make implicit proliferation threats in alliance consultations. As I discuss in the conclusion, however, the threat-assurance trade-off casts doubt on the contemporary efficacy of this strategy for Japan beyond the 1960s.

This chapter examines how variation in nuclear latency shaped the effectiveness of Japan's nuclear gambits from 1957 to 1970. The first part of the chapter briefly assesses the failed attempt by Japanese leaders to renegotiate the US security pact in 1957–1960. The second part unpacks Satō's effort in 1964–1970 to entangle Japan's nonproliferation promises with the negotiations over US extended deterrence and the reversion of Okinawa. As Japan moved into the fissile material sweet spot, Satō found that he could make implicit threats and withhold assurances to gain leverage in negotiations over the alliance. The final part of the chapter uses this evidence to evaluate the book's hypotheses.

The Security Pact Crisis, 1957–1960: Low Latency

In 1957, the first major crisis in the alliance between Japan and the United States emerged over defense commitments and the Ryukyu Islands. I examine this episode in two sections. The first reviews the genesis of the alliance to identify the fault lines in the relationship. The second section focuses on the negotiations over the US-Japan security pact that lasted from 1957 until 1960. This episode sets a baseline to explore how the subsequent growth of Japan's nuclear energy program shaped negotiations over the same set of issues less than five years later.

Origins and Fault Lines, 1951–1957

The US-Japan alliance originated as a means for former combatants to pursue a common set of interests. In the aftermath of the Second World War, Japan remained under occupational control by the United States until 1951. The terms of surrender required Japan to disband its military forces and rely on the United States for protection against external threats. During this time, Japan needed extensive American assistance to rebuild the country. Elites in Washington and postwar Tokyo wanted to rebuild Japan as a liberal democratic mercantile hub in East Asia. Despite Tokyo's considerable dependence on Washington, a common set of interests and the strategic value of Japan created a strong foundation for the alliance.[2]

Beyond this shared ground lay several conflicting issues that came to the fore during discussions over the postoccupation treaty alliance in the summer of 1951. When Prime Minister Shigeru Yoshida sat down with John Foster Dulles to finalize the return of sovereign administration, both sides agreed that a tight nexus between the American security umbrella and Japanese economic growth constituted the core of the alliance. Japan would remain dependent on US forces for its defense. Yoshida believed this would free up resources for Japan to invest in economic growth.[3] However, Dulles insisted on retaining territorial control over the Ryukyu and Bonin Islands in the Western Pacific. The United States had acquired these islands at great cost during the war. Most important, a critical military base now sat on Okinawa. Dulles ended up giving "an important sop to Yoshida by holding the bases but recognizing Japan's 'residual sovereignty' in the islands," according to Walter LaFeber (1998: 290). This symbolic phrase allowed the United States to maintain control over the islands indefinitely. Yoshida also preferred Washington continue to shoulder the defense burden. But Dulles signaled that Japan needed to rearm and contribute to its defense at some point in the future. Although Yoshida and Dulles were able to reach a compromise and sign a formal treaty in September 1951, territorial control of the Western Pacific islands and defense burden sharing became fault lines in the alliance.

Tumult over Treaty Renewal, 1957–1960

The first crisis in the alliance emerged over these issues several years later. According to the provisions laid out by Yoshida and Dulles, the US-Japan Security Treaty had to be renewed by 1960. Trouble started to brew in 1957 when Prime Minister Kishi Nobusuke assumed office and passed the American ambassador in Tokyo a list of Japanese stipulations for renewal. The prime minister requested the return of Okinawa and the Bonin Islands to Japanese control and sought greater independence from American foreign policy.[4] LaFeber (1998: 316) argues that Kishi "wanted a new understanding of the entire issue of security." These demands stemmed from two problems. First, vocal segments of the Japanese public and political elite viewed the occupation of the Western Pacific islands as intolerable subordination. Second,

Eisenhower's New Look defense policy raised the prospect that Tokyo might be entrapped in a nuclear conflict with the Soviet Union. Under the New Look reorientation, the United States reduced its troop footprint in Japan and left behind an overwhelming contingent of air force personnel. If a conflict escalated to nuclear exchange, this force ratio signaled to the Japanese that the United States would use their local bases to wage such a war against the Soviet eastern flank. Kishi set out in 1957 to solve these problems by renegotiating terms of the alliance.

With support from former premier Yoshida, Kishi then suggested that Japan might pursue an independent nuclear deterrent capability. In January 1957, Yoshida laid out the case for Japan to acquire nuclear weapons as an option to counter entrapment scenarios from the American New Look defense reorientation (Welfield 1988: 110–11, 157). At a Diet committee meeting soon after, Kishi modified his past stance against Japan acquiring nuclear weapons. According to a cable from the US ambassador in Tokyo, Kishi "testified that the Japanese constitution does not bar possession of nuclear weapons 'for defensive purposes. . . . In view of progress of science, we must have effective power to carry out modern warfare within scope self-defense.'"[5] The cable went on to emphasize that Kishi "assured Diet committee he had no intention of arming Self-Defense Forces with nuclear weapons or reversing opposition to US stationing of nuclear units in Japan."[6] The remarks signaled that proliferation could be legal under Article IX of Japan's constitution, which permitted the buildup of military force only for defensive purposes. Some historians, notably Walter LaFeber (1998) and John Welfield (1988), view this implicit threat of proliferation as being part of a deliberate gambit. However, there is insufficient evidence in the archival record to determine if Kishi was using the prospect of Japanese proliferation strategically to underwrite his demands. We only know that his remarks coincided with the start of a campaign to change the security relationship with the United States and resolve territorial problems relating to the Ryukyu and Bonin Islands.

The Yoshida-Kishi threat resonated within the US intelligence community. In one of the earliest National Intelligence Estimates on nuclear proliferation, American analysts interpreted the remarks as an indicator that Japan might launch a nuclear weapons program. The estimate determined that "Japan's defense planners and a small but influential conservative elite view domestic production of nuclear weapons as essential to Japan's defense and to the establishment of Japan as a leading power in Asia. These views have been circulated in the Diet and are probably supported by Prime Minister Kishi."[7] Given the strong domestic opposition to nuclear weapons in Japan, however, the analysis surmised that "the Japanese government will probably take the initiative in building public support for nuclear weapons production," most likely under the guise of work being done on peaceful uses of nuclear technology.[8] "Thus the chances now appear at least even that Japan will undertake the initial steps in a nuclear weapons production program within five years," the estimate concluded.[9] Elite chatter in Tokyo about the legality of producing nuclear weapons thereby led US intelligence analysts to overestimate Japan's proclivity for the bomb.

The deeper problem was that diplomatic maneuvering based on Japan's nuclear options rested on an empty technical foundation. The country had no nuclear fuel cycle technology at all. Even under the most permissive conditions, the US intelligence community estimated that it would take almost ten years for Japan to produce nuclear weapons.[10] Japan started its nuclear energy program in 1956 with the backing of the United States. It was almost entirely dependent on foreign assistance when Yoshida and Kishi attempted to strengthen their position. Washington exerted too much control through technology transfers and uranium fuel supply at this stage. If the United States cut off assistance and pressured other foreign suppliers to follow suit, Japan would be left with a stillborn nuclear energy project (Gilinsky and Langer 1967: 1–4, 15–26). In this sense, the United States could essentially thwart Japan from proliferating for a long period of time. As a result, Japan did not have the nuclear latency necessary to send credible signals in the late 1950s. Yoshida and Kishi made the untimely decision to flirt with the bomb when other states could still deny Japan the ability to realize this option.

The distant prospect of Japan going nuclear did little to sway the political leadership in Washington. Kishi visited the White House on June 19 to present his demands about the Western Pacific islands and bargain over the renewal of the security pact. In a preparatory position paper for President Eisenhower, Secretary of State Dulles underscored that "this is not the time to renegotiate any of the specific provisions of the present Treaty. . . . The United States cannot relinquish administrative rights over these islands so long as the threat and tension in the Far East continue."[11] Dulles and other senior US officials seemed to brush off the allegation from the intelligence community that there was an "even" chance of Japanese proliferation—no mention of it appears in the available archival record.[12] Given Eisenhower's infamously sanguine views on ally proliferation, it is also possible that this alarm bell from Langley failed to rouse the White House.[13] Japan was simply too far away from the bomb for the issue to put pressure on a president with rather weak nuclear nonproliferation preferences.

Eisenhower stonewalled Kishi at their meeting on June 18. The prime minister raised the "territorial problems" with the Western Pacific islands, noting that the Japanese people did not understand "why there is a need for the United States to hold political and administrative power in Okinawa just because it is a military base."[14] The president underscored that the US military needed "to be able to react swiftly in the event of attack without interference. But we will talk over this problem and try to be helpful."[15] Kishi tried again with Dulles the next day, asking "for the return of such territories as have always been Japanese."[16] The response from Dulles was unequivocal: "We do not see any possibility of relinquishing control in Okinawa because our responsibilities for the defense of Japan, ourselves and other free nations."[17] Upon his return to Japan, the prime minister started to lose domestic support and faced electoral challenges in the Japanese Diet. Eisenhower seized on this weakness in October 1958. American officials gave Kishi "a new draft treaty little changed from the 1952 pact," LaFeber (1998: 318) finds. The draft did contain more explicit promises from the United States to defend Japan. But this security commitment came with a catch: the US military needed to use its bases on the Western Pacific islands to meet this obligation.

The Japanese public responded to this draft treaty with a series of riots and protests over the next few years. In January 1960, Kishi flew to Washington to sign the treaty. According to LaFeber (1998: 319–20), "The 1960 treaty, unlike the old, explicitly committed the United States to defend Japan, and to consult with the Japanese before putting forces into action under the pact's provisions." However, Kishi had not obtained any concessions over the Western Pacific islands or the future of economic contributions to the alliance. As US assistant secretary of state Graham Parsons privately bragged to the British, the 1960 treaty "gave Washington everything it wanted."[18] Premier Kishi's inability to bargain with the United States for a more equitable alliance treaty and the ensuing domestic unrest in Japan ended his political career.

The first alliance crisis between Japan and the United States establishes a useful analytic baseline. The allies negotiated over a set of issues—Okinawa and defense commitments—that would re-emerge several years later. In addition, the asymmetric nature of the alliance relationship carried over into the 1960s. Although Japan's economy grew at a rapid clip, Tokyo remained highly dependent on Washington for security support and economic trade. Finally, Japanese leaders failed to gain any leverage from toying with the notion of an independent nuclear deterrent. The episode therefore sets the foundation to explore how future increases in latency shaped Japan's bargaining strategy toward the United States. But one key qualification is in order: the United States would become increasingly opposed to ally proliferation after Eisenhower left office. This factor arguably made it easier for the next generation of Japanese leaders to leverage latency against Washington.

Satō's Subtle Nuclear Gambit, 1964–1970: Medium Latency

In November 1964, Satō Eisaku assumed leadership of the Liberal Democratic Party (LDP). As prime minister, he set out to strengthen the relationship with the United States while securing the return of the Western Pacific islands.[19] In contrast to his predecessors, however, Satō inherited a medium level of latency from Japan's nuclear energy program. He leveraged this growing capacity to build the bomb as a bargaining chip over six stages of negotiations with US officials from 1964 until 1970.

Nuclear Drivers and Political Barriers in Japan, 1964

Satō became prime minister just as Japan's nuclear energy program began developing the capacity to produce fissile material, albeit for peaceful purposes. In the early 1960s, "Japanese officials strongly felt it imperative that Japan establish its own nuclear fuel cycle in order not to depend heavily on foreign resources and services for its nuclear power production," Akira Kurosaki (2017: 60) argues. By mastering the back end of the fuel cycle, Japanese leaders hoped to offset the lack of substantial uranium reserves in the country. To this end, Japan initially focused on developing several types of plutonium production and fast breeder reactors, along with reprocessing technology.

By 1964, Japan had made significant progress in developing its civil nuclear enterprise. In November, the Office of Scientific Intelligence at the Central Intelligence Agency provided a detailed study on the state of Japan's nuclear fuel cycle capabilities.[20] Construction was underway at the Tokai-mura nuclear energy complex on a British-supplied Calder Hall–type graphite moderated reactor. Once completed, this nuclear power plant would be capable of producing electricity and large amounts of plutonium from natural uranium fuel. Japan's first indigenous heavy-water moderated research reactor went critical in 1962; seven other research reactors came online with foreign assistance between 1961 and 1964. Tokyo was also supporting research on advanced fast breeder reactors and planning to build another large nuclear power plant based on the US light-water-type reactor. Thousands of Japanese nuclear physicists and engineers had been trained to operate and build nuclear power plants as part of ambitious plan to expand atomic energy production.

On the back end of the fuel cycle, the US intelligence report underscored that Japanese scientists had separated small amounts of plutonium in laboratory experiments to study its peaceful uses in fast breeder reactors. One of the key industry stakeholders, the Japan Atomic Fuel Cooperation, solicited bids from foreign suppliers to accelerate the construction of a reprocessing plant at Tokai-mura, eventually choosing a French vendor in 1964. This commercial-scale plant was expected to be capable of processing almost one ton of spent fuel per day. Japan was also developing the front end of the fuel cycle, building uranium refinement and fuel fabrication facilities, as well as researching enrichment techniques. With financial support from Tokyo, the Japanese nuclear industry was rapidly marching up the latency continuum. But the November 1964 study emphasized that Japan had so far only developed nuclear technology for peaceful purposes.

In contrast to Kishi's tenure, Japanese leaders now faced strong incentives to avoid any indication that they were interested in atomic weapons. On the international front, Japan's postwar rise as a mercantile state made nuclear armament unattractive for the government in Tokyo. Foreign trade enabled the Japanese economy to grow at a rapid clip in the 1960s. This prosperity ushered in an era of political dominance for Satō and his ruling LDP. But political survival thereby came to rest on keeping the Japanese export juggernaut in motion. Building atomic weapons might have imperiled this economic strategy, triggering sanctions or even trade embargoes from nations worried about a nuclear-armed Japan.[21]

The civil nuclear program in Japan also relied on foreign firms to supply assistance and materials. Beyond help from British and French nuclear firms to build the Tokai-mura nuclear power plant and reprocessing plant, Japan had to import most of its uranium and heavy water from Canada and the

United States. The 1964 CIA report emphasized that these suppliers required Japan to accept safeguards over virtually its entire nuclear fuel cycle at the time. For example, under the terms of the 1958 US-Japan nuclear cooperation agreement, Washington could exercise veto power over Japanese plans to reprocess spent fuel of US origin. If Tokyo violated these agreements to jump-start a military program, the Japanese nuclear enterprise would likely be cut off from critical foreign vendors. Japan's dependence on uranium fuel made proliferation an existential threat to the commercial viability of the nuclear power industry.

On the domestic front, elite empowerment and public opposition to atomic weapons further curtailed Satō's nuclear options. By the mid-1960s, Japan's nuclear energy program was being driven forward by a powerful constellation of actors. This group consisted of bureaucratic institutions with control over government resources, the electric power and nuclear manufacturing industries, as well as scientific research centers. Kurosaki (2017: 51) finds that, despite parochial policy differences, these elites all "shared a professional interest in continuing civilian nuclear energy development." Moreover, the stakeholders started to gain autonomy from Tokyo, creating "a 'sub government' in the civilian nuclear-power field" (Kurosaki 2017: 51). Any attempt from Tokyo to leverage latency for military purposes would be met with considerable resistance from the elite stewards of Japan's nuclear energy program.

As the only population to suffer nuclear bombardment, the Japanese public was firmly opposed to the military uses of nuclear technology. Despite concerns about nuclear fallout in the aftermath of the 1954 Daigo Fukuryū Maru accident, popular support grew for the civil nuclear energy program, given its economic potential. This prevailing sentiment was codified in the 1955 Atomic Energy Basic Law, which limited Japan's nuclear energy program to peaceful purposes and prohibited any military applications. Japan's so-called nuclear allergy remained strong in the early 1960s, creating an electoral bulwark against atomic weapons (Mochizuki 2007). Public opinion was so opposed to the bomb that the Japanese government had not even formalized the role of US extended nuclear deterrence in the alliance when Satō came into power in 1964 (Hoey 2016a; Kurosaki 2020). Any leader who espoused arming Japan with its own atomic weapons would face considerable resistance from the public electorate in Japan.

These barriers to the bomb made it difficult for Japanese leaders to leverage latency in an explicit manner. Japan already seemed committed to

nuclear restraint when Satō took the reins in November 1964. Public proliferation threats or overt mobilization campaigns were likely to trigger costly
blowback from other nations, elite stakeholders, and the general public. But
Tokyo could still play the nuclear card against Washington by making implicit threats to reconsider arming Japan with nuclear weapons down the
road. The key was to carefully exploit American concerns about the future
of Japan's nonproliferation policy, sending signals in private and linking the
nuclear issue to deeper problems in the alliance.

Satō's First Summit in Washington, January 1965

In December 1964, Satō seized an opportunity to set this strategy in motion. Washington had recently become worried that Tokyo might reconsider
its nuclear options for two reasons. First, US officials believed that China's
nuclear test in October 1964 could tip other nuclear dominoes around the
world, perhaps starting in East Asia with Japan (Miller 2014a). Tokyo now
had a real reason to toy with idea of building the bomb. Second, Washington
feared that the political barriers to proliferation in Japan might erode in the
years ahead. This prospect was alarming because Japan's civil nuclear enterprise would soon be capable of building atomic weapons. On December 12,
a background paper on proliferation trends from the State Department wove
together both concerns:

> [Japan] has the industrial plant, technological capacity, and economic
> base to create a deliverable nuclear *force*, probably comparable to any in
> the world except those of the United States and the Soviet Union. . . . The
> principal obstacles now apparent to such a course are all subject to change.
> If only because of its formidable potential if it should decide to enter the
> nuclear weapons field, Japan *should* be closely watched and more carefully
> treated over the next several years.[22]

The report estimated that Japanese leaders were likely to continue relying on
the US nuclear umbrella in the immediate aftermath of China's nuclear test.
However, it went on to anticipate that there would "also be some fairly strong
support for the creation by Japan of a nuclear deterrent of its own."[23] The
extent of this support, officials at the State Department argued, would depend on the credibility of US security commitments, as well as "the degree

of satisfaction (or, conversely, of frustration) which Japan is deriving at that time from its over-all relationship with the United States."[24] Indeed, both factors would soon become central in negotiations over the future of the US-Japan alliance.

Satō appears to have taken advantage of American concerns about proliferation in two ways. First, after becoming prime minister in November, he quickly pressed US ambassador Edwin Reischauer to schedule a summit with President Lyndon Johnson in Washington, citing China's nuclear test as one reason why the two leaders needed to meet as soon as possible (Hoey 2015: 8). Second, once the summit was scheduled for mid-January, Satō appears to have led a quiet campaign to sow doubt about Japan's future nuclear options. "According to intelligence reports," a senior technical adviser from the US Arms Control and Disarmament Agency noted on December 31, "Prime Minister Satō and other leaders of the dominant LDP Party have been privately urging that Japan soon undertake a crash program to develop nuclear weapons."[25] Beyond these internal deliberations, Satō sent clear signals in his meetings with US officials. On December 29, "Satō privately told U.S. Ambassador Reischauer that Japan could easily build such weapons, and that the Japanese public would have to be educated to accept them."[26] In the lead-up to the summit, Satō drove this point home again on January 4, telling the ambassador that the nuclear threat from China made it "only common sense for Japan to have nuclear weapons."[27]

The stage was set for Satō to play the Japanese nuclear card in the upcoming summit at the White House. Specifically, Japan needed leverage to firm up the US extended nuclear deterrent commitment. "Satō wished to keep his options open," Fintan Hoey (2015: 9) argues, so he "manoeuvred to induce the United States to provide a nuclear umbrella while keeping the alternative of developing an independent deterrent further down the road." Ayako Kusunoki (2008: 31) concurs, pointing out that Satō "hinted at ambitions of nuclearization, but he knew beforehand that Washington would react unfavorably to such desires. . . . Instead, his talk of such may have been an effort to get an ironclad American guarantee of protection from external threats." US officials also anticipated that Satō would at least float the idea of restoring territorial control of the Western Pacific islands to Japan.[28] By keeping the nuclear chatter private, Satō started to walk a fine line between making veiled proliferation threats while still keeping Japan ostensibly committed to the peaceful uses of nuclear technology.

The summit discussions in Washington from January 11 to 13 validated Satō's initial approach to alliance diplomacy. At the main morning meeting with President Johnson on January 12, Satō underscored that one of the "greatest problems" centered around China, especially given Japan's lack of nuclear weapons.[29] He asked Johnson "whether the United States would come to Japan's assistance under the [security] Treaty in the event of nuclear, no less than conventional, attack on Japan."[30] Johnson confirmed that Japan would be covered under the US nuclear umbrella, in part because he "did not want to increase the number of nuclear powers."[31] The president underscored that "if Japan needs our nuclear deterrent for its defense, the United States would stand by its commitments and provide that defense."[32] Extracting this explicit extended nuclear deterrent commitment from Johnson appears to have been one of Satō's principal goals in the talks. Later in the day, the prime minister told Secretary of State Dean Rusk that he was "fully assured" by the president's guarantee.[33] According to Hoey (2015: 11), returning to Japan with this ironclad nuclear commitment from Johnson was "a signal achievement" for Satō.

After securing the US nuclear umbrella, Satō raised the status of the Western Pacific islands in an afternoon discussion on foreign policy issues. The prime minister acknowledged that the US military installations on Okinawa were necessary to shield Japan from potential threats. "Due to U.S. commitments under the U.S.-Japan Security Treaty," Satō explained, "the Chinese Communist nuclear explosion had not had great impact in Japan."[34] However, he underscored a major problem with the current arrangement: the vast majority of Japanese people "ardently" aspired to reclaim sovereignty over the islands. "It had been twenty years since the U.S. assumed control there," Satō told Johnson. "He was sure that the President understood what the feelings of the people of Okinawa and Japan on this matter are."[35]

The prime minister then linked reversion to the viability of US defense commitments. Returning the islands, Satō claimed, "would enable the United States to carry out its security mission more effectively."[36] Rusk pushed Satō to clarify this link, asking him to what extent China's nuclear test had changed public perception of the alliance, notably over the US military presence on Okinawa. Satō responded that most Japanese people continued to support the US-Japan Security Treaty and oppose nuclear weapons. "Although he could see why it might be argued that if China has nuclear weapons, Japan should also," the prime minister added, "this was not Japan's policy."[37] He made a similar request to Rusk on the final day of the summit, suggesting that some of the smaller islands be returned to Japan. "This, however, was met with stony silence," Hoey (2015: 10) finds. Satō was starting to weave together the fate of Okinawa, Japan's nonproliferation policy, and the broader alliance relationship. The Johnson administration was not ready to give up control of the Western Pacific islands at this stage. But the summit set the foundation for Satō to continue pursuing his quest to wrest back control of Okinawa.

Tokyo Links Nonproliferation to Reversion, 1965–1967

After the summit, the basic contours of a deal over the Ryukyu Islands started to come into focus from 1965 to 1967. In June 1965, the Johnson administration shifted US nonproliferation policy toward a more proactive approach. The goal was to seek stronger promises of nuclear restraint from countries, especially allies such as Japan that had built extensive civil nuclear programs. In the wake of China's nuclear test, Secretary Rusk had tasked Llewellyn Thompson with leading a committee to assess proliferation risks and formulate policy options for countries of concern. Thompson's reports were eventually fed into the Task Force on Nuclear Proliferation—more commonly known as the Gilpatric Committee (Brands 2006; Miller 2018: 52). As part of this broader policy review, Washington updated its assessment of Japan's nuclear latency in June 1965.

From a technical perspective, the Thompson report emphasized that Japan would soon have the capacity to produce enough fissile material for atomic weapons. Construction was almost complete on the British Calder Hall–type power reactor at Tokai-mura. "The Japanese could operate this reactor to produce sufficient plutonium for an estimated 30 weapons per year beginning in late 1966."[38] Japan lacked the capacity to reprocess large amounts of irradiated fuel, as the chemical reprocessing plant was in the design stage. However, the report identified an alternative pathway to the bomb. "The Japanese are now operating a laboratory facility for studies on chemical separation processes."[39] The concern was that the lab could be used on "a makeshift basis" to extract small quantities of plutonium.[40] As a result, the report estimated that Japan was the on the cusp of being able to extract plutonium in significant quantities.

US officials worried that, once the larger Tokai-mura reprocessing plant came online in 1969 or 1970, the Japanese nuclear program would start churning out enough fissile material for a small nuclear force every year. Japan had clear plans to use this plutonium for peaceful purposes, fueling fast reactor experiments and a large breeder reactor.[41] But this looming increase in latency led the Thompson report to estimate that "political considerations aside, [Japan] could test its first nuclear device as early as 1971 without violating existing reactor safeguard provisions, thereafter producing an estimated 10–30 weapons annually."[42] In addition, Japan had founded a "relatively sophisticated space program" with US assistance that would have to capability to produce "as many as 100 nuclear-equipped [medium-range ballistic missiles] MRBMs by 1975."[43] The report concluded that the barriers to the bomb in Japan would soon be purely political. "A realistic assessment of Japan's prospects in the nuclear weapons field must thus recognize Japan's capacity to build its own nuclear force as a near-certainty; the important question is whether the decision to develop this potential is likely to be made."[44]

The Japanese leadership seemed unlikely to make such a decision. But Satō's nuclear chatter in the lead-up to the January 1965 summit created the perception among US officials that Tokyo might reconsider its defense posture down the road, particularly if the alliance weakened. The Thompson report found that Japanese opposition to nuclear weapons was starting to diminish. Further advances in China's nuclear force threatened to create greater public support for a Japanese nuclear deterrent.[45] Japan's nuclear future appeared to "largely depend" on the health of the alliance with the United States.[46] The report emphasized Japanese confidence in the US nuclear deterrent and the alliance relationship as two key factors that had inhibited proliferation thus far.[47] As part of a general push to make the US nuclear umbrella more credible, the Johnson administration adopted the report's recommendations to deepen security cooperation with Japan. In this context, simmering questions about US control over the Ryukyu Islands loomed over the alliance, potentially opening the door to a nuclear-armed Japan.

In the summer of 1965, US officials started to seek stronger nonproliferation commitments from Japanese leaders. The economic and political consequences of proliferation were already high for Japan. Yet Washington feared that these costs might not restrain Japan's budding nuclear latency over the long run. In addition, the Japanese nuclear energy program was building indigenous facilities outside of existing safeguards. Once operational, these assets could be used as part of a parallel military effort without violating agreements with foreign suppliers. The Johnson administration therefore wanted to convince Tokyo to champion an emerging global "antiproliferation" effort—what would soon become the NPT. If Japan joined the vanguard of this movement, the Thompson report predicted, "Its involvement would tend to commit Japan more firmly to a non-nuclear role, in a context which would enhance its stature on the international scene."[48] Signing an international treaty to forgo nuclear weapons would further raise the potential costs of proliferation for Japan.

The United States circulated an early draft of the nonproliferation treaty to Japan in 1966. Much to Washington's surprise, Tokyo rejected the treaty. The main objection came from the nuclear energy industry, which opposed the economic costs of complying with intrusive verification measures. Japanese politicians demanded assurances that the NPT would not restrict any peaceful uses of nuclear technology. Other Japanese leaders argued that Japan's nuclear latency gave them leverage to negotiate for a better agreement. As Foreign Vice Minister Takeso Shimoda privately told McGeorge Bundy in February 1966, "Countries which have the capacity to produce nuclear weapons but do not want to do so should have more weight accorded their views."[49] In early December, Ushiba Nobuhiko, Satō's deputy vice minister for foreign affairs, requested firmer US security guarantees in exchange for joining the NPT. Security commitments were important, he told American diplomats, because "Japan has very strong views against being permanently classified as a second-rate power through signing the treaty and foregoing nuclear weapons."[50] Other Japanese officials echoed similar concerns and demands throughout 1966 and 1967. As Ayako Kusunoki (2008: 44) concludes, Japanese leaders "sent a consistent message to the United States: It was going to be difficult to convince Japan to sign the NPT."

Japan's reluctance to join the NPT coincided with a major debate in Tokyo over national security. In April 1966, a special report from the Central Intelligence Agency flagged that the Japanese were in serious deliberations about their requirements for defense. The intensity of the debate was unprecedented for the postwar era. Despite maintaining support for the US-Japan alliance, government leaders were "stressing that Japan must make a great effort to provide for its own defense."[51] The debate focused on the extent to which Japan should strive for greater independence in military affairs. "The acquisition of a nuclear capability, despite continuing public sensitivities," the report highlighted, was "being increasingly aired as a logical corollary of an independent force posture."[52] The prime minister seemed to be supporting this line of discussion, as he was "quite circumspect in reaffirming past renunciation of nuclear arms."[53] Moreover, the report concluded that Satō had "been careful not to close the door to a future nuclear weapons program."[54]

By the spring of 1967, Japanese opposition to the NPT had dovetailed with pressure on the United States to return the Western Pacific islands. According to an April 1967 cable from the American Embassy in Tokyo, Japan's adverse reaction to the NPT appeared "to reflect the deep and abiding Japanese sensitivity to anything identifiable as discrimination against Japan."[55] This in turn meant that US officials had to be prepared to offset this perceived imbalance, especially as the Japanese public demanded their leaders "do something" about Okinawa. In particular, the cable noted, "US policy towards the Ryukyu Islands appears to be nearing the limits of its current viability, and urgent attention should be given to the development of alternatives which will permit the US to accommodate Japan's desire for the return of administration of the Ryukyus."[56] In August, the Office of the Secretary of Defense concurred. "We are confronted by a clear cut Japanese request to resolve the Ryukyu and Bonins question," the Pentagon underscored, noting the need to retain "the most important U.S. military base in the Western Pacific" on Okinawa.[57] The strategic utility of Okinawa led the Joint Chiefs of Staff to oppose any change to the status quo. Other US officials identified an alternative solution. Since the Bonins and several smaller islands were "of little or no importance militarily," the Pentagon suggested that Washington could "negotiate the return of these islands as a package with the Ryukyus."[58] The Johnson administration was now prepared to consider returning control over some of the Western Pacific islands if an acceptable deal could be reached.

Satō's Second Summit in Washington, November 1967

In mid-November 1967, Satō arrived in Washington to push the reversion issue forward at another summit with Johnson. Japanese and American officials had spent several weeks staking out their respective positions. The Johnson administration would give up the Bonin Islands while longer discussions began over how to return Okinawa. However, US officials stressed that reversion remained conditional on preserving the American military base system on Okinawa, including the ability to move nuclear weapons through Japanese territory. In addition, Johnson wanted to obtain greater Japanese financial support for US-led regional security operations.

At the State Department, Secretary Rusk also saw the reversion issue as an opportunity to secure Japan's adherence to the nonproliferation treaty, which would open for signature in 1968.[59] Satō appeared amenable to these conditions, having gone to great lengths to convince the Americans that Japan would support US military access rights in the Ryukyus. But he held back on making specific foreign aid or nonproliferation commitments in advance of the summit, perhaps as a way to retain leverage as the negotiations played out (Buckley 1995: 114; Hoey 2015: 30–33).

The first meeting on November 14 began as each side expected, with Johnson offering to return the Bonin Islands and table negotiations over Okinawa. The president then pushed Satō to provide more Japanese foreign aid in Southeast Asia and help the United States solve its trade imbalance problems. Satō steered the talks toward the Ryukyus. He told Johnson that it was "especially important to avoid any mistakes in handling the question of reversion because quite frankly, any mistakes could lead to undesirable consequences which would adversely affect future United States-Japan relations."[60] In particular, Satō reemphasized that Japan would continue to forgo nuclear weapons, relying instead on the US nuclear umbrella for security. Since these security arrangements were "an absolute necessity for Japan," the prime minister explained, "Okinawa and the Bonins must be viewed by Japan in these terms."[61] Returning the islands on terms acceptable to both countries would strengthen the security ties at the core of US-Japan alliance. But the meeting ended without Satō making much progress on the reversion issue with Johnson.

The rest of the summit proved to be more productive. Later in the afternoon, Secretary of Defense McNamara asked Satō how the Japanese people were reacting to China's nuclear capabilities. The prime minister lamented that his "government had not done enough to educate the masses" about the nuclear threat from China; but quickly noted that the "Japanese were well protected by the U.S. nuclear umbrella and Japan had no intention to make nuclear weapons."[62] McNamara then drew a link between the US extended deterrent commitment and the reversion issue:

The Ryukyus were bound to revert to Japan. The question was not one of reversion but of bases and the Mutual Security Treaty, as well as the president's statements about responding to nuclear blackmail. These all carried unwritten assumptions that Japan would act in a way which would permit the use of bases . . . Japan must permit the U.S. to operate militarily in the Ryukyus in ways which might involve operations requiring nuclear weapons to be placed there and combat operations to be conducted from there.[63]

McNamara knew that the Japanese public would not readily support this type of US military presence. "It would take time for Mr. Satō educate his people," he admitted.[64] Meanwhile, diplomats could work out the military and political details to satisfy the interests of both countries. Satō agreed with this general plan. However, he noted the need to "give some hope to the people of Japan that reversion was coming."[65] McNamara offered to support reversion in general terms, conditional on being able to preserve US military capabilities in the Ryukyus.

The final set of meetings on November 15 firmed up this approach to reversion. Satō wanted to issue a joint communiqué announcing that both leaders had "agreed to make efforts to reach, in a few years, agreement on a date satisfactory to the two governments on the return of administrative rights to Japan."[66] Secretary Rusk proposed a watered-down version with language that left the United States with considerable room to maneuver over the terms. In his final talk with Johnson, Satō also asked the president to "reconfirm" the US nuclear security commitment to defend Japan.[67] After reiterating his pledge, Johnson launched into another attempt to elicit economic aid from Japan. The prime minister deflected these requests, politely listening to the president without agreeing to any concrete deliverables.

The summit was a minor diplomatic success for Satō. Having already stoked concerns in Washington about reversion and the future of Japan's national security policy, the prime minister used a light touch in the discussions with the president and his cabinet. Hoey (2015: 37) argues that "Satō was able to return to Japan with what he needed: significant forward movement on the reversion issue." The Bonin Islands would revert within a year. The prime minister had reframed the reversion issue, convincing US officials that they had to determine "when" rather than "if" Okinawa would revert to Japanese control. This alone was "a significant concession to the Japanese position," Hoey (2015: 37) notes. In exchange, Satō made few concessions. According to Buckley (1995: 119), "The United States gave more than it got over the Okinawa question. The Japanese government could hardly complain at the gains it made at the expense of the United States from Satō's visit in the autumn of 1967."

A few weeks later, Satō addressed Japan's nuclear policy in a statement to committee members at the Diet. The Washington summit had left Satō with the impression that he needed to cultivate Japanese support for US military forces in the Ryukyus. But the prime minister faced opposition on this front, especially over the question of hosting US nuclear weapons on Japanese soil. In an apparent effort to quell domestic criticism, Satō announced, "We will not possess nuclear [weapons], nor will we produce them, nor will we allow nuclear [weapons] to be introduced [into Japan]. These are the three principles with respect to nuclear weapons."[68] He also referenced President Johnson's assurances that the United States would defend Japan against any attack. However, the nonintroduction principle seemed to be incongruous with US efforts to maintain its nuclear umbrella over Japan. Satō attempted to square this circle at his annual speech to the Diet in January 1968, where he announced the Four Pillars of Nuclear Policy for Japan. The three nonnuclear principles constituted one pillar, along with reliance on the US nuclear umbrella, support for global nuclear disarmament, and investment in the peaceful uses of nuclear energy technology (Kusunoki 2008: 37–42).

Back in Washington, US officials interpreted the prime minister's remarks as a ploy to gain an advantage in upcoming negotiations over military access rights on Okinawa (Buckley 1995: 119). Satō had made a public commitment to secure reversion without allowing nuclear forces to be introduced on the island. Moreover, the timing of this announcement coincided with Japan's official refusal to sign the nonproliferation treaty when it opened for signature in the summer of 1968. According to Kusunoki (2008: 25), Satō was deliberately linking these decisions together. Japan had little desire to develop atomic weapons. Indeed, in September 1968, a top-secret Japanese study strongly recommended against Japan building the bomb for a variety of reasons (Kase 2001; Kurosaki 2017: 52–54). But holding out on the NPT could give Japan leverage over the Okinawa issue. Satō wanted to keep his nuclear options open, Hoey (2016b: 169) argues, because "he still cherished hopes of leveraging Japan's nuclear renunciation to the benefit of the reversion of Okinawa." American scholars and officials reached similar conclusions at the time. As George Quester (1970: 771) argued, "Japan indeed clearly signaled that concessions might be required to win approval of the NPT." Similarly, an American diplomat concluded in December 1968 that "we have reached the point of no return on the reversion issue."[69] Japan's accession to the nonproliferation regime was now intertwined with the reversion of Okinawa. But Satō would have to wait until the incoming Nixon administration entered office to negotiate the agreement.

Securing the Return of Okinawa from Nixon, 1969

In early 1969, Satō's reversion strategy entered its final phase. President Nixon was less concerned with proliferation than his predecessor. But Japan's nuclear latency still cast a shadow over US deliberations about Okinawa. The prime minister met outgoing Ambassador Johnson on January 13 to emphasize the importance of obtaining an agreement over Okinawa within the year. He told the ambassador that Japan's three nonnuclear principles were "nonsense," to the "astonishment" of those in the room.[70] On January 20, a review of US foreign policy for Nixon determined that Japan was unlikely to build to bomb in the near term. "Nevertheless, the Japanese leadership is expected to keep its options open indefinitely," the report concluded.[71] This was problematic in the context of Okinawa, the study emphasized, because "failure to reach agreement on reversion could constitute a turning point for Japan by stimulating the more aggressive, nationalist forces."[72] In turn, the report worried, such "a Japanese decision to plot a more independent military course would entail serious consideration of nuclear arms development."[73] The United States could avoid these adverse outcomes by returning Okinawa to Japan.

By the spring, Nixon was ready to cut a deal over reversion that met most of Satō's long-standing demands. After a lengthy evaluation, the president issued a top-secret memorandum on US policy toward Japan in late May 1969. The United States was willing to return Okinawa provided an agreement could be reached with the Japanese government "on the essential elements governing U.S. military use."[74] In addition, Nixon would withdraw US nuclear weapons from Okinawa. But this concession came with an old catch: Washington wanted to retain "emergency storage and transit rights" for its nuclear forces.[75] Over the summer, National Security Advisor Henry Kissinger worked with Secretary of State William Rogers to translate this guidance into diplomatic strategy for several high-level meetings in Tokyo. As Kissinger aptly summed up, "Our negotiating posture should reflect the fact that we will agree to reversion provided the price is right."[76]

When Secretary Rogers arrived in Tokyo over the summer, Satō led an effort to make Japan's NPT accession conditional on the United States returning Okinawa. According to Kusunoki (2008: 45), Japanese leaders "expected that signature of the NPT would prove a useful bargaining chip in achieving a nuclear-free Okinawa." After an initial meeting with Rogers, Satō admitted in his diary, "I wanted to entangle the Okinawa problem and the nonproliferation treaty, I am sure I was able to deepen [Rogers's] understanding."[77] When Rogers then met with Foreign Minister Aichi, he reported that "references to Okinawa arose as by products of discussion ... of Aichi's explanation of [Japan's] attitude on NPT."[78] Rogers also found it prudent to inform Aichi that Nixon's lukewarm stance on the NPT did not apply to Japan. "Whatever information may have been conveyed to GOJ [government of Japan] that President not interested in this is not repeat not true, and the President does indeed hope Japan will sign [the NPT]. U.S. did not want GOJ to feel it being pressured to do so, but the Secretary made clear that U.S. did hope GOJ would sign."[79] In response, Aichi suggested that Japan would sign the NPT after a deal was reached on Okinawa.

Satō's Third Summit in Washington, November 1969

Satō met with Nixon to finalize the reversion agreement during a summit at the White House in November 1969. In preparation for the meeting, US officials anticipated that Satō would try to use the nonproliferation treaty as leverage over Okinawa. "Japan will probably sign the NPT in the near future," a background paper from the Arms Control and Disarmament Agency noted in early November.[80] "A final decision, however, may well be dependent upon finding a formula for the question of nuclear weapons on Okinawa that Satō can accept."[81] Indeed, Satō had privately decided to support Japan's accession to the NPT months earlier. But he planned to play this card during reversion negotiations with Nixon (Hoey 2016b: 170). A few days before the summit, Secretary Rogers received a briefing memorandum that underscored, "The Japanese have not yet made up their minds to sign [the NPT]. You might reemphasize to Aichi the importance that the US attaches to the treaty and to early Japanese signature. The President will be making similar points to Satō."[82]

However, Satō's push to "entangle" the nonproliferation treaty with Okinawa appears to have been unnecessary at this late stage of diplomacy.

The United States was already prepared to return Okinawa and remove its forward-deployed nuclear weapons. On the first day of the summit, Nixon dangled these favorable terms for reversion in an attempt to induce Japanese cooperation over trade and security issues. Satō unexpectedly found himself under pressure to curb the export of Japanese textiles. Even more surprising to Satō, Nixon muddled his message on nonproliferation. According to the official memorandum of conversation, Nixon encouraged Japan "to develop a significant military capability. He did not mean that this should include a nuclear capability."[83] But other US officials in the room contend that Nixon made an off-the-record remark to Satō, hinting that he would "understand" if Japan built the bomb after the United States pulled out its nuclear weapons from Okinawa (Hoey 2015: 109–10; Schaller 1997: 218). After the meeting, State Department officials were so alarmed by Nixon's comment that they pulled Satō aside to reinforce US nonproliferation policy toward Japan.

By the end of the summit, Satō and Nixon had reached an agreement over reversion. The United States would return Okinawa and remove its nuclear weapons from the islands. Japan would continue to rely on the US nuclear umbrella for protection. But Satō was pressured into signing a secret waiver that granted the United States access rights to reintroduce nuclear weapons in an emergency situation (Hoey 2016b: 171). In exchange for nonnuclear reversion, Nixon also demanded a quid pro quo over Japanese trade policy. Satō reluctantly agreed to curb textile exports. On the nonproliferation front, Satō informed Nixon that Japan would sign the NPT, but felt it was unnecessary to do so "in haste" with an early signature. Nixon concurred, noting that Japan "must do so in its own time, when it felt it best to do so."[84] With all the major issues resolved, the president and prime minister held a joint preference to announce the return of Okinawa.[85]

Satō arrived back in Tokyo having achieved a significant victory for Japan: the return of Okinawa without US nuclear weapons. At the final summit with Nixon, Satō nailed down favorable terms without giving up much except a promise to curtail textile exports and join the nonproliferation treaty. The prime minister soon pushed the Diet to sign the NPT. After several months of legislative wrangling, Japan became a signatory to the treaty on February 3, 1970. In exchange for US extended nuclear deterrence commitments and the return of Okinawa, Japan bound its nuclear energy program to the nonproliferation mast.

Bargaining in the Sweet Spot

Japan illustrates how an ally can use its peaceful nuclear energy program as a bargaining chip in negotiations with the United States. Table 3.2 summarizes the outcome of each compellence episode I assessed in this chapter.

In the first episode (1957–1960), Japanese leaders failed to elicit changes in the US alliance architecture. As expected by the too little (H1) hypothesis, Japan's low level of latency undercut threat credibility. The infant state of the atomic energy program meant that Japanese leaders lacked the technical foundation to produce fissile material, let alone a fully fledged nuclear force. The prospect of Japan charting its own nuclear course à la France did not loom over US officials until almost a decade later. Moreover, Japan's initial investment in nuclear technology was apparently not costly enough to convey possible weapons aspirations. Washington brushed off the notion that Japan would field an independent nuclear deterrent as an infeasible bluff.

Table 3.2 Compellence Outcomes for Japan

Episode (dates)	Latency	Outcome	Details	Theory support
Security pact crisis (1957–1960)	Low	Failure	Washington unequivocally denied Tokyo's requests to revise the security treaty or return the Western Pacific islands to Japanese control. Japan was unable to attain any real concessions from the United States.	Strong (H1)
Satō's Okinawa gambit (1964–1970)	Medium	Success	Japanese leaders persuaded the United States to comply with demands for stronger security guarantees and the territorial reversion of the Bonin and Ryukyu Islands. In 1965, Prime Minister Satō successfully extracted an ironclad extended nuclear deterrent commitment from Washington. Under the Johnson and Nixon administrations, the United States also agreed to return all the Western Pacific islands, including Okinawa, under terms favorable to Japan.	Strong (H3)

The success of Satō's campaign less than a decade later (1964–1970) supports the sweet spot hypothesis (H3). The prime minister persuaded the United States to meet Japan's demands for stronger security commitments and reversion of the Western Pacific islands. However, historians debate the degree to which Japan's latency contributed to this outcome. Some skeptics (Kurosaki 2017, 2020) contend that international and domestic factors preordained Japan's accession to the NPT, which may have made it difficult for Satō to leverage latency at all (A1). Others (Hoey 2015, 2016b; Kusunoki 2008) argue that Satō played the nuclear card to great effect in discussions with American leaders, even though the final quid pro quo with Nixon focused less on nonproliferation than expected. This latter position aligns with my argument that states can use modest amounts of latency to wrest concessions from great powers. Japan's nuclear energy program cast a shadow over deliberations with US officials because it was on the cusp of producing plutonium. This medium level of latency enabled Satō to surmount the threat-assurance dilemma in three ways.

First, the mobilization of Japan's nuclear program for peaceful purposes presented Satō with an opportunity to put pressure on the United States. Industry stakeholders were driving the rapid growth in latency to reap economic benefits from the nuclear fuel cycle. However, the dual-use nature of nuclear technology triggered ticking clock concerns about proliferation in Washington. Once reprocessing operations began at the Tokai-mura plant, Tokyo would find itself sitting on enough fissile material for a small nuclear arsenal. American officials wanted to secure greater nonproliferation assurances from Tokyo before Japan acquired this higher level of latency in the 1970s. Satō and his cabinet appear to have taken advantage of this civilian-led growth in the nuclear program, using it to make implicit threats more credible while readily committing Japan to nuclear restraint.

Second, Japan's pattern of building vulnerable nuclear facilities in plain sight made it possible to use the nonproliferation treaty as a commitment device. The Japanese nuclear industry depended on bilateral supply contracts to import technology and materials from foreign nuclear vendors. This development strategy facilitated Japan's rapid ascent into the fissile material sweet spot during the 1960s. But it also set the foundation for other nations to intervene against Japan for using its safeguarded civilian facilities to build nuclear weapons. Joining the NPT at this stage of development would bring all of Japan's nuclear assets under verifiable safeguards, including indigenous facilities being built outside of foreign supply contracts. In this sense, accession to the treaty would increase the costs of proliferation for Japan. Satō could therefore offer to make this credible nonproliferation assurance conditional on the reversion of Okinawa.

Third, elite empowerment and public activation over nuclear issues in Japan enhanced the credibility of Satō's signals. In the early 1960s, Tokyo vested elite stakeholders with the resources and autonomy necessary to build Japan's nuclear program. The public also came around to supporting nuclear energy in response to outreach efforts from government and industry. When Satō became prime minister, he inherited these strong state commitments to continue marching up the latency continuum for peaceful purposes. This propelled Japan's civil nuclear mobilization effort forward, giving the prime minister enough latency to cultivate concerns about proliferation. But nuclear elites and the Japanese public also constrained Satō's freedom of action—they created formidable barriers to the bomb. In the end, domestic politics helped the prime minister to walk a fine line between making implicit proliferation threats and ironclad nonproliferation promises.

The threat-assurance trade-off suggests that leveraging latency became far less viable for Japanese leaders after Satō's success. Over the next five decades, Japan's nuclear energy program matured into one of the most advanced enterprises in the world. On the one hand, this high level of latency led to periodic concerns in Washington and Beijing about whether Tokyo might build the bomb. Former Japanese officials occasionally stoked this fire by claiming that Japan's nuclear energy program provided virtual deterrent and hedging benefits. On the other hand, however, Japanese leaders assiduously avoided using the nuclear program as a bargaining chip. This reluctance may have stemmed from the significant costs associated with making threats or assurances on the cusp of the bomb. Instead, Japan continued to strengthen its commitments to the global nonproliferation regime.

4

West Germany

In 1955, the Federal Republic of Germany (FRG) launched an atomic energy program after freeing itself of postwar constraints on nuclear technology development. Over the next fifteen years, the country built a fleet of nuclear power plants, pioneered uranium enrichment techniques, and mastered plutonium-reprocessing technology. West Germany accumulated nuclear latency in plain sight as it developed these capabilities for ostensibly peaceful purposes. After a brief military flirtation with the French and Italians in 1957–1958, German leaders avoided any nuclear weaponization activities that might ignite an international crisis or political turmoil at home. But Bonn soon discovered that Soviet and American fears of German proliferation could be exploited as a diplomatic lever. Much like Satō in Japan, West German leaders relied on the dual-use nature of civil nuclear technology to underwrite implicit threats and back demands on the international stage. Unlike Japan, however, the Federal Republic faced formidable challenges as it attempted to wrest concessions from both superpowers.

West German leaders leveraged latency against the United States and Soviet Union on three successive occasions from 1961 to 1969. In the first episode (1961–1963), Chancellor Konrad Adenauer led an effort to strengthen West Germany's position within the North Atlantic Treaty Organization (NATO) while forcing concessions from the Soviets over reunification. My theory expects that the Adenauer government should have struggled to make its threats credible at this early stage of nuclear technology development. In the second episode (1963–1966), the government of Ludwig Erhard launched a campaign to secure German participation in NATO nuclear sharing arrangements. West Germany's atomic energy program moved into the fissile material sweet spot during this era. According to my theory, Bonn should have been able to surmount the threat-assurance trade-off at this level of latency and wrangle concessions from Washington and Moscow. The Federal Republic remained in the sweet spot for the third episode (1966–1969), when Bonn pushed back against the superpower fait accompli over the Treaty on the Non-Proliferation of Nuclear Weapons (NPT), demanding

Leveraging Latency. Tristan A. Volpe, Oxford University Press. © Oxford University Press 2023.
DOI: 10.1093/oso/9780197669532.003.0004

core changes to the treaty and additional assurances from the Americans. If the book's central argument is correct, West German leaders should have had just enough nuclear latency on hand to extract concessions from the superpowers at this stage. Table 4.1 summarizes the historical contours and theoretical expectations of each episode I analyze in this chapter.

Table 4.1 Compellence Cases by West Germany

Episode (dates)	Latency	Target	Demands	Expected outcome
Adenauer's gambit (1961–1963)	Low	United States (ally) Soviet Union (adversary)	Bonn wanted Washington to support greater integration of West Germany within the NATO command structure and demanded access to nuclear weapons under MLF arrangements. Bonn demanded Moscow make diplomatic concessions over the fate of divided Berlin and East Germany. German leaders wanted to "get something" from the Soviets in return for reaffirming nonnuclear status.	Failure
Erhard's NATO push (1963–1966)	Medium	United States (ally) Soviet Union (adversary)	Bonn again pushed Washington to support West German participation in a multilateral nuclear force and firm up FRG's role in NATO nuclear strategy. Bonn demanded Moscow support the reunification of Germany or at least make tangible diplomatic concessions over the issue.	Success
Kiesinger's NPT campaign (1966–1969)	Medium	United States (ally) and Soviet Union (adversary)	Bonn demanded Washington and Moscow make the NPT more flexible with modifications and new provisions, such as protections for peaceful nuclear energy programs, changes to verification protocols, as well as the inclusion of limited duration and withdrawal clauses. Bonn also requested US assurances that the NPT would not limit nuclear consultations among allies.	Success

The three compellence episodes provide valuable historical and theoretical insights. West Germany is the only latent nuclear power that challenged two superpowers—an ally and an adversary—at the same time.[1] Scholars have long investigated how the issue of Bonn's nuclear status lay at the heart of American and Soviet efforts to establish détente in the 1960s (Trachtenberg 1999; Schrafstetter and Twigge 2004; Gavin 2012; Lutsch 2019). In contrast to skeptics of compellence with nuclear latency, I show that German leaders were ultimately able to manipulate superpower concerns about proliferation as a diplomatic asset. However, Bonn faced limits on leveraging latency in the shadow of superpower collusion—West German leaders were unable to secure critical concessions despite being in the fissile material sweet spot. From a research design perspective, West Germany's steady accumulation of nuclear latency also establishes important within-case variation. This allows me to analyze how low and then medium levels of latency shaped the threat-assurance trade-off for German leaders while holding most other factors constant. I draw heavily on declassified intelligence estimates and memoranda of conversation to tease out the role that West Germany's growing nuclear potential played in negotiations with the United States and Soviet Union over NATO force posture and the global nonproliferation regime.

This chapter assesses West Germany's strategy of bargaining with nuclear latency in five parts. In the first part, I identify the origins of the strategy amid the peaceful rebirth of the German nuclear program and security crises of the late 1950s. The second part examines Adenauer's attempt to leverage a low level of latency against the superpowers in the early 1960s. In the third part, I detail how moving into the fissile material sweet spot impacted Erhard's quest to enhance West German influence over NATO nuclear strategy. The fourth part explores whether nuclear latency enabled Bonn to extract concessions from Washington and Moscow over the NPT. The fifth part evaluates the degree to which the evidence from each episode supports my theoretical claims, especially compared to alternative arguments.

The Initial Nuclear Forays, 1952–1961

West Germany's approach to leveraging latency against the superpowers originated in the late 1950s amid the *Sputnik* and Berlin crises. I examine the genesis of this strategy in two sections. The first traces out Chancellor Adenauer's effort to free the Federal Republic of stringent postwar constraints on nuclear technology and launch an atomic energy program. The second section examines how Bonn explored its nuclear options in response to a credibility crisis within the NATO alliance architecture. Blowback from a short-lived plan to consider building the bomb with France and Italy led West German leaders to focus on developing nuclear technology for peaceful purposes. But the mere prospect of the Federal Republic acquiring nuclear weapons set off alarm bells in Moscow, which played a key role in sparking the Berlin crisis. Bonn came to realize that the threat of proliferation could be wielded against the Soviets.

The Rebirth of Nuclear Latency in Postwar West Germany

In the aftermath of the Second World War, the Allies imposed stringent limits on nuclear technology development in the Federal Republic of Germany. During negotiations over the end of Allied rule and the foundation of the European Defense Community (EDC), West German chancellor Adenauer found himself under pressure to renounce atomic weapons and the underlying capacity to make them. The Americans joined with the British and French to compel Adenauer into issuing a "voluntary" renunciation of atomic weapons and nuclear latency in a letter to be filed with the EDC treaty in May 1952. Under the terms of the agreement, West Germany would have been prohibited from manufacturing atomic weapons and producing more than half a kilogram of fissile material per year (Küntzel 1995: 3). However, this nuclear abstinence pledge never took effect. When France failed to ratify the EDC treaty, Adenauer's letter was rendered null and void (Bluth 1995: 16–17; Bozo 2016: 31–34; Winand 1996: 54–63).

Several years later, Adenauer persuaded the Allies to lift all restrictions on West Germany's development of nuclear technology for peaceful purposes. The Paris modifications to the Brussels Treaty in October 1954 paved the way for the Federal Republic to regain sovereignty and join NATO. Adenauer agreed to "voluntarily" renounce the manufacture of atomic weapons on German territory. This left the door ajar to build the bomb outside of Germany as part of a collaborative effort with other Western European nations. West Germany would also refrain from the production of fissile material for military purposes. But the chancellor firmly rejected any limitations on fissile material production within the civilian nuclear fuel cycle. The modified Brussels Treaty granted the Federal Republic a blanket waiver to develop "all" nuclear technologies and materials, so long as they were for "civilian purposes or for scientific, medical, and industrial research."[2] Given the dual-use nature of nuclear technology, the treaty set the legal foundation for West Germany to start marching up the latency continuum.

German scientists were eager to be free of the postwar nuclear technology restrictions for purely peaceful research reasons. Led by Werner Heisenberg and his Max Planck Institute, German nuclear scientists wanted to expand their work on uranium enrichment, build research and power reactors, and eventually reap economic benefits from the plutonium fuel cycle. From the outset, these technical elites wanted to ensure that the West German nuclear enterprise remained committed to nonmilitary activities. A few days after Adenauer signed the revised Brussels Treaty in late October 1954, Heisenberg met with American, British, and French scientists to discuss West Germany's nuclear plans. "Germany would not develop an atomic weapons program," he reiterated, even though German scientists were drafting plans to pioneer new uranium enrichment technology and build a natural uranium research reactor for studying chemical separation techniques.[3] Heisenberg understood that this civil nuclear research program could be diverted into a weapons-production effort. He promised to keep his ally counterparts informed of progress as West Germany developed nuclear fuel cycle technology. At home, Heisenberg pushed West German leaders to make public announcements about the peaceful nature of the nuclear program (Carson 2010: 245; Eckert 1990).

As soon as the Paris Treaty came into force in May 1955, Adenauer worked with Heisenberg to launch a major nuclear development project. The effort focused on building multiple research centers where scientists could master nuclear technology. Amid this period of solid economic growth for West Germany, Cathyrn Carson (2010: 251) notes, "The government proved willing to fund new construction (and personnel and equipment) on a scale previously unseen." The nuclear program also enjoyed strong support from German politicians. As the top-ranking Christian Democrat, Adenauer forged a partnership with the Christian Social Union by selecting Franz Josef Strauss to head the newly formed Ministry for Atomic Affairs in October 1955. Flush with funding and political backing, scientists and industry quickly established research centers at Karlsruhe, Jülich, and Geesthacht in 1956. Over the next year, Germany brought its first research reactor online near Munich, prospected for uranium, and helped to establish the European Atomic Energy Community (EURATOM) multinational nuclear research organization with Belgium, France, Italy, Luxembourg, the Netherlands. The Federal Republic had committed itself to joining the vanguard of the atomic energy movement (Mahncke 1972; Krige 2016: 49–77).

By the end of the decade, German scientists were on track to start mastering the nuclear fuel cycle for civilian purposes. However, West Germany's atomic energy program remained at a low level of latency. In July 1958, a US national intelligence estimate on nuclear proliferation highlighted several constraints on Bonn's capacity to build the bomb. Despite the progress on research reactors, West Germany had yet to initiate construction on large power reactors. Moreover, the Federal Republic lacked suitable sources for mining uranium, hampering its capacity to produce fissile material. The intelligence assessment estimated that it would take the West Germans until "about 1962–64" to fully make up "their postwar lag in scientific and military research." In the meantime, Germany could partner with other Western European allies, notably France and Italy, to jointly produce atomic weapons. The report concluded that an agreement to combine the "technological and industrial capacities of the Germans" with the French nuclear program "would mean the emergence of a major 'fourth power' in Europe."[4] Indeed, the prospect of West Germany pursuing such a European deterrent had recently become more likely in a wake of several strategic shocks.

Adenauer's Nuclear Probes

In October 1957, the Soviet Union demonstrated the success of its ballistic missile program by launching the *Sputnik* satellite into orbit. Moscow now had the capacity to strike at the continental United States with nuclear forces (Freedman 2003: 131–44). This growth in Soviet military power led West German and other European leaders to question the credibility of US extended deterrent pledges (Bluth 1995: 29–30; Tertrais 2004). Under Eisenhower's New Look defense reorientation, the United States had come to rely on nuclear weapons to underwrite security commitments to the Federal Republic and other NATO allies. But the dawn of the missile age in the fall of 1957 tore a hole in the US nuclear umbrella. From Adenauer's vantage, it no longer seemed reasonable to assume that Washington would come to the defense of Bonn or Berlin if it meant the annihilation of American cities. As a result, Bonn probed the possibility of building the bomb in collaboration with Paris and Rome.

The idea of augmenting the French nuclear program with German resources had first been floated in early 1957 amid fears of US troop withdrawals from Europe. It gathered additional momentum after *Sputnik*. In November 1957, French state secretary Maurice Fauere proposed the notion to a receptive Adenauer. Detailed discussions continued at a lower level led by Strauss, who had become minister of defense, and his French counterpart, Jacques Chaban-Delmas. The Italians eventually joined the effort, leading to the F-I-G Agreement among France, Italy, and Germany for the collaborative development of various weapons. Plans for a joint nuclear force were kept secret. According to a cable from the US Embassy in Paris, a French official admitted in the winter of 1958 that "possibilities of cooperation in fabrication of atomic weapons in France had definitely been discussed during Bonn talks."[5] Signed in April 1958, the agreement set the foundation for Italy and especially Germany to provide technical expertise and financial resources in exchange for access to nuclear warheads developed in France. However, General Charles de Gaulle suspended all cooperation over atomic weapons upon assuming power in June 1958, putting an end to France's flirtation with a European nuclear deterrent (Ahonen 1995: 33; Bozo 2020).

The Adenauer administration faced significant blowback at home. In April 1957, the West German scientific community revolted against an attempt to recruit talent for the potential Franco-German nuclear weapons program. Eighteen prominent German nuclear scientists, including Heisenberg, Max Born, and Otto Hahn, penned a public statement declaring that none of them would participate in the creation, testing, or deployment of any type of nuclear weapon.[6] The so-called Göttingen Manifesto galvanized elite and mass public opposition to building the bomb in the Federal Republic (Cioc 1988: 43–44, 72–80). Rumors about plans to produce atomic weapons with France and Italy in the winter of 1958 further widened the gap between German scientists and the political leadership in Bonn. "From this point on," Alex Bollfrass (2017: 181) argues, "it would have been extremely difficult to mobilize the scientific and nuclear engineering expertise of the [Göttingen] signatories for an indigenous weapons program." The revolt constrained West German leaders from using the nuclear energy enterprise to support military applications. This domestic opposition to the bomb would become important as German scientists developed dual-use nuclear capabilities in the years ahead.

On the international stage, the short-lived European nuclear plan created the impression that West German leaders wanted the bomb in some form.

In February 1958, Jean Laloy, the French Foreign Ministry's director of European affairs, told US officials that the French were becoming "greatly concerned over prospect that West Germans will acquire their own atomic capability through participation in French program."[7] He believed that Strauss and a select group of West German military elites were "pushing hard for this," and underscored that the French Foreign Ministry "would be very receptive" if Secretary of State Dulles were to express "reservations and concern" over the prospect of a joint atomic weapons program.[8] In fact, Dulles had already discussed the F-I-G proposal with Adenauer, suggesting instead "a nuclear weapons authority" as the "best way to keep the situation under control as regards the undue spreading of nuclear weapons."[9] These suspicions about West Germany's atomic ambitions would linger for years, ultimately returning to fore as the German nuclear energy program developed more latency in the 1960s (Burr 2018).

At the time, however, the Eisenhower administration was sanguine about the prospect of West Germany acquiring nuclear weapons. This view stemmed from the notion that nuclear sharing arrangements were the best way for Washington to strengthen the US security architecture in Western Europe (Trachtenberg 1999: 197). In this context, Bonn's consideration of a European deterrent led Eisenhower and other US officials to double down on nuclear sharing projects (Ahonen 1995: 35). In December 1957, the Americans laid out the new NATO nuclear stockpile plan, which proposed to make atomic weapons available to allies during an emergency (Trachtenberg 1999: 194). Over the next year, German forces were trained to use nuclear munitions and given access to NATO operational plans. At a National Security Council meeting in July 1959, Eisenhower even toyed with idea of covertly giving the Germans sensitive information that would enable them to develop nuclear weapons on their own.[10] This suggestion was abandoned in favor of a December 1960 plan to field an independent European nuclear force under control of the NATO commander—the infamous Multilateral Force (MLF).[11] As a result, under Eisenhower, the Americans became increasingly supportive of European and even West German nuclear ambitions (Gavin 2012: 38; Trachtenberg 1999: 215).

By contrast, Soviet officials were far more alarmed by the prospect of German nuclear armament. From Moscow's perspective, the main concern was that Bonn could use nuclear weapons as a shield to pursue an aggressive foreign policy untethered from NATO (Trachtenberg 1999: 146). This fear emerged as soon as the Federal Republic freed itself from the postwar nuclear technology restrictions. In December 1955, the Politburo instructed the Soviet ambassador in Bonn to make the West German rearmament effort and nuclear energy program top priorities for intelligence collection (Zubok 1993: 7). Given West Germany's low level of latency, however, the Soviets were primarily worried about Bonn acquiring atomic weapons via nuclear sharing arrangements within NATO. In the spring of 1957, for instance, Adenauer set off alarms in Moscow when he told Soviet ambassador Smirnov that West Germany was on the cusp of initiating a nuclear weapons program—an apparent allusion to the trilateral agreement being hashed out with France and Italy (Zubok 1993: 7–8).

The situation had become intolerable for the Soviets by the fall of 1958. The Americans were pressing ahead with the NATO stockpile plan, including the effort to train the German air force in nuclear strike operations (Trachtenberg 1999: 256). In November, Nikita Khrushchev threatened to expel the Western powers from Berlin unless a settlement was reached to constrain West Germany. Keeping atomic weapons out of Bonn's reach was central to this gambit.

The Americans and West Germans were aware of Soviet concerns. As the Berlin crisis unfolded, Western leaders determined that fear of a nuclear-armed Federal Republic was driving Khrushchev's calculations.[12] Eisenhower and his top cabinet officials believed that West Germany's nuclear status could be used to balance Soviet power and demonstrate American resolve. The Federal Republic need not be kept from building up military power and even arming itself with nuclear weapons, Eisenhower believed, because a strong West Germany could keep the Soviet Union in check. As a result, "The U.S. government was not prepared to push for concessions in this area," Trachtenberg (1999: 281) argues, so "the Berlin Crisis brought no change in Eisenhower's nuclear sharing policy." With little resistance from Washington, Adenauer dug in his heels, refusing to make any compromises over West Germany's nuclear status. He even exploited Soviet concerns by pushing back against his 1954 nuclear abstinence pledge. Because it engendered such a strong reaction from Moscow, "The threat of some form of West German nuclear capability was seen as a powerful diplomatic lever in negotiations with the Soviets over German reunification," Susanna Schrafstetter (2004: 120) finds. However, the Adenauer government would soon find itself under pressure from the new Kennedy administration to curtail its nuclear options.

Adenauer's Nuclear Gambit, 1961–1963: Low Latency

Under Adenauer's leadership, the Federal Republic attempted to leverage its status as a non-nuclear-weapon state to elicit concessions from both the Soviet Union and the United States from late 1961 until mid-1963. Bonn devised this subtle coercive diplomatic campaign in reaction to several major US foreign policy shifts in 1961, notably Kennedy's opposition to West German proliferation and negotiations over Berlin with the Soviets. The Adenauer government used the dual-use nature of nuclear technology to nurture suspicions in Washington and Moscow. The chancellor even fired several "shots across the bow," implicitly threatening to renege on the non-proliferation commitments in the 1954 Brussels Treaty if the United States sold out West German interests to the Soviets. In line with my theory, however, this effort failed to change American or Soviet foreign policy because the Federal Republic had no viable path to the bomb at the time. The West German atomic energy program remained at a low level of latency. The superpowers were therefore in an advantageous position to further curb Bonn's nuclear options with the Limited Test Ban Treaty in 1963.

Kennedy Strengthens US Nonproliferation Policy

In January 1961, John F. Kennedy took over the reins at the White House. He updated US nonproliferation policy for two reasons. First, the Kennedy administration wanted to transition US nuclear strategy from maximum retaliation to flexible response. Washington needed centralized control over NATO nuclear operations to make this latter approach work. National nuclear forces in the hands of smaller European allies would make it difficult for the Americans to wage a discriminate nuclear war (Gavin 2012: 38). Second, the president and his top advisers feared that a nuclear-armed West Germany would curtail American freedom of action and foment instability with the Soviet Union. Once Bonn counterbalanced Moscow with a small nuclear force, the argument went, West German leaders would be able to pursue a more independent foreign policy. They might even become emboldened to push for reunification, dragging the United States into a dangerous crisis with the Soviets.[13] The Kennedy administration also understood that the West German civil nuclear program would eventually give Bonn the technical option to build the bomb in the distant future. This led strategists to worry about proliferation becoming "inevitable" in the absence of active measures.[14]

Kennedy codified his opposition to the prospect of German proliferation with a substantial shift in US nuclear policy. In April 1961, Secretary of State Dean Rusk concluded a policy directive designed to move the United States away from the selective proliferation and permissive nuclear sharing plans of the Eisenhower administration.[15] Going forward, Washington would oppose its allies acquiring national nuclear forces and maintain veto authority over the use of force in NATO. The MLF no longer presaged an independent European deterrent; it was now just a tool to dampen any lingering demands for nuclear weapons in Bonn. In stark contrast to their dealings with Eisenhower, West German leaders suddenly found themselves the focus of Kennedy's new nonproliferation effort.[16]

The change in US policy set the stage for the Americans to use West Germany's nuclear status as an inducement to resolve the Berlin crisis. Khrushchev turned up the heat soon after Kennedy's inauguration, threatening to "liquidate" the Western powers from Berlin unless an agreement was reached by the end of the year. Throughout the summer and fall, it became clear that the Soviet urgency stemmed from their perception of Bonn's nuclear ambitions. In July, Soviet ambassador Mikhail Menshikov told several US officials that "the reason they thought a peace treaty now was essential because things were going on in Germany which must be stopped. There was a revanchist group in Germany which was arming Germany and seeking thermonuclear weapons."[17] Foreign Minister Gromyko drove this point home to Rusk, telling him that an agreement over Berlin had to include provisions for the "prevention of spread national nuclear weapons and of transfer possession or control such weapons to West Germany."[18] Moscow "placed utmost emphasis on this question," he reiterated to Kennedy.[19] Once again, the Berlin crisis centered on Soviet fears of a nuclear-armed Federal Republic.

Unlike his predecessor, however, Kennedy was prepared to stabilize relations with the Soviets by burning the German nuclear card. At a meeting with Khrushchev in Vienna over the summer of 1961, the president admitted "that the US is opposed to a buildup in West Germany that would constitute a threat to the Soviet Union," and suggested that a nuclear test ban treaty could help to "impede such proliferation."[20] Of course, Kennedy wanted to extract concessions from Moscow in return. He refused to let the Soviets trade "an apple for an orchard" when Khrushchev pushed him on the German nuclear issue in October.[21] Eisenhower had wanted to hold back this offer until a deal could be reached over German reunification. "But now the Federal Republic's non-nuclear status would be part of an arrangement that would settle the crisis and secure the status quo in Berlin and in central Europe as a whole," Trachtenberg (1999: 328) argues. This represented an adverse change in the US bargaining posture for Bonn. The Kennedy administration was ready to accept the perpetual division of Germany. Even more alarming, Washington now wanted to reach an agreement with Moscow over Berlin based on locking in West Germany's nuclear abstinence pledge.

Bonn Leverages West Germany's Nonnuclear Status

In the wake of Kennedy's foreign policy shifts, Bonn became increasingly worried that Washington might sell out the Federal Republic to establish détente with Moscow. As the Berlin Wall started to go up in August 1961, West German leaders grew disheartened with the Kennedy administration for not taking a more hard-line stance. Although Adenauer was willing to accept the reality of a divided Germany, he suspected Kennedy might cut a deal with the Soviets at Bonn's expense. The chancellor also refused to budge on the nuclear issue. He continued to demand West German access to nuclear weapons under the NATO sharing arrangements put in place under Eisenhower. In November 1961, elections in the Federal Republic ushered in a new cabinet around Adenauer, with Foreign Minister Gerhard Schröder joining the inner circle alongside Minister of Defense Strauss. As talks over Berlin continued between Washington and Moscow, Adenauer's core leadership group set out to carefully leverage American and Soviet concerns about West German proliferation.

The contours of Bonn's bargaining strategy came into focus for US officials by the end of the year. After the German election in November, sources for the Central Intelligence Agency painted a detailed portrait of deliberations within Adenauer's cabinet about how they should push back against the Americans and Soviets. According to the declassified report, the entire cabinet agreed that "West Germany's position in NATO must be further strengthened," especially amid efforts from the Soviets "to force concessions from the West likely to limit West Germany's power."[22] The Federal Republic needed to keep its nuclear options open, the cabinet members concurred, because this threat could be wielded against the superpowers. But Strauss and Schröder disagreed about how to execute this strategy.

Strauss wanted to pressure Washington into abandoning its veto over NATO nuclear forces. In line with his previous efforts from 1956 to 1958, he saw the French option as the key lever for compelling the Americans to share operational control over nuclear forces deployed in the defense of Western Europe. Unless Washington revised its nuclear sharing posture, Strauss argued, "The Germans and French should cooperate to produce atomic weapons of their own."[23] However, the main problem with this approach was the apparent lack of interest on the French side. Strauss had already reached out on several occasions to judge the possibility of resuming Franco-German nuclear cooperation in 1960–1961. He returned home without any making any tangible progress (Ahonen 1995: 38).

By contrast, Foreign Minister Schröder allegedly believed the threat of West Germany going nuclear would be a more effective diplomatic lever. Rather than flirt with the French again, he argued that "the Germans should retract their pledge not to produce ABC [atomic, biological, chemical] weapons."[24] The prospect of the Federal Republic fielding its own nuclear deterrent would "impress" the Soviets, Schröder claimed, because such a force was more likely to be used in defense of Europe than the American arsenal. "If faced with a German atomic capability," he thought, "the Soviets would be prepared to make major concessions in negotiations with West Germany. Otherwise, any concessions the Soviets made would be made to the Western powers without primary attention to the interests of West Germany."[25] The implication was that the Federal Republic needed to weaken its nonproliferation commitments, or perhaps even take steps toward the bomb.

Schröder's plan, however, was infeasible. West German leaders faced formidable barriers to leveraging latency in the early 1960s. On the technical front, the Federal Republic lacked the capacity to build the bomb within a reasonable amount of time. Although Bonn was supporting efforts to master the front and back ends of the nuclear fuel cycle, the atomic energy enterprise remained at a low level of latency. The US intelligence community reiterated this point in several proliferation assessments. In September 1960, for instance, American analysts estimated that it would take West Germany six to eight years to build the bomb. "The obstacles are considerable," the report emphasized, pointing to the lack of large fissile material production capabilities in Germany.[26] Over the next year, the West Germans made modest progress on developing gas centrifuges for uranium enrichment. An updated National Intelligence Estimate (NIE) in 1961 calculated that it would now take Bonn four to five years to acquire a nuclear weapon.[27]

Despite this bump in capability, the West Germans remained on the lower end of the latency continuum.

In addition, developing nuclear weapons would likely create a serious political crisis for the Federal Republic. On the international stage, West Germany risked triggering preventive war with the Soviet Union if it initiated a weapons production program. The civil nuclear energy program was being built in plain sight. It would likely be difficult to mask military activities from the Soviets, especially for an extended length of time. Moreover, the West Germans believed that clear steps toward the bomb "would be an almost intolerable provocation of the Soviet Union," according to declassified US intelligence reports from this era.[28] Within the Federal Republic itself, American analysts believed that a nuclear weapons program would likely create "serious political dissension" from elites and the general public.[29] As a result, leveraging German proliferation in any sort of explicit or tangible fashion promised to ignite a crisis with the Soviets and domestic revolt at home.

Adenauer's inner circle seemed to have been aware of these limitations. In a private conversation with Otto Haxel in late 1961, Strauss admitted that "he was not as stupid as to presume that Germany could afford to build its own nuclear weapons."[30] Instead, Radkau and Hahn (2013: 121) find that he merely "wanted to have the capability for doing so as a bargaining chip in international negotiations. 'As a politician, you do not relinquish something like that just for nothing.'" Indeed, the West Germans had recently pitched this basic idea to US officials in June. Amid discussions about ongoing negotiations with the Soviets over Berlin, German ambassador Wilhelm Grewe pushed the Americans to hold back on reaffirming West Germany's status as a non-nuclear-weapon state. The German government "felt that this was something which should be kept in store for possible later use," he argued, "and not included as commitment vis-à-vis Soviets, who are here giving nothing in return."[31] Despite proposing more aggressive plans, Strauss and Schröder appear to have adopted a similar posture by the fall of 1961. They agreed "to oppose all proposals for regional disarmament or any limitations on German armaments" until there was "increased German integration into the NATO command structure."[32] In essence, Bonn wanted to use its nonnuclear status as a bargaining chip.

This strategy required little concrete action by the West Germans. The civil nuclear energy program was already on a trajectory that would give the Federal Republic weapons-production options by the end of the decade. Even if German scientists and the public writ large opposed nuclear weapons,

Bonn would still end up sitting on a bomb in the basement. The Soviets and Americans were well aware of this fact. Moscow had long wanted to neutralize this looming threat. Khrushchev's provocations over Berlin were vivid reminders of how seriously the Soviets took the West German nuclear issue. But this created an opportunity for Bonn. As part of Adenauer's "policy of strength" toward the Soviets, the idea was that West Germany should keep it nuclear options open to make Moscow "feel the squeeze of the German 'sword of Damocles,'" Andreas Lutsch (2016a: 41) argues. "In other words, even though German policymakers regarded the nuclear option de facto as unfeasible, a seeming state of 'nuclear latency' should keep Moscow in uncertainty in regard to Bonn's intentions" (Lutsch 2016a: 41). Adenauer extended this approach to put pressure on the Americans as well. Given Kennedy's opposition to proliferation, Catherine Kelleher (1975: 279) argues that the West German diplomatic approach rested upon "finding ever new ways to trade upon the commitment not to develop nuclear weapons now or in the future." At such a low level of latency, however, it remained to be seen whether this gambit would be effective.

Shooting Blanks across the Bow

Chancellor Adenauer attempted to exploit American opposition to German proliferation at a meeting with President Kennedy in late November 1961. The purpose of the visit was for the two leaders to discuss the ongoing American-Soviet talks over the Berlin crisis (Bark and Gress 1989a: 482–83). The chancellor arrived at the White House worried that the Kennedy administration was on the verge of giving up major concessions to the Soviets. On the American side, Kennedy's "suspicions about West Germany's nuclear ambitions informed his discussions," William Burr (2018) notes. After discussing a variety of issues, Kennedy asked Adenauer how he felt about the "desirability" of Western Germany continuing its pledge to forgo nuclear weapons. The chancellor underscored that when he made this statement in 1954, "Mr. Dulles had come up to him and said that this declaration was of course valid only as long as circumstances remain unchanged. Nevertheless, the Chancellor said, Germany had not undertaken anything in this respect as yet."[33] Adenauer seemed to be casting doubt on the viability of his 1954 commitment to forgo arming the Federal Republic with atomic weapons.

Kennedy made it clear that any steps toward a German bomb would be incompatible with the US security architecture in Europe. He told Adenauer that "if Western Germany were to begin nuclear experimentation, the danger of war would sharply increase without providing additional security."[34] In response, the chancellor stated that "Germany was not considering any nuclear experimentation."[35] This unequivocal statement stood in contrast to his veiled threat to abandon the nuclear abstinence pledge in the Brussels Treaty. Later in the conversation, Adenauer again downplayed the prospect of Bonn going nuclear, assuring Kennedy that he was under no pressure to change the Federal Republic's stand on manufacturing nuclear weapons.[36] But the chancellor suggested that such pressure could emerge in the future unless West Germany gained greater control over US nuclear forces stationed in the country. "The Germans are ready to receive them," he noted of the American nuclear weapons promised under the NATO stockpile plan.[37] Adenauer asked Kennedy to "make clear" to Strauss what was "actually available," emphasizing that "it would greatly strengthen his hand to know."[38] The president promised to set up briefings from the Defense Department on the status of US nuclear forces in Europe.

After returning to Bonn, Adenauer found out that his gambit had backfired. In an interview five days later with Aleksei Adzhubei, editor of the widely read Soviet periodical *Izvestia*, Kennedy expressed his willingness to reach an agreement with Moscow on Berlin and the larger German nuclear question. "Now we recognize that today the Soviet Union does not intend to permit reunification," the president admitted, before noting that "without nuclear capability, with very few divisions today, I don't believe West Germany is a military threat."[39] Kennedy went on to underscore that the United States would "not give nuclear weapons to any country, and I would be extremely reluctant to see West Germany acquire a nuclear capacity of its own."[40] According to Dennis Bark and David Gress (1989a: 483), "Those were the most conciliatory words spoken by an American president since World War II." To Adenauer, the interview amounted to a public repudiation of his diplomatic foray.

Although Kennedy took a hard-line stance toward Bonn, his top diplomats recognized the value of playing the German nuclear card against Moscow. During talks in Geneva over the winter of 1962, Rusk warned Gromyko that Soviet pressure on West Germany could end up leading Bonn toward the bomb. The best way to dampen this risk, he argued, was to settle the Berlin crisis while reaching a nonproliferation agreement. Rusk made this linkage explicit in a working paper he delivered to Gromyko in late March. The so-called "Principles Paper" offered the Soviets a quid pro quo deal. If Moscow recognized American (and NATO) equities in West Germany and Berlin, then Washington was ready to assuage concerns about the "non-diffusion of nuclear weapons"—an implicit nod to the Federal Republic's nuclear status. The "nuclear diffusion" principle in the paper offered to limit US nuclear sharing plans, as well as further lock in West German nonproliferation commitments.[41]

Rusk and his advisers even made a similar case to West German officials. In early March, Roy Kohler, assistant secretary of state for European and Eurasian affairs, briefed Foreign Minister Schröder and State Secretary Karl Carstens in Lausanne about Rusk's plan to make nonproliferation conditional on settling Berlin. Carstens questioned whether it was "wise to link Berlin to the disarmament question," as the Soviets could use nonproliferation as an excuse to intervene in Berlin.[42] "It would work the other way around," Kohler argued, because "these supplementary arrangements would operate to hold the Russians to any agreement on Berlin."[43] Once the Federal Republic reaffirmed its non-nuclear status, he suggested, the Soviet Union would be less likely to risk disturbing this favorable status quo. In any case, Kohler emphasized, "It was his view that they should get something in return for a non-diffusion formula."[44] Carstens later told Rusk that he was "impressed by this argument."[45]

But the notion of letting the Americans trade away West Germany's nuclear options sent shockwaves through the Adenauer government. In early April, West German leaders finally got their hands on the Principles Paper after Rusk delivered a copy to Ambassador Grewe. Carstens, Schröder, and other "soft-liners" supported the deal (Bark and Gress 1989a: 485). But Adenauer was outraged. He had long wanted to extract concessions from the Soviets before offering them a firm nonproliferation assurance. When Assistant Secretary of Defense Paul Nitze met with Adenauer in Bonn a few days later, the chancellor said he was "shocked by the latest messages from State about negotiations with the Soviets on Berlin."[46] The decision to include a nonproliferation arrangement, Adenauer argued, was a "poor" way to work out the Berlin issue, because "the Soviets pocket any concessions which we offer without giving anything in return."[47] Adenauer reiterated his concerns in a letter to Kennedy, which went unanswered. The Americans kept the nonproliferation principle as the centerpiece in talks with the Soviets over Berlin.

When Rusk arrived in Bonn with a delegation over the summer of 1962, Adenauer again attempted to weaken West Germany's nonproliferation commitment in the Brussels Treaty. By this point, Rusk and other officials in the Kennedy administration were growing concerned about whether Bonn would accept the "nondiffusion" formula being hashed out with the Soviets. In late June, the secretary met with Adenauer and Schröder, telling them that the United States opposed "national nuclear capabilities" as the way to strengthen the credibility of NATO's defense posture.[48] Schröder stressed that American conventional power was "absolutely necessary," along with West German participation in a "multilateral project" for sharing nuclear forces.[49] But Adenauer recounted how, in 1954, while renouncing the manufacture of atomic weapons in West Germany, "Secretary of State Dulles had said to him that the rebus sic stantibus doctrine would of course apply."[50] The chancellor emphasized that he had indicated his awareness of this escape clause should there be a fundamental change of circumstances. Yet Adenauer did not specify whether the conditions had indeed changed enough to warrant the Federal Republic abrogating its treaty commitments. Nor did he spell out how Bonn would build the bomb, given the low level of German latency at the time.

Adenauer's remark reinforced concerns among Kennedy administration officials that West Germany might pursue nuclear weapons in the future. "My visit to Bonn removed any doubt I might have had as to the inevitable growth of German pressure for nuclear weapons," Rusk reported back in a sensitive telegram to Kennedy, "unless there are multilateral arrangements in NATO or Europe."[51] He emphasized how Adenauer "asserted in the most positive terms that his 1954 declaration renouncing the production of nuclear weapons was made under and subject to then prevailing conditions (rebus sic stantibus)," while Schröder "wrestled very hard" to keep open nuclear sharing options.[52] Several days later, Rusk and Kohler were frank in expressing their concerns about West German proliferation to British officials in London. Rusk reiterated that he had "gained clear impression Germans want to reserve their position on nuclear question for [the] future." Kohler concurred, pointing out that the "Germans themselves in Bonn had been careful to say there were no pressures for national program 'as of now.'"[53] He lamented that they were "convinced that pressures for national program inevitable in Germany if alternative not found," specifically through a multilateral solution such as the MLF.[54]

Despite these concerns, Kennedy and Rusk still sought to cut a deal with the Soviets that involved strengthening West Germany's nonproliferation commitment. Adenauer sent a loud signal that was received in Washington. But it was not enough to change US policy. "The key point here," Trachtenberg (1999: 347) argues about the chancellor's gambit, "is that even his open opposition to the Kennedy policy did not lead the Americans to shift course. In the talks with Russia, the US proposals remained on the table." Part of the reason stemmed from value the Soviets placed on keeping nuclear weapons out of German hands. "It is our problem number one," Soviet ambassador Dobrynin repeatedly told Rusk during Berlin negotiations in August 1962.[55] Moscow wanted to reach an agreement on global nonproliferation, plus another deal that would specifically prohibit the Federal Republic from acquiring nuclear weapons through ally transfer or indigenous development. Washington was willing to curb Bonn's nuclear options, but only as part of a general treaty that kept hope alive for the MLF. As Kohler and Rusk had admitted earlier in the summer, US officials were eager to avoid creating long-term pressures for nuclear weapons in Germany.

The Adenauer campaign also failed because West Germany's civil nuclear enterprise remained at a low level of latency throughout this period. The chancellor was adept at exploiting the dual-use nature of nuclear technology to nurture suspicions among American and Soviet officials. But it was not clear how he planned to follow through on the "rebus sic stantibus" escape clause. Bonn could not actually build in the bomb in the early 1960s— a point reiterated by every available US intelligence assessment of West Germany's nuclear program at the time. By the summer of 1963, the Federal Republic still lacked the capacity to produce enough fissile material for an independent nuclear deterrent. "Although West Germany has the industrial potential, personnel, and technological skills to enter the nuclear weapons field," an NIE determined in June, "the obstacles to undertaking such a program are substantial."[56] The assessment again underscored the absence of fissile material production capabilities beyond experiments with plutonium and gas centrifuges. These technical barriers could erode over time, however, because West Germany was seeking "to become a world leader in the nuclear sciences" for peaceful purposes.[57] If the nuclear energy program built large power reactors and plutonium-reprocessing facilities in the years ahead, the assessment pointed out, it would bring the Germans to the "threshold" of the bomb.[58] As talks with the Soviets intensified in 1962–1963, American

officials were therefore in a prime position to lock in West Germany's nonnuclear status before it marched further up the latency spectrum.

Franco-German Civil Nuclear Cooperation and the Test Ban Fait Accompli

In the meantime, the Kennedy administration worried that West Germany's
atomic energy program could provide Adenauer cover to toy with the French
nuclear option again. Throughout 1962, US diplomats accumulated evidence
that "a conscious effort [was] underway to develop closer cooperation between France and Germany in the atomic energy field," as the American embassy in Bonn reported at the end of the year.[59] This civilian effort in part
reflected de Gaulle's larger effort to pull the Federal Republic closer to France
and away from the United States. The French revolt culminated in Adenauer
and de Gaulle signing the landmark Franco-German friendship treaty in
January 1963 (Gavin 2002; Harrison 1981; Kaplan 1999: 99–111).

Back in Washington, Kennedy and other officials were worried that this
shift might breathe new life into efforts by West German leaders to develop
nuclear weapons with the French. When the British defense minister met
with Kennedy and McNamara in September 1962, he found them "resentful
and distrustful of both French and German intentions."[60] The president told
him that if the Germans actually followed through with Adenauer's threat to
abrogate the 1954 Brussels Treaty, the United States might have to "haul out"
its forces from Europe.[61] Yet American diplomats and intelligence analysts
found no indications that the Germans were going to embark on such a quest,
either alone or with the French.[62] Cooperative research between French
and German nuclear scientists remained segregated from possible military
applications. Given the intrinsic duality of the technology, some US officials
apparently feared the Franco-German civilian nuclear effort was setting the
foundation for a joint military program.

Although Adenauer fell short in his goal of changing US policy in the
Berlin talks, he did create incentives for the Kennedy administration to
avoid antagonizing the Federal Republic. To ward off abandonment fears and
shore up the NATO defense posture, the United States recommitted itself to
maintaining conventional forces in Germany on a continual basis. On the
nuclear front, Kennedy and Rusk refused to give up the MLF in negotiations
with the Soviets over establishing a global nonproliferation treaty—they

saw it as critical for alleviating any proliferation pressure in Bonn (Gavin 2012: 46; Miller 2018: 48). If the European multinational force project failed, one US official argued, West Germany "would sooner or later begin to move towards a national nuclear capability."[63]

The problem was that Moscow rejected any type of nuclear sharing arrangement in Europe, fearing it would bring the West Germans closer to atomic weapons. From the Soviet perspective, Ambassador Dobrynin told Rusk, the MLF was "only a first step toward full proliferation," even though the Americans would retain operational control.[64] The Americans were willing to curb West Germany's nuclear options, but their position over the MLF plan did not change from 1961 to 1963. As a result, talks between the Americans and Soviets over what would later become the NPT stalled out under Kennedy.

Instead, Washington and Moscow reached an informal arrangement over Berlin that utilized the Limited Test Ban Treaty (LTBT) to solidify Bonn's status as a non-nuclear-weapon state. Finalized over the summer of 1963, the atmospheric nuclear test ban had little impact on the United States and Soviet Union, who were already moving their testing enterprises underground. But it erected an early nonproliferation barrier for future nuclear aspirants, making it harder for these signatories to cross the weapons acquisition threshold in vivid fashion.[65] The most pressing targets were China and West Germany. In Politburo discussions about the utility of the LTBT for the Soviet Union, Deputy Foreign Minister Vasilii Kuznetsov explained that "the main goal" was "to bind West Germany's hands, to prevent it from obtaining nuclear weapons."[66] The ban treaty represented a comprise position. It would dissuade the West Germans from testing atomic weapons while sidestepping the sticky MLF issue that had thwarted progress toward the larger nonproliferation regime.

Adenauer took a symbolic last stand against signing the treaty. He knew that the effect of the LTBT "would be to yet further lock in Germany's non-nuclear status," Trachtenberg (1999: 394) argues. As the chancellor told McNamara in August 1963, the treaty appeared to be "a gain for the USSR" at the expense of West Germany.[67] But Adenauer had few levers of power at his disposal to resist Washington or Moscow. He had already tried to push back on the Kennedy administration by threatening to renege on the 1954 nuclear forbearance commitment. This gambit created greater suspicion of West Germany's atomic weapons aspirations. Yet it ultimately rang hallow because there was no clear path to the bomb for Bonn in the early 1960s. The

West German civil nuclear program was years away from building enrichment or reprocessing facilities. Franco-German cooperation in the nuclear field was focused on civilian research. Any overt mobilization campaigns risked triggering a crisis with the Soviet Union. By the end of summer, the Federal Republic acceded to the LTBT. Adenauer's "policy of strength" had failed to elicit concessions or substantial policy changes from the Americans or Soviets.

Erhard's Push for Nuclear Influence, 1963–1966: Medium Latency

In the fall of 1963, leadership changes on both sides of the Atlantic set the stage for another round of diplomacy over West Germany's nuclear status. Ludwig Erhard succeeded Adenauer as chancellor of the Federal Republic in October 1963. As an Atlanticist who favored close relations with the United States, Erhard empowered Schröder to continue in his cabinet as foreign minister. On November 22, Lyndon Johnson became president after Kennedy's assassination.

At first, this transition seemed to bode well for Bonn's quest to secure nuclear sharing arrangements. In contrast to Kennedy, Johnson initially supported the MLF as a tool to keep the Germans close and away from nuclear weapons of their own. But China's nuclear test in October 1964 led the president to freeze the MLF as he adopted stronger nonproliferation measures toward adversaries and allies alike. By the spring of 1965, the Johnson administration decided to withdraw support for the MLF in favor of concluding a nonproliferation treaty with the Soviets. Over the summer, American officials began admitting in public that they might sacrifice multilateral force options in NATO to achieve a global nonproliferation agreement.[68]

Johnson's sudden about-face on US nuclear policy caught the Germans by surprise. The president had backtracked and then quashed the MLF in a unilateral manner without consulting the Erhard government. From Bonn's perspective, Washington appeared to be colluding again with Moscow to present another fait accompli, this time over the core prohibitions in the nonproliferation treaty (Brands 2007: 404; Lutsch 2016a: 47). The immediate fear was that the Soviets would succeed in their long-running effort to box the Germans out of NATO nuclear strategy altogether. In negotiations over the NPT at the time, Soviet diplomats argued that even allowing the Germans into NATO consultations about nuclear strategy would be tantamount to giving them access to atomic weapons.[69] As a result, Bonn set out to improve the Federal Republic's position within the NATO alliance architecture.

Nuclear Signals and Nonproliferation Linkages

The Erhard government launched a concerted campaign to secure German nuclear interests over the summer of 1965. In July, Schröder publicly refused to offer German support for the draft nonproliferation treaty unless several conditions were met by the Americans and Soviets. First, taking a page out of Adenauer's playbook, the foreign minister made FRG accession conditional on the reunification of Germany. This symbolic demand was designed to indicate that Bonn would not reaffirm its 1954 nuclear forbearance obligations unless it received something of substance in return. Second, Schröder offered to strengthen nonproliferation commitments to NATO allies—but not the Soviets—in return for German participation in a multilateral force. Even though the MLF appeared to be dead, Bonn was making a last-ditch attempt to revive it, or at least receive firm assurances on Germany's role in NATO nuclear strategy going forward (Küntzel 1995: 44–46; Lutsch 2016a: 44).

West German leaders attempted to exploit the Johnson administration's strengthened nonproliferation stance in private discussions throughout the latter half of 1965. Ambassador Heinrich Knappstein told Secretary Rusk that the draft NPT agreement was "unacceptable" because it privileged preventing proliferation over alliance cohesion and failed to address "the problem of reunification."[70] Rusk flatly refused "to accept a linkage" between the nonproliferation treaty and German reunification; he argued that it was in the interest of all NATO allies "not to have more *national* nuclear forces."[71] The ambassador responded that this was precisely "why a program of joint [nuclear] ownership in the Alliance was significant," hinting the MLF would help to keep Bonn away from the bomb.[72]

Erhard drove this point home at a White House summit in December 1965, where he pushed Johnson to support "a fully integrated system" of nuclear sharing within NATO. Even though many Germans found nonproliferation attractive, the chancellor noted, "It was impossible to assume that Germany will go forever without a nuclear deterrent."[73] Erhard went on to backstop this threat by musing about how "some nuclear scientists had told him that in the not too distant future nuclear weapons could be produced much more cheaply and technological aspects mastered more easily."[74] Unless the Federal Republic gained greater influence over NATO nuclear strategy, the chancellor intimated, it might be tempted to explore alternative arrangements as the technical barriers to the bomb fell in the years ahead.

The Erhard government managed to send a clear signal to US officials in Washington. After the December summit, the State Department issued a report on the challenges it faced persuading "key nuclear capable countries" such as West Germany to accept the draft text of the NPT. Bonn seemed to highly value its political relationship with Washington, the report noted, and remained content to forgo the bomb in exchange for protection under the US nuclear umbrella. However, analysts in Foggy Bottom worried that the demise of the MLF and concurrent rise of the NPT was putting pressure on West German leaders to seek some measure of equality with their nuclear-armed allies in Europe. "The Germans have indicated their reluctace [sic] to sign new non-proliferation commitments until the nuclear sharing question has been settled to their satisfaction within the alliance."[75] The State Department recommended a search for alternative arrangements to satisfy Bonn's push for greater voice within NATO nuclear strategy. "It is not possible to close all doors to West Germany and at the same time expect a stable situation to result."[76]

The Triumph of NATO Nuclear Consultations over Hardware Solutions

In contrast to the Adenauer era, the steady maturation of the West German nuclear energy program helped to underwrite Bonn's conditional threats over the NPT. By the spring of 1966, the US intelligence community concluded that the Federal Republic had acquired a medium level of latency. According to an NIE compiled at the request of defense secretary McNamara in April, it would take the West Germans about "two years" to produce enough plutonium for a nuclear weapon. They benefited from having "a larger nuclear research and power program than any other country not already possessing nuclear weapons."[77] Scientists were researching various enrichment methods to fuel power reactors in Germany, with the ultracentrifuge process moving beyond the experimental stage. West Germany had made major progress on mastering the back end of the fuel cycle for peaceful purposes. The plutonium research facilities at Karlsruhe were now "among the best in the

Western world."[78] A larger reprocessing plant would still be needed to make additional increases in plutonium production capacity. But West Germany "unquestionably" had the "technical and economic capability" to build the bomb within a few years.[79]

Although the Federal Republic was in the fissile material sweet spot for bargaining with nuclear latency, US intelligence analysts judged it would not actually build the bomb, even if the MLF continued its slow death. The April 1966 NIE determined that West German leaders would "almost certainly" avoid starting "a national nuclear weapons program."[80] Earlier intelligence reports from American diplomats in Bonn underscored that "there would be vehement opposition to the idea among important sectors of the public."[81] Moreover, it would be difficult to keep a nuclear weapons program secret, the US Embassy in Bonn noted, because "our intelligence activities and those of the Soviets (who have an estimated 20,000 operatives in Germany) . . . are directed with great intensity toward discerning any such move."[82] In lieu of a covert weapons program, though, the NIE determined that Bonn would "probably want to keep open what options it can for the eventual production of nuclear weapons."[83] The civil nuclear energy enterprise was central to this development strategy, as it would "continue to increase the country's nuclear resources and improve its technology." Bonn could then "carry on research applicable to nuclear weapons, but without committing itself to a weapons program. In all this, West Germany will be seeking to hedge against the uncertainties of its own and Europe's future."[84]

The problem for the Erhard government was that this hedging strategy no longer appeared to be conditional on the revival of multilateral force options within NATO. In a notable departure from prior intelligence assessments, the 1966 NIE concluded that the death of the MLF would do little to alter West Germany's proliferation calculus. "We do not believe that West German sentiment in favor of a national nuclear weapons program will be significantly strengthened if Bonn fails to obtain a 'hardware' solution to the problem of nuclear sharing in the Alliance."[85] The United States did not need to keep hope alive for the MLF solely to stave off German nationalist flirtations with the bomb. Given McNamara's keen interest in the NIE, it is reasonable to assume that he and other top US officials were aware of this key shift, which would have gutted the credibility of Erhard's bargaining approach. The protests and implicit threats from Bonn over the MLF therefore had little impact on the American position.

By mid-1966, it became clear that Erhard and Schröder had failed to wrest back American support for nuclear sharing options within NATO. Their subtle attempt to leverage latency fell short in part because US officials saw little risk of West Germany going nuclear, despite the country's budding capacity to produce fissile material. By abandoning support for NATO "hardware" arrangements such as the multilateral force, Washington could move closer to concurrence over the NPT with Moscow. Moreover, growing British opposition to the MLF and the French withdrawal from NATO command in February 1966 took critical ally support off the table as well (Bluth 1995). "This outcome was a heavy blow for German decision-makers and administrative elites," Lutsch (2016b: 541) argues, "who had demanded some form of hardware solution for years." In an apparent rebuke of my sweet spot hypothesis, Bonn was not able to use its budding latent nuclear capabilities to secure greater control over NATO nuclear forces.

Despite this defeat, West Germany managed to wrangle a small but important concession from the United States. In exchange for accepting the demise of the MLF without further protest, the Federal Republic would gain a permanent seat on NATO's Nuclear Planning Group (NPG)—a nascent consultative venue where allies could share information and coordinate nuclear defense plans. Defense secretary McNamara had floated the idea of formalizing consultations with Western European allies in mid-1965 to enhance the credibility of NATO's nuclear posture and mend defense relations with Bonn (Bluth 1995: 180–81). The Johnson administration soon backed the NPG's creation to assuage German demands for influence over the formulation of NATO nuclear strategy (Haftendorn 1996: 161; Kaplan 1999; Schwartz 2003: 49–63). Chancellor Erhard made this linkage explicit in his final meeting at the White House in September 1966 when he told the president that the Germans "would have to know which voice they would have in nuclear strategy. Nobody was expecting a 'hardware solution' any longer. What was needed and desired was a common solution under NATO."[86] As Hal Brands (2007: 408) concludes, "Johnson accepted this quid pro quo; in return for a private understanding that the MLF was dead, Germany became a permanent member of the NPG in late 1966."

The rest of the summit turned into a disaster for Erhard, who bungled a high-profile promise to bring home economic relief from the payments Bonn made to offset the cost of stationing US troops on West German soil.[87] Failure to resolve this monetary dispute with Johnson overshadowed the chancellor's minor achievement on the nuclear front. Back in Bonn, German participation in the consultative NPG was largely viewed as a "consolation prize" given out in lieu of the MLF (Heuser 1997: 139). This concession was not enough to keep Erhard in power. His government fell in December 1966. But in the decades ahead, the NPG would become a key lever for Germany to influence the provision of US extended nuclear deterrence and advance the European integration project through NATO.[88] Despite the defeat of Erhard's effort to secure "hardware" options, the chancellor did at least accomplish his secondary goal of ensuring that the Federal Republic would not be excluded from US and NATO nuclear strategy.

Kiesinger's Campaign to Shape the NPT, 1966–1969: Medium Latency

In December 1966, a new government formed in Bonn. Kurt Georg Kiesinger from the Christian Democrats (CDU) became chancellor in alliance with the Christian Social Union (CSU), recalling noted nuclear advocate Franz Joseph Strauss to government as finance minister. The so-called Grand Coalition split power with the Social Democrats, elevating former West Berlin mayor Willy Brandt to the foreign minister post.

Upon entering office, the Kiesinger government was confronted with a draft of the nonproliferation treaty hashed out by the United States and the Soviet Union. Bonn quickly launched an intensive diplomatic campaign to shape the provisions of the NPT (Bark and Gress 1989b: 60–63; Küntzel 1995: 69–81). By this point, William Gray (2008: 244) notes, West Germany had little interest in building the bomb, "But formally renouncing the right to do so was another matter entirely."[89] West German leaders again leveraged the country's nonnuclear status, this time to elicit changes in the draft text of the NPT.

The ultimate success of this effort was remarkable. Because the Federal Republic had not yet joined the United Nations, it was excluded from the actual NPT negotiations taking place in Geneva. Bonn also faced long odds in persuading Washington and Moscow to make concessions, considering the superpowers both wanted to advance a strong treaty.[90] Yet the Kiesinger government managed to get almost everything it demanded, including foundational clauses over treaty verification, duration, abrogation, as well as the development of enrichment and reprocessing technology for peaceful purposes (Lanoszka 2018b: 71–78; Lutsch 2016a: 47). I show how the latent weapons capability lurking within West Germany's atomic energy program played a role in this outcome.

The NPT Fait Accompli and German Demands for Accession

At the outset, the ability of West German leaders to influence the nonproliferation treaty appeared destined to fail. In late 1966, the superpowers presented Bonn with a fait accompli over Articles I and II of the draft NPT (Küntzel 1995: 94). These core provisions were designed by Washington and Moscow to inhibit the foreign transfer or indigenous acquisition of nuclear weapons. The Soviets had softened their stance toward the "no transfer" clause to permit NPG-style consultations, which enabled them to erect the two main nonproliferation pillars of the treaty in close collusion with the Americans.[91] Once this draft agreement was in place, Secretary Rusk briefed NATO allies before unveiling it at the United Nations disarmament talks in Geneva—the main multilateral venue for negotiating the NPT text. West German officials were only brought into the process after the superpowers had hashed out provisions intended in large part to solidify the Federal Republic's status as a non-nuclear-weapon state.

American diplomats encountered resistance in Bonn as they rolled out the tentative nonproliferation treaty. In late December, Ambassador McGhee attempted to sell the draft text to Kiesinger. But the chancellor expressed concern that "keeping the door open" to future nuclear options would be difficult once West Germany signed the treaty.[92] German ambassador Knappstein repeated this line to Secretary Rusk one week later. "The Germans fear that most if not all of the available options for participation in nuclear defense would be closed."[93] As McGhee reported back to Washington, West German officials felt frustrated and "boxed in" by the superpowers for presenting "Germany with a fait accompli in the NPT with which it has no choice but to comply."[94] By January 1967, however, the Kiesinger government's vague concerns about "keeping nuclear options open" had morphed into a more concerted effort to advance three major demands.

First, Bonn pushed Washington to protect atomic energy enterprises in the nonproliferation treaty. The Germans found themselves in alignment with many other non-nuclear-weapon states that were demanding access to peaceful nuclear technology in the NPT negotiations.[95] At this stage in early 1967, the draft text did not yet include any provisions about the peaceful uses of nuclear technology. In an extensive discussion with William Foster, director of the Arms Control and Disarmament Agency (ACDA), Ambassador Knappstein repeatedly asked if the treaty would permit West Germany to develop nuclear technology as part of its atomic energy program, noting that various statements "gave them the impression that a number of options or possibilities would be kept open."[96] Foster emphasized that the treaty would only "state what is prohibited," so atomic energy activities not mentioned "would be kept open."[97]

Several weeks later, Brandt laid out the geopolitical concerns lingering behind this request at a meeting with Rusk, Foster, McGhee, and other top US officials in Washington. The main problem with the draft, he stressed, was that "the NPT should not be used as an instrument of discrimination against the FRG in the peaceful development of atomic energy."[98] Brandt pointed out that the Soviets were continuing to "question the peaceful purposes of the German nuclear program," and worried that they might use the NPT as a tool to curtail nuclear technology development in the Federal Republic.[99] The Germans wanted bilateral assurances from the Americans that "full and untrammeled cooperation" would be permitted in the peaceful atomic assistance arena, plus treaty commitments ensuring their right to civil nuclear energy endeavors.[100]

Second, the Federal Republic requested the verification protocols in the treaty be modified to protect their atomic energy assets from Soviet espionage and sabotage. The EURATOM consortium already sent inspectors from Western European countries to implement peaceful use safeguards in many West German civil nuclear facilities.[101] Bonn's concern with the NPT was that it would require verification through the International Atomic Energy Agency (IAEA), which might send inspectors from Russia or other Warsaw Pact countries. Access to nuclear facilities, the Germans argued, could create a vector for adversarial agents to collect sensitive information or even cripple critical infrastructure.[102] "If we get IAEA controls over civilian fields," Brandt pointed out, "any advantages the Germans may have attained would be exposed. He was concerned about industrial espionage."[103] The Americans were sympathetic, but had to convince the Soviets, who remained strongly opposed to giving the Germans "special treatment" to use EURATOM in lieu of the IAEA. From Moscow's perspective, Bonn might leverage this exception to reject cooperation with the IAEA altogether.[104] Washington would therefore have to fight a lengthy diplomatic battle on behalf of the Federal Republic.

Third, the Kiesinger government wanted assurances that the NPT would not prohibit or otherwise limit nuclear consultations among allies. Knappstein worried that the Soviets could interpret the Article I prohibition on "indirect" transfer of nuclear weapons to include activities in the NPG. He asked whether the NPG would even be permitted in the NPT, and, if so, how far consultations could go without coming into conflict with the treaty. This point of clarification seemed relatively easy for US officials to meet, considering it had been central to the superpower negotiations over the "no transfer" formula in Articles I and II. Foster emphasized that Moscow was "under no illusions that the treaty can be used to forbid it. The Russians of course do not like it, but consultation is understood to be beyond the limitations of the treaty so long as it does not lead to decisions or control over the weapon."[105] Knappstein and later Brandt still pushed the Johnson administration to provide them with firmer commitments. The Germans were "concerned about nuclear blackmail," Brandt pointed out, and needed ironclad assurances that the Soviets would not be able to use the NPT to box them out of the NPG.[106] In addition, Bonn worried that the NPT might inhibit the long-term prospects of European integration by prohibiting a united continental superstate from arming itself with nuclear weapons (Gray 2008: 246).

The Americans complied with the requests from Bonn over the winter and spring of 1967. The archival evidence suggests that German latency played an indirect role in the negotiations at this stage. Although other non-nuclear-weapon states were making similar demands in the negotiation process (especially over access to peaceful nuclear technology), West Germany's support was essential for the viability of the NPT. The key was that concerns lingered in Washington and especially Moscow about the military utility of Bonn's ostensibly peaceful enrichment and reprocessing facilities. The United States could not afford to have an ally with a burgeoning atomic energy enterprise abstain from the NPT to keep the door open on nuclear options, as Kiesinger had intimated. "We still must be particularly careful with the Germans," Walt Rostow emphasized at the White House.[107] Without the Federal Republic onboard, there would be no path to conclude the NPT. "For the immediate future," Ambassador McGhee stressed, "we should do everything possible to provide answers to the seemingly unending series of questions raised by the Germans—public and private—on the NPT."[108]

The United States went to great lengths to allay the fears of West German leaders. In late February, ACDA and the State Department drew up a memorandum that codified the NPT interpretation points raised by the Germans, including "the peaceful applications of atomic energy," the exploitation of international inspections for "industrial espionage," and "allied consultations on nuclear defense."[109] At German insistence, the Americans reworked Article III on safeguards to bring EURATOM into compliance with the IAEA verification system envisioned in the NPT. President Johnson even pushed the UN Disarmament Conference to formulate a new provision stipulating that "the full benefits of peaceful nuclear technology" be made available to all the signatories of the NPT.[110] Yet even after wresting these concessions from Washington, West German officials continued to express reservations and demand additional modifications to the draft treaty text.

Final Concessions and Clarifications

By late April 1967, Johnson's patience was wearing thin with the Kiesinger government. When the president arrived in Bonn to mourn the death of Adenauer, he hoped to nail down German's position on NPT. As Johnson noted in a private discussion with Kiesinger, the lack of German support for the treaty had become one of his main concerns in the alliance relationship. The chancellor "saluted" the president for meeting the West German requests, but questioned "if the FRG could accept the Treaty out of the consideration of its relationship with the Soviet Union."[111] Hard-line elements within the Bundestag remained opposed to the NPT, the chancellor noted, so it would be necessary for the Americans to make additional modifications to win over their support. In particular, Kiesinger "felt strongly that the Treaty should be of a limited duration," reviewed and extended every ten years, rather than remaining in force indefinitely.[112] Johnson pointed out that the United States had already "changed the treaty text 25 times, just for the benefit of the FRG"—a complaint he repeated in frustration several times.[113] The chancellor refused to budge. He informed the president that "some subjects should be explored in greater depth" due to the poor "quality" of US consultations over the NPT.[114] Johnson was taken aback by this diplomatic barb. His rejoinder did little to change the fact that Kiesinger had moved the goalpost over NPT accession. The president returned to Washington without firming up Bonn's concurrence with the treaty.

Over the next eight months, US officials incorporated the latest batch of demands from West Germany into the nonproliferation treaty. The Soviets initially remained opposed to letting the Federal Republic employ a joint

EURATOM-IAEA arrangement to verify compliance with the NPT. "We must push the Russians hard to meet German concerns regarding Article III," Rostow recommended in November 1967: "Not to do so would give the Germans an excuse for rejecting the Treaty, and would seriously damage our relations with them."[115] By mid-January 1968, the Soviets relented under pressure from the Americans. Officials from ACDA told West German diplomats that the Soviets only accepted the EURATOM-IAEA inspection protocols after being told that the Americans "could go no further" with Article III.[116] The NPT draft tabled by the superpowers also included provisions limiting the duration of the treaty and enabling members to withdraw. As the US ambassador to NATO explained to Western European allies on January 18, the treaty "contained major change of limiting duration to 25 years. While US, for its part, favored unlimited duration, we had been induced, as result of wide-spread support among allies for limited duration, to press Soviets on this point as well."[117] Working in conjunction with other key non-nuclear-weapon states, West Germany had persuaded the United States and Soviet Union to make major alterations to the NPT (Gray 2008: 247; Schrafstetter and Twigge 2004: 185).

The Kiesinger government still found little reason to celebrate its diplomatic accomplishments, largely because domestic politics precluded full-throated support for the NPT. When the chancellor convened his defense council to review the January draft of the NPT, a secret source informed the Americans that the atmosphere was "heavy and despondent."[118] Nuclear hard-liners from the CSU—notably Strauss—remained opposed to signing the treaty. Even members from Kiesinger's own CDU were ambivalent about the NPT. To keep the Grand Coalition from splitting apart, Kiesinger and Brandt needed to delay support for the NPT while extracting more concessions. Despite agreement that Soviet movement over Article III "represented progress," the source reported that the council decided to push back against the perceived "inflexibility" of some treaty provisions.[119] With the contours of the NPT coming into final focus, the officials realized that this would be the last major request they could make of the United States— the Federal Republic could not "stand in the way" much longer.[120]

Bonn soon pressed for more revisions in private communiqués to American diplomats. On February 10, Brandt informed Rusk that his government appreciated the improvements to the latest version of the treaty that took "into account German wishes." But the foreign minister requested that the procedural rules of the NPT be made "more flexible," especially for the provisions on duration, extension, and withdrawal.[121] Over the spring, concerns re-emerged about the viability of the Nuclear Planning Group under the NPT, leading Bonn to request additional assurances about nuclear defense arrangements.

The Johnson administration again went through the laborious process of addressing the final requests from West Germany. Legal language modifications and the inclusion of NPT review conferences helped to deal with the "flexibility" issue.[122] At the NATO defense ministers meeting in May 1968, the US defense secretary privately reiterated that the NPT would not interfere with the NPG.[123] At German insistence, the Johnson administration also planned to reaffirm US security commitments to NATO when the NPT opened for signature later in the summer.[124] By this point, the State Department reported, US officials had "conducted hundreds of consultations with the Germans" to address their "serious objections to the Treaty text, most of which have been met. Essentially, however, they remain lukewarm."[125] Bonn still worried that Moscow might use the treaty to harm German security interests, even though there were few concessions left to extract on this front. Johnson pointed this out at a bilateral meeting with German officials in July. The president "jokingly" expressed his surprise with German reluctance to sign the NPT, "since he understood the Germans had practically written the Treaty as it stands now."[126]

The president's remark belied the fact that the superpowers had presented a fait accompli over Articles I and II, only leaving open space for West Germany to bargain over secondary provisions in the treaty (Lutsch 2016a: 47). Within these parameters, however, the Kiesinger government extracted notable concessions designed to assuage the security and economic interests of the Federal Republic. As the first round of countries signed the NPT in early July, Bonn could take some measure of solace in the success of this diplomatic effort to shape the final agreement.

Elite coalition politics drove West Germany's subsequent seventeen-month delay in signing the nonproliferation treaty. Because the NPT text was now set in stone, Kiesinger and Brandt pivoted away from "treating the Federal Republic's nonnuclear status as an object of barter, something that would be acknowledged only in exchange for concessions," Gray (2008: 249) argues. But some hard-line members of the Grand Coalition wanted to continue pursuing a transactional approach toward NPT accession. In late July, for instance, Strauss was still probing Rusk for possible quid pro quo side trades over the NPT, albeit in a semiofficial capacity. "The Soviets gave up nothing but got everything," he lamented, "including a permanent right of accusing the FRG of doing things it should not do under the treaty."[127] Chancellor Kiesinger found himself struggling to maintain the Grand Coalition as Strauss and other hard-liners threatened to resign from the cabinet if the Federal Republic signed the NPT. In August, the Soviet military intervention in Czechoslovakia provided a useful pretext for Kiesinger to pause NPT deliberations.

The arrival of the Nixon administration in Washington reignited the hopes of hard-liners who wanted to make additional demands before signing the NPT. To be sure, the Germans had already extracted concessions over the treaty text from the Johnson administration. But Bonn soon found that Washington had reached it limit—no new efforts were made to elicit the Federal Republic's signature. In February 1969, for example, Secretary of State Willian P. Rogers rebuffed fresh demands over the NPT from German ambassador Carl Lahusen, underscoring that "the project had become pretty well jelled" under the previous administration.[128] Even National Security Advisor Henry Kissinger, with his infamously cool view of the NPT, told the Germans that Washington expected the Federal Republic to sign the treaty. As Schrafstetter and Twigge (2004: 193) conclude, "The opponents of the treaty badly overestimated the German bargaining position and failed to extract any [additional] concessions from Washington" at this late stage. West German elections in October 1969 paved the way for accession by ushering in a new government led by Brandt that favored the NPT. After opponents in the CDU and CSU were swept aside, the Federal Republic signed the NPT on November 28, 1969. This put a definitive end to Bonn's use of nuclear latency as a bargaining instrument.

The Limits on Leveraging Latency

West Germany's diplomatic track record reveals the upper limits on leveraging latency to change the status quo in the face of joint superpower opposition. When Adenauer flirted with the European nuclear option in the late 1950s, he enjoyed tacit approval from Eisenhower, who wanted to use German nuclear ambitions to put pressure on the Soviets. Subsequent shifts in US nuclear policy under Kennedy and Johnson drove Bonn to use nonproliferation assurances to gain influence within the Western alliance as well. It is hardly surprising that West German leaders found it difficult to achieve all their diplomatic goals, considering the German nuclear question lay at the heart of superpower efforts to establish détente. Yet I find that variation in nuclear latency—specifically the jump into the fissile material sweet spot—made it possible for West Germany to achieve several tactical victories against Washington and Moscow during the latter half of the 1960s. Table 4.2 summarizes the outcome of each compellence episode I assessed in this chapter.

Table 4.2 Compellence Outcomes for West Germany

Episode (dates)	Latency	Outcome	Details	Theory support
Adenauer's gambit (1961–1963)	Low	Failure	Washington rebuffed Bonn's demands, refusing to give up veto authority over the use of force in NATO and diluting support for the MLF. But the United States reiterated its conventional force commitment to FRG. In direct opposition to Adenauer's requests, the superpowers also reached an arrangement over Berlin that utilized the LTBT to solidify West Germany's status as a non-nuclear-weapon state.	Strong (H1)
Erhard's NATO push (1963–1966)	Medium	Partial success	Bonn failed to wrest back American support for nuclear sharing options within NATO, as Washington abandoned "hardware" solutions such as the MLF. But West Germany was successful in gaining a permanent seat on NATO's Nuclear Planning Group. Superpowers began drafting foundational text of the NPT without acceding to West Germany's demands over reunification.	Modest (H3)
Kiesinger's NPT campaign (1966–1969)	Medium	Success	Superpowers presented a fait accompli over core articles of the NPT. But Washington incorporated almost every demand from West Germany into the final treaty text, even pushing the Russians hard to accept modified EURATOM-IAEA inspection protocols.	Strong (H3)

At a low level of latency, the Adenauer government failed to extract any tangible concessions from either the United States or Soviet Union (1961–1963). This first episode offers strong support for the too little hypothesis (H1). As my theory expects, the Federal Republic lacked the fissile material production capabilities necessary to make Adenauer's implicit proliferation threats credible in the eyes of the Americans. The chancellor's private musings about the "rebus sic stantibus" escape clause from the 1954 Brussels Treaty had the intended effect of stoking proliferation concerns in Washington. But rather than comply with West German demands, the Americans colluded with the Soviets to solidify Germany's nonnuclear status under the LTBT before the country marched further up the latency continuum.

In the second episode (1963–1966), the Erhard government met with mixed results in its attempt to improve West Germany's influence over NATO nuclear strategy. The demise of nuclear sharing plans under the MLF represented a clear defeat for Bonn. This outcome appears to lend modest support to the claim from skeptics that latency is not a suitable means for bargaining with superpowers. Moreover, securing a permanent seat on NATO's Nuclear Planning Group was considered a minor consolation prize in some quarters of Bonn. Yet the NPG still reflected a successful quid pro quo deal. The episode therefore offers modest support for my sweet spot hypothesis (H3). Bonn faced a mild threat-assurance trade-off at this medium level of latency. West Germany's atomic energy enterprise had the capacity to produce enough fissile material for a bomb within a few years. Taking a page out of Adenauer's playbook, the Erhard government attempted to make German support for the NPT conditional on nuclear sharing arrangements in NATO. Offering up such a nonproliferation assurance was relatively easy at this stage. The problem was that the West German leaders failed to convince the Americans that they might exploit the weapons potential within the peaceful nuclear program if the MLF died. The episode reveals that leveraging latency in the sweet spot may sometimes just yield limited benefits rather than total success.

The third episode (1966–1969) provides strong support for my theory. The Federal Republic was squarely in the fissile material sweet spot during this period. In line with skeptics (A1), some scholars (Gavin 2012: 97; Gerzhoy 2015) contend that the superpowers coerced West German leaders into signing the NPT and offered no benefits for accession. The Kiesinger government confronted a superpower fait accompli over the NPT, to be sure. The core nonproliferation commitments in Articles I and II were effectively set in stone from the outset. But the episode demonstrates that Bonn went on to leverage its latency to shape many of the secondary provisions in the treaty and wrest additional assurances from the superpowers. As Alexander Lanoszka (2018b: 71) argues, "Washington and (Moscow) made various concessions to Bonn so as to gain West Germany's signature on the NPT." In a similar vein, Brands (2007: 412) concludes that smaller powers such as West Germany were able "to exert considerable pressure on US and Soviet policy" through the NPT negotiation process. The mild nature of the threat-assurance trade-off helps to explain this outcome. West German leaders had enough latency on hand to give their demands considerable heft. This made complying with German requests "vital to the success of the Treaty," Walt Rostow admitted in late 1967.[129] At the same time, the Federal Republic was far enough away from the weapons threshold that Bonn could reaffirm its nuclear forbearance commitments via NPT accession.

German political leaders never again leveraged latency after signing the NPT in October 1969 (Heuser 1997: 141). The atomic energy enterprise continued to expand its uranium enrichment and plutonium-reprocessing capabilities throughout the 1970s. But this growing capacity to produce fissile material offered few benefits at high potential cost for leaders in Bonn and later Berlin after reunification. On the global stage, Germany went on to strengthen its nonproliferation commitments beyond the obligations in the NPT, steadily enmeshing the civil nuclear program within new bilateral agreements and multilateral treaties. At home, public opposition to nuclear weapons and atomic energy eventually dovetailed with the loss of elite support for the nuclear energy industry. This movement culminated in the decision by Chancellor Angela Merkel to phase out all nuclear power plants after the 2011 Fukushima nuclear accident—an unprecedented step to start divesting Germany from some of its core latent nuclear assets. As a result, any German leader tempted to leverage latency would have had to grapple with the ramifications of triggering an international crisis and domestic revolt. Occasional flirtations with the French about reviving the European deterrent option always fizzled out, even after the most recent crisis in alliance credibility under the Trump administration. Bonn's old playbook of nurturing nuclear suspicions therefore became an artifact of the early Cold War and a *verboten* topic best left in the shadows.[130]

5

North Korea

Over the last four decades, the Democratic People's Republic of Korea (DPRK) repeatedly leveraged its nuclear program as a blunt coercive instrument against the United States. In the early 1990s, Pyongyang threatened to produce plutonium for nuclear weapons unless Washington provided energy assistance. During the Six-Party Talks a decade later, the North Koreans returned to concession-seeking diplomacy by restarting their mothballed plutonium facilities, producing large quantities of fissile material, and even testing a nuclear device in 2006. After these negotiations reached an impasse, North Korea avoided diplomacy until February 2012, when it agreed to a moratorium on nuclear activities and missile launches in exchange for food aid from Washington.[1] But a satellite launch in April 2012 and another nuclear test in February 2013 left US officials wondering "why Pyongyang would edge close to a deal and then rip it to pieces within days," according to a Reuters report (Quinn 2012).[2] Subsequent efforts to resume negotiations fell apart when North Korea conducted its fourth nuclear test in January 2016 (Gale and Lee 2016). The brief bout of diplomacy at the 2018 Singapore Summit made it clear that North Korea had little interest in trading away its nuclear weapons or the underlying production complex (Jackson 2018: 184–87).

North Korea's steadfast development of an atomic arsenal raises the question of why Pyongyang used its nuclear program as a bargaining chip at all. Given the opaque nature of the regime, North Korean intentions can be difficult to estimate with confidence. But the historical record suggests that the ruling Kim regime long desired nuclear weapons to offset conventional inferiority and guard against ally abandonment. Beset by insecurity after the Korean War, North Korea solicited atomic assistance from the Soviet Union to train nuclear scientists and engineers (Szalontai and Radchenko 2006). Kim Il Sung then founded the Yongbyon nuclear research complex and unsuccessfully attempted to import sensitive nuclear technology from allies and partners (Mansourov 1995). As the Cold War ended, Pyongyang found itself struggling to survive amid the loss of Soviet protection. Nuclear weapons

Leveraging Latency. Tristan A. Volpe, Oxford University Press. © Oxford University Press 2023.
DOI: 10.1093/oso/9780197669532.003.0005

could shield North Korea from far more powerful adversaries—the United States and the Republic of Korea (ROK)—and perhaps even catalyze additional support from China. By contrast, the mere capacity to build the bomb provided Pyongyang with few immediate security benefits. Drumming up the threat of proliferation heightened crisis instability with Washington and Seoul, which arguably made North Korea less secure (Cha 2002: 223).

Despite facing incentives to build the bomb as quickly as possible, North Korea appears to have pursued compellence with nuclear latency for two reasons. First, coercive diplomacy helped Pyongyang to protect and expand its nuclear program during periods of vulnerability. By cutting a deal with the United States in 1994, for instance, North Korea reduced the threat of military action against the exposed Yongbyon plutonium complex, opening room to develop other strategic assets in secret. After the exposure of its hidden uranium enrichment program in 2002, Pyongyang dusted off the blackmail playbook in part to ward off sanctions from Washington and deflect pressure from Beijing. Leveraging latency in this manner reflected a central tenet of North Korean strategic thought—the counterintuitive notion that coercing stronger states with explicit threats and brinksmanship tactics was the best form of protection (Jackson 2017, 2018: 36–40).

Second, the Kim regime's survival came to depend on extorting concessions from foreign governments. During the Cold War, Moscow and Beijing propped Pyongyang up with economic and military assistance (Gelman and Levin 1984; Oberdorfer 2002: 154). This patronage was crucial to sustaining the small cadre of political and military elites who ran the country (Byman and Lind 2010; Haggard and Noland 2017: 2). After the collapse of the Soviet Union, however, North Korea lost its main foreign aid patron (Haggard and Noland 2017: 70–72). The dramatic shortfall in material support—especially energy imports—from Moscow crippled the North Korean economy, leaving the military without enough heavy fuel oil to operate.[3] But Pyongyang soon found that it could use the threat of proliferation to compel economic concessions from the United States and its allies.

North Korea may have stumbled onto the blackmail potential of its nuclear program by accident in the early 1990s. "There is no evidence that Pyongyang saw the nuclear program as a bargaining chip at its inception," Don Oberdorfer (2002: 249–50) points out, "but the record is clear that by the 1990s it had learned the program's value in relations with the outside world." Indeed, Pyongyang was well versed at identifying American and South Korean pressure points, and then exploiting these vulnerabilities with coercive diplomatic campaigns (Michishita 2009). "The identification of the nuclear issue as a priority for the United States," Scott Snyder (1999: 85) argues, "provided North Korea with significant, otherwise unavailable leverage" over Washington. Looking back over Pyongyang's diplomatic track record in the 1990s, Stephen Walt (2006: 153) also underscores that the nuclear program helped North Korea to become "the undisputed world champion in the 'effective use of blackmail' category." Compelling concessions from the United States and its allies was more than just a tactical twist in North Korea's nuclear program. It seems to have become an essential element of the Kim regime's survival strategy for two decades.

When did compellence with nuclear latency work for North Korea? In line with the Goldilocks principle, Pyongyang was in the best bargaining position as its plutonium production assets came online in the early 1990s. North Korea could issue a credible threat of proliferation backed by a relatively low-cost assurance to freeze fissile material production at Yongbyon in exchange for concessions. Once North Korea's nuclear program left this sweet spot by producing large quantities of plutonium, it became increasingly costly and unattractive for the Kim regime to reverse course or even freeze these activities. North Korea then crossed the weapons threshold in 2006 when it tested a nuclear explosive device. North Korean officials may have liked to pretend that they were still a latent nuclear power during subsequent discussions. But the operational nuclear weapons enterprise no longer provided them with a viable means to make credible nonproliferation assurances. Table 5.1 summarizes the two episodes of compellence with nuclear latency that I analyze in this chapter.

North Korea's compellence episodes are important to study for policy and theoretical reasons. Analysts and decision-makers often debate whether Pyongyang used nuclear negotiations to buy time or probe détente with the United States and its allies. My bargaining framework suggests that North Korea need not have made a binary choice between deception and deals. But the threat-assurance trade-off explains why it became harder for Pyongyang to employ coercive diplomacy as a ruse at higher levels of latency. Indeed, North Korea exhibits dramatic within-case variation in latent and eventually operational nuclear capabilities across the two episodes. In the first nuclear crisis from 1991 to 1994, North Korea used its medium amount of latency to compel energy concessions from Washington. Pyongyang employed similar coercive bargaining tactics with its nuclear program during the second crisis from 2002 until 2008. But North Korea struggled to manage

Table 5.1 Compellence Cases by North Korea

Episode (dates)	Latency	Target	Demands	Expected outcome
First nuclear crisis (1991–1994)	Medium	United States (adversary)	North Korea demanded political, economic, and energy concessions from the United States and its regional allies, such as heavy fuel oil, modern light-water nuclear reactors, and security assurances.	Success
Second nuclear crisis (2002–2008)	High; nuclear test in 2006	United States (adversary)	North Korea demanded political and economic concessions from the United States, notably normalized relations, security guarantees (including a nonaggression pact), economic aid, and energy resources (especially heavy fuel oil). North Korea also put pressure on China to moderate its support of US nonproliferation efforts in the Six-Party Talks. But Beijing was an outside intervener in the crisis, not the primary target of compellence.	Failure

the threat-assurance trade-off as the nuclear program matured into an operational military capability—going from a high level of latency to crossing the weapons threshold with the 2006 nuclear test. This controlled comparison enables me to assess the book's argument. I find that the sweet spot (H3) and too much (H2) hypotheses outperform alternative explanations.

The First Nuclear Crisis, 1991–1994: Medium Latency

The first crisis over North Korea's plutonium program in the early 1990s illustrates how a weak adversary can leverage a modest amount of latency to compel concessions from a great power. Pyongyang managed to resolve the tension between making proliferation threats and nonproliferation assurances credible because its nuclear program was in the fissile material sweet spot. Coercive diplomacy between the United States and North Korea unfolded in four stages between 1991 and 1995.

Yongbyon under Pressure

During the first stage, North Korea came under pressure from the United States to curb its budding plutonium program. Throughout the 1980s, Washington had closely watched the North Koreans construct an indigenous plutonium production reactor at the Yongbyon nuclear research complex north of Pyongyang (Richelson 2006: 346–48). In 1985, North Korea reluctantly acceded to the Treaty on the Non-Proliferation of Nuclear Weapons (NPT) in exchange for Soviet assistance with finishing the reactor project.[4] By the end of the decade, it became clear to the US intelligence community that North Korea was also building a large reprocessing plant next to the Yongbyon reactor.[5] Pyongyang delayed negotiations to bring the facility under safeguards, which raised concerns about potential military activities at the site.[6] In early 1991, Washington watched with growing alarm as work on the reprocessing plant and several support facilities neared completion. North Korea was quickly moving into the fissile material sweet spot, as it would soon be able to produce significant quantities of fissile material at the Yongbyon complex.

In response, the United States led a diplomatic campaign to persuade North Korea to roll back its plutonium production capabilities. During the fall of 1991, Washington coordinated with Seoul to offer Pyongyang greater security and economic benefits in exchange for cooperation on the nuclear issue. As an internal paper on US-ROK positions made clear in August 1991, Washington and Seoul planned to "make use of all possible diplomatic means and international pressures to bring North Korea to implement fully the provisions of the IAEA safeguards agreement . . . and forego the reprocessing and enrichment of nuclear materials."[7] After George H. W. Bush announced the withdrawal of all US tactical nuclear weapons from South Korea in September, US officials wanted to sell this move as an inducement "to demand that the North Koreans go beyond their international obligations and desist from reprocessing—something they are legally able to do," according to recommendations from a Pentagon policy memorandum.[8] In December, the National Security Council laid out the final "'game plan' to bring North Korea's nuclear weapons program under control," which combined "escalating international pressure with concrete inducements for Pyongyang."[9]

Over the winter, the US strategy yielded promising results at first. Negotiations between Seoul and Pyongyang produced the South-North Joint

Declaration on the Denuclearization of the Korean Peninsula, under which both countries agreed in January 1992 to forgo nuclear reprocessing and uranium enrichment facilities. On January 7, Seoul and Washington canceled the Team Spirit joint military training exercise, which Pyongyang had long viewed as a rehearsal for invasion. In return, North Korea announced that it would sign a safeguards agreement with the International Atomic Energy Agency (IAEA) by the end of the month. The Bush administration then agreed to a meeting at the senior political level with the North Koreans, where Under Secretary of State Kanter extracted a promise that North Korea would quickly ratify the safeguards agreement, shining much-needed light on the track record of activities at Yongbyon (Cha 2012: 251; Oberdorfer 2002: 260–67).

Yet progress came to a halt as North Korea delayed ratifying the safeguards agreement, which kept IAEA inspectors out for several months. During this period, US officials became increasingly "concerned about clear indications of North Korean stalling," as a Defense Department memorandum from February 1992 noted.[10] "North Korea's intentions remain unclear," another memorandum prepared for the North Korea Deputies' Committee at the NSC pointed out in March.[11] But the report highlighted that there were "indications of an internal debate that may be slowing decisions; the North may perceive some political advantage in delay; or it may be playing for time to destroy, dismantle, or convert sensitive facilities before allowing inspections to take place."[12] Washington began preparing various options to turn up the diplomatic pressure on Pyongyang.

After stalling for months, North Korea ratified the safeguard agreement in early April, paving the way for IAEA teams to inspect the Yongbyon nuclear complex in the spring of 1992. In its formal declaration of nuclear facilities and materials to Vienna, Pyongyang claimed to have produced about ninety grams of plutonium—a small quantity—during a single reprocessing campaign in 1990 (Sigal 1999: 39). But IAEA inspectors soon uncovered evidence that North Korea was lying about its past track record of plutonium production. On-site inspections of Yongbyon revealed two facilities near the reprocessing plant that appeared to be storage sites for holding large amounts of nuclear materials. Even more alarming, the IAEA's analysis of environmental samples collected from Yongbyon indicated that North Korea had conducted four distinct plutonium-reprocessing campaigns in 1989, 1990, 1991, and early 1992 (Mazarr 1995: 45, 84; Oberdorfer 2002: 274–75). By attempting to conceal these activities, the North Koreans left open the possibility that they were hiding a secret reserve of plutonium, perhaps with enough fissile material for one or two atomic weapons.

For the United States, the production of large amounts of plutonium constituted a major redline in negotiations—a point US officials had driven home to the North Koreans on several occasions. With backing from Washington, the IAEA demanded that North Korea allow for special inspections to determine exactly how much plutonium had been produced at Yongbyon. Pyongyang refused to provide Vienna with more information or additional access (Gordon 1993). But the North Koreans kept all the IAEA surveillance devices in place—an array of video cameras, unique seals, and other instruments to detect the diversion of spent fuel from the reactor to the reprocessing plant. "North Korea was engaged in show-and-tell," Leon Sigal (1999: 38–39) argues, "revealing enough to demonstrate willingness to make a deal while withholding enough to retain its bargaining leverage." The deliberate effort to maintain transparency at Yongbyon seemed to serve several purposes. First, it helped to stabilize the nuclear crisis in the wake of the plutonium production cover-up. Second, it set the stage for Pyongyang to take verifiable steps toward—but not across—the fissile material redline in clear view of the IAEA. By the end of 1992, North Korea found that it could use the plutonium program put pressure on the United States.

Turning the Table

The second stage of the crisis began in winter of 1993 as North Korea shifted toward an overt coercive bargaining strategy, starting with an explicit threat to mobilize the plutonium program. After months of resisting cooperation with the IAEA, Pyongyang announced on March 12, 1993, that it would withdraw from the NPT in ninety days. By exercising the exit clause in the treaty, North Korea set off a countdown clock to the production and weaponization of fissile material.

Pyongyang's pressure tactic created a renewed sense of urgency in Washington to resolve the nuclear issue before it was too late. Officials in the new Clinton administration interpreted the withdrawal announcement as an ultimatum designed to pull them into direct bilateral diplomacy with the North Koreans. As Joel Wit, Daniel Poneman, and Robert Galluci (2005: 37) recount, Pyongyang appeared to be "setting the stage to negotiate with the United States on a package that would secure the greatest benefits on the easiest terms possible." In response, Washington devised a diplomatic plan that focused on demanding nonproliferation assurances from Pyongyang, notably that North Korea return to the NPT, comply with the IAEA, verifiably declare all nuclear activities, and ship all plutonium and spent fuel out of the country (Sanger 1993).

North Korea's gambit proved to be effective at bringing the United States to the negotiation table. "By hinting that it might be willing to remain in the NPT and allow IAEA inspections if the United States met certain conditions," Drennan (2003: 168) argues, "Pyongyang maneuvered Washington into doing what it had long refused to do: enter into a bilateral diplomatic process with North Korea." When negotiations began in June 1993, North Korean chief delegate Kang Sok-ju issued a clear set of threats, assurances, and demands to the US delegation, led by chief negotiator Robert Gallucci (Sigal 1999: 63–65). Kang emphasized that "Pyongyang had the 'capability' to build such weapons, but going that route made little sense since the United States had a large nuclear arsenal," Wit, Poneman, and Gallucci (2005: 53) recall, underscoring that "Kang proposed a deal. If the United States stopped threatening North Korea, his country would commit itself never to manufacture nuclear weapons." Kang also requested energy assistance, including heavy fuel oil and modern light-water nuclear reactors, in exchange for the nonproliferation promise.

The basic contours of North Korea's offer fit with the American goal of limiting plutonium production at Yongbyon. But Gallucci made clear that US cooperation depended on the North Koreans first taking tangible steps to forgo its fissile material capabilities. Pyongyang needed to make a credible nonproliferation commitment before Washington would provide any energy concessions or take the threat of economic sanctions off the table. Kang bluntly told Gallucci that North Korea would "proceed to extract enough plutonium from its spent fuel rods to build one or two weapons" if the United States resisted (Wit et al. 2005: 55). From the US vantage point, it seemed that the North Koreans were trying to extract the greatest package of concessions possible. Diplomacy broke down as Pyongyang refused to take concrete steps away from the bomb.

After negotiations deadlocked, North Korea manipulated three aspects of its nuclear program to gain additional leverage over the United States. First, Pyongyang continued to hold hostage the spent fuel rods, which contained critical information about the history of plutonium production at Yongbyon. Once these rods were dissolved and reprocessed, it would be difficult for the IAEA to estimate how much fissile material had been produced in the past. Second, North Korea informed the IAEA that the Yongbyon reactor would be shut down to remove the spent fuel. Unless North Korea allowed the IAEA on-site access to monitor this defueling process, the United States would not know if the spent fuel rods were diverted to the plutonium-reprocessing plant.

Third, Pyongyang exploited IAEA inspections as a channel for sending both assurances and threats to Washington. North Korea allowed the IAEA to perform maintenance and even install new monitoring equipment at Yongbyon, keeping the main elements of its nuclear program out in the open for Washington to track. But then in March 1994, inspectors discovered that North Korea had quietly doubled its capacity to reprocess plutonium at Yongbyon. Washington viewed this expansion in latency as "a ploy to build up negotiating leverage" because it "meant that Pyongyang might ramp up its nuclear weapons program rapidly if diplomacy failed," according to Wit, Poneman, and Gallucci (2005: 144). If the United States continued to rebuff North Korea's demands, Pyongyang signaled it was prepared to march toward the bomb on short notice.

Plutonium Brinkmanship

North Korea started to mobilize its plutonium production program during the third stage of the crisis in the spring of 1994. By this point, Washington had resisted Pyongyang's demands for over a year. Concessions from the United States continued to hinge on North Korea making a credible promise to freeze and dismantle the plutonium program at Yongbyon. Pyongyang began marching toward the fissile material redline set by Washington in an effort to break the deadlock. "It was a provocative way to draw attention to its nuclear potential and away from its nuclear past," Sigal (1999: 113) notes. But this tactic pulled the United States to the brink of preventive war.

In April 1994, North Korea announced that it would discharge the spent fuel rods from the Yongbyon reactor in preparation for a major reprocessing campaign. Similar to the NPT withdrawal crisis, Pyongyang sought to re-assert "control of negotiations through the creation of perceived deadlines by which [Washington] should respond," Snyder (1999: 81) points out. Drennan (2003: 179) underscores that North Korea was becoming "partic-ularly adept at creating artificial 'deadlines' . . . to which the United States felt compelled to respond to keep the situation from deteriorating further." For instance, the defueling process put pressure on Washington to strike a deal before North Korea destroyed the historical record of its past reprocessing activities by discharging the rods without the IAEA present. Even more worrisome, Pyongyang started another countdown clock, this time to the recovery of plutonium from the rods after cooling them off for several months in a storage pod at Yongbyon. North Korea officials also linked the looming fissile material production campaign to demands for concessions from the United States.

On May 12, North Korea began to unload fuel from the reactor without IAEA inspectors present. Pyongyang claimed it was preserving the historical information of past irradiation history in the rods. But the North Koreans hoped the unsupervised defueling "would both force the [United States] to react and increase Pyongyang's bargaining leverage by presenting a fait accompli that [Washington] would need to pay a higher diplomatic price to reverse," according to Snyder (1999: 81). North Korean officials made explicit the coercive nature of the mobilization process, telling their American counterparts that the discharge campaign would take about two months to complete, which left enough time for both sides to reach an agreement (Wit et al. 2005: 171).

But when the IAEA team arrived several days later on May 19, it became apparent that the North Koreans had accelerated their march toward plutonium production (Gordon 1994). Inspectors "discovered that Pyongyang's unloading of the spent fuel was proceeding at twice the expected rate since it had two, not just one, machines to discharge the fuel," Wit, Poneman, and Galluci (2005: 182) recount, so "it looked as though the rods would be removed in a matter of weeks." In June, while the United States considered how to respond to the crisis, the IAEA approved independent sanctions against North Korea. Pyongyang withdrew from the IAEA and expelled inspectors from Yongbyon (Sigal 1999: 120–21).

In response, the United States considered a preventive strike against a range of North Korean nuclear and regime targets. Yet the potential costs of retaliation from North Korea were deemed to be extremely high (Carter and Perry 2000: 130–31). When President Bill Clinton asked General Gary Luck, the commander of United States Forces Korea, whether the United States could successfully perform such a mission, General Luck replied, "Yes, but at the cost of a million [civilian casualties] and a trillion [dollars in economic damage to South Korea]" (Wit et al. 2005: 181). The United States backed away from the preventive strike option, but boosted military capabilities in the region, and prepared to levy harsh sanctions on the Kim regime.

Endgame

The final stage of the crisis played out between the summer and fall of 1994. As Washington and Pyongyang teetered on the brink of war, North Korea appeared eager to find a way back to negotiation table before the situation escalated out of control. The unexpected visit of former US president Jimmy Carter with Kim Il Sung provided an offramp for Pyongyang to offer a promise of nuclear restraint (Sigal 1999: 131–33). The two sides returned to the bargaining table and reached a deal. North Korea agreed to freeze operations at Yongbyon, seal the reprocessing facility for eventual dismantlement, store and ship its spent fuel out of the country, halt construction of two large reactors, and remain party to the NPT. As Secretary of State William Christopher (1995: 6) summarized in congressional testimony, "North Korea's capacity to separate plutonium was ended," and it was "obligated to fully disclose its past nuclear activities." Cooperation with the IAEA at each step provided a credible system of verification for the United States. In return, the United States agreed to the phased delivery of $50 million in heavy fuel oil each year, $4 billion in modern proliferation-resistance nuclear reactor technology, the relaxation of economic and political barriers, and a formal assurance against the threat or use of nuclear weapons against the DPRK. The final Agreed Framework signed by North Korea and the United States on October 21, 1994, formalized this bargain.

North Korea was able to strike a low-cost and high-reward deal because it could reassure the United States by freezing operations at Yongbyon. This was a modest price to pay. North Korea avoided military attack and reaped badly needed energy assistance. Washington believed that Pyongyang was unlikely to cease plutonium production if it wanted nuclear weapons in the near term. The United States also insisted upon several hand-tying mechanisms to increase the costs of reneging on the Agreed Framework while boosting the benefits of sustained cooperation. As Ambassador Gallucci (1994: 12) admitted in December 1994, "We entered into discussions . . . without any uncertainty or delusions about past North Korean behavior." He argued that the Agreed Framework was "not based upon trust," but rather a tit-for-tat structure "so that we can withhold cooperation at any point that we determine that North Korea is not meeting its obligations under the agreement" (1994: 12). The American negotiators decomposed the terms of the deal into a series of smaller steps, with the burden of up-front performance falling on the North Koreans. To receive the first shipment of heavy oil, for example, North Korea had to verifiably halt all its declared nuclear operations. Larger benefits would only come several years later when the United States "had an opportunity to judge [North Korea's] performance and its intentions," as Secretary Christopher (1995: 7) underscored. To receive the full package of energy assistance, Pyongyang had to uphold its complete promise to disable the Yongbyon complex. The deal bound the Kim regime to its nonnuclear promise for as long as North Korea valued the energy subsidies more than acquisition of nuclear weapons.[13]

The Second Nuclear Crisis, 2002–2008: High Latency and Weapons Acquisition

Less than a decade later, North Korea found itself embroiled in another nuclear crisis with the United States. Washington's discovery of hidden uranium enrichment facilities in the fall of 2002 led Pyongyang to fall back on leveraging latency again. Over the next six years, North Korea ramped up pressure on the United States with vivid mobilization tactics, even going so far as to test a nuclear weapon in 2006. Yet this compellence campaign unraveled once North Korea ultimately refused to give up its fissile material production capabilities or small atomic arsenal. In line with this book's core argument, the dilemma between making threats and assurances credible became too difficult to resolve once Pyongyang built the bomb. The four main stages of the second nuclear crisis from 2002 to 2008 illustrate how the severity of the threat-assurance trade-off undermined North Korea's coercive diplomatic strategy.

Exposure, Remobilization, and Intervention

In October 2002, a small team of US officials arrived in Pyongyang with evidence that the North Koreans were covertly marching toward the bomb again, this time with a hidden uranium enrichment program (Chinoy 2009: 117). Vice Foreign Minister Kang Sok Ku deflected the allegation, only to admit that "for the DPRK to engage in dialogue with the United States, it needed leverage—either from uranium enrichment or nuclear weapons," as one member of the US delegation recounted (Pritchard 2007: 39). In the wake of exposure, the North Koreans were trying to turn the nuclear program back into a bargaining chip. Kang "was in effect putting the uranium issue on the table," Mike Chinoy (2009: 122) argues, "sending a strong signal that if Washington were willing to engage in a broad negotiation . . . then the North was ready to address U.S. worries about the uranium program." Yet the Bush administration worried that bilateral diplomacy would just be a ruse for North Korea to buy time and deflect international pressure. Washington refused to negotiate and terminated the provision of energy assistance in the Agreed Framework.

North Korea responded by remobilizing its dormant plutonium production assets. Once the United States cut off the flow of heavy fuel oil in December 2002, Pyongyang declared the Agreed Framework void, and announced the resumption of operations at Yongbyon. North Korea removed or disabled IAEA seals and monitoring equipment on all the mothballed nuclear facilities, and expelled inspectors at the end of the month. North Korean officials then informed the IAEA that they planned to reprocess the old stock of spent fuel that had been sitting in the cooling pond next to the reactor since 1994; they also initiated the lengthy process of restarting the Yongbyon reactor (Samore 2004). On January 10, 2003, North Korea turned up the pressure even more by withdrawing from the NPT altogether. In an apparent effort to dampen blowback and restart negotiations with Washington, Pyongyang underscored that its nuclear activities would "be limited to the peaceful purpose of electricity production at the present stage," and offered to prove that they would "not make nuclear weapons" (KCNA 2003). As one North Korean official made explicit about the Yongbyon restart and NPT withdrawal, "These are just tactics . . . to improve our negotiating position" (Chinoy 2009: 152).

But the plutonium brinkmanship campaign failed to coax Washington into opening bilateral discussions. Instead, the United States set the stage for multilateral diplomacy with the help of North Korea's last major power partner—China. The Bush administration wanted Beijing to intervene and change the nuclear calculus in Pyongyang (Bechtol 2010: 80; Snyder 2003). In contrast to prior eras, China faced stronger nonproliferation incentives and wielded more influence over North Korea (Medeiros 2007). Beijing saw a nuclear-armed North Korea as a liability with the potential to drive crisis instability and regional arms races (Feng 2006). China could intervene against North Korea in three ways. First, Beijing provided political cover for Pyongyang at the United Nations, so it could threaten to stop shielding North Korea from harsh Security Council sanctions. Second, North Korea's experience during the Korean War created the belief that China might bail it out again in a future conflict. Beijing could manipulate this expectation by taking steps to curtail military support.

The third and most influential lever came from North Korea's dependence on China for energy assistance. Energy problems in the DPRK steadily worsened throughout the 1990s, even with the additional supply of heavy fuel oil from the Agreed Framework. As North Korea suffered more severe fuel oil shortages, regime survival continued to hinge on securing foreign sources of energy, with almost all petroleum imports coming from China after the collapse of the Agreed Framework. According to Julia Joo-A Lee (2009), Beijing ramped up its energy assistance to Pyongyang in an effort to gain greater influence over the North Korean leadership. By making North Korea more dependent on China, Beijing increased its capability to use the supply of oil as a means to threaten and punish Pyongyang. Yet Beijing was only willing to go so far, as turning the oil spigot off for a long time could trigger regime collapse in North Korea.

The power to hurt North Korea made China an ideal intervener for Washington to bring into nuclear negotiations. In the aftermath of North Korea's withdrawal from the NPT, President George W. Bush and other high-level US officials led a sustained campaign to elicit support from China's leaders (Bechtol 2010: 80; Chinoy 2009: 146; Snyder 2003). Beijing was receptive and undertook an intensive effort to shape North Korean behavior over the nuclear issue (Pollack 2011: 144). After denouncing Pyongyang's nuclear activities, China voted in support of an IAEA resolution referring North Korea to the UN Security Council in February 2003. Beijing also flexed its coercive levers, denying requests for military hardware from North Korea and even cutting off oil supplies for three days in March (Watts 2003). But these actions had little impact. The mobilization of Yongbyon continued at the same steady pace throughout the winter of 2003.

Multilateral Diplomacy and Plutonium Production

The crisis moved into its second stage in spring of 2003. Unable to elicit nuclear course corrections from Pyongyang, Beijing worked with Washington to host a trilateral summit in late April. The lead North Korean negotiator opened with an explicit quid pro quo offer. Pyongyang was willing to dismantle its nuclear program with international inspectors present. In exchange, North Korea "demanded major concessions from the United States, such as normalized relations, economic aid, security guarantees, and a nonaggression pact," according to Chinoy (2009: 171). The North Korean delegation also announced that they were already reprocessing the spent fuel rods at Yongbyon, further underscoring the urgency of acceding to their demands in a timely fashion.

But the US delegation refused to put any concessions on the table until North Korea gave up its nuclear program. Washington felt it had been burned by Pyongyang's nonproliferation promises before. US officials insisted that North Korea had to go to greater lengths to make its nonproliferation promises credible by dismantling the nuclear program in a "verifiable and irreversible" manner (Cha 2012: 255–56, 290–91). Despite mediation efforts from Chinese officials, the negotiations made little progress, leading President Bush to admonish North Korea for moving "back to the old blackmail game," in an *NBC News* interview (Brokaw 2003). On the last day of the summit, US officials remained adamant that they would not reward North Korea for simply halting the production of fissile material—the nuclear program would need to be dismantled first. North Korean diplomats threatened to cross the weapons threshold and even implied that they might transfer nuclear technology and materials out of the country.[14]

After failing to make any progress at the April summit, North Korea redoubled its efforts at Yongbyon. In July, North Korea announced that it had finishing reprocessing all of the spent fuel rods at Yongbyon. To underscore the looming nature of the proliferation threat, North Korean officials also informed their American counterparts that they were taking steps to weaponize the fissile material (Chinoy 2009: 178). By the end of the summer, Washington had little choice but to resume nuclear negotiations with Pyongyang.

China mediated the opening round of the Six-Party Talks in August 2003, which now included South Korea, Japan, and Russia alongside North Korea and the United States. The North Korean delegation again demanded that the United States resume shipments of heavy fuel oil and food aid, compensate them for the loss of electricity under the collapsed Agreed Framework, conclude a nonaggression treaty, and open diplomatic relations. Although the North Koreans denied having a uranium enrichment program, they did offer up a nonproliferation promise. In exchange for the concessions, North Korea would refreeze operations at Yongbyon, invite the IAEA back, resolve concerns over ballistic missile development, and dismantle all declared nuclear facilities. The US team stuck to Washington's hard-line position: North Korea had to "completely, verifiably, and irreversibly dismantle" its nuclear program before the United States would consider making any concessions (Chinoy 2009: 184). Diplomacy ended when the North Koreans responded with explicit threats to acquire nuclear weapons.

During the winter of 2004, North Korea brandished its most significant plutonium production campaign to date. In January, Pyongyang invited an unofficial delegation of US experts to tour facilities at the Yongbyon nuclear complex. Without IAEA inspectors on the ground, North Korea used the visit to reveal information about its growing fissile material stockpile. For instance, North Korean officials highlighted the importance of including Siegfried Hecker from Los Alamos National Laboratory in the group, noting his expertise in plutonium metallurgy. "Hecker's presence will allow us to tell you everything," one North Korean diplomat told the US delegation, before adding that "the time that has been lost [in dealing with us] has not been beneficial to the U.S. side. With an additional lapse in time, our nuclear arsenal could grow in quality and quantity" (Hecker 2004). To make this claim credible, the North Koreans led the Americans through several facilities at Yongbyon, showing off the removal of all fuel rods from the storage pod, the unfrozen plutonium production reactor, and even a purported sample of plutonium in the reprocessing laboratory. Yet the visit did not break Washington's bargaining stance. US officials refused to table any concessions until North Korea dismantled its nuclear program. Diplomacy bore little fruit over the next year.

In February 2005, Pyongyang upped the ante again with a series of proliferation provocations. The DPRK Ministry of Foreign Affairs announced that North Korea would suspend its participation in the Six-Party Talks "for an indefinite period" until Washington was ready to make concessions. Even though the KCNA (2005) statement went on to underscore that North Korea had "manufactured nukes [sic] for self-defence," it still held out the promise of resolving the nuclear issue through diplomacy. North Korea then launched another mobilization effort in the spring of 2005. Preparations began to remove a fresh batch of fuel rods from the plutonium production reactor for reprocessing. A senior North Korean official admitted to a visiting American scholar that Pyongyang was planning "'to unload the reactor to create a situation' to force President Bush to negotiate on terms more favorable to North Korea," according to the *New York Times* (Sanger 2005). In May, North Korea fired multiple short-range ballistic missile tests into the Sea of Japan, accelerated preparations at a suspected nuclear weapon test site near Kilchu, finished unloading all the spent fuel rods, and announced resumed construction on the 50 MW reactor.

Under renewed pressure from China, North Korea came back to the Six-Party Talks in July 2005. But after twenty days of negotiations, Washington and Pyongyang were headed toward deadlock again, so all parties agreed to a brief recess in August. During the break in diplomacy, North Korea invited back the unofficial US delegation of experts to Pyongyang. Upon arrival, the North Korean director of nuclear facilities told the visitors that they could not visit Yongbyon "because of the elevated radiation levels resulting from the reprocessing activities that were then under way," as Charles Pritchard recounts (2007: 117). To substitute, the director provided technical information on the plutonium production campaign. He made four major claims: (1) they had operated the small Yongbyon reactor at full power from February 2003 to March 2005; (2) the spent fuel rods from the reactor were unloaded in April 2005 to extract plutonium; (3) they had already reloaded the reactor in June 2005 with fresh fuel; (4) the fuel fabrication facility was being refurbished in preparation for additional reprocessing (Hecker 2005). As Narushige Michishita (2009: 169) aptly sums up, "The North Koreans were playing a game of coercion with the Americans." Indeed, several members of the US delegation came away with the impression that Pyongyang was using the visit to harden its position during the recess (Pritchard 2007: 117).

The Six-Party Talks resumed in September 2005 as North Korea continued to ramp up operations at Yongbyon. With the plutonium production campaign hanging over the summit, the United States and North Korea sketched out the contours of a satisfactory solution to the nuclear crisis. A joint statement on September 19 announced a preliminary quid pro quo deal. North Korea affirmed it "was committed to abandoning all nuclear weapons and existing nuclear programs and returning, at an early date, to the NPT and to IAEA safeguards."[15] In exchange, the United States along with China, Japan, South Korea, and Russia all underscored "their willingness to provide energy assistance to the DPRK . . . and agreed to discuss, at an appropriate time, the subject of the provision of light water reactor to the DPRK."[16] But in a supplemental statement, the United States defined "an appropriate time" as occurring only "when the DPRK has come into full compliance with the NPT and IAEA safeguards, and has demonstrated a sustained commitment to cooperation and transparency."[17] The American position had hardly changed: Washington still refused to table concessions until Pyongyang dismantled its nuclear weapons enterprise. The North Koreans were quick to reject this qualification (Michishita 2009: 170). Diplomacy deadlocked yet again.

Freezing Finances and Building Bombs

The third stage of the crisis began in September 2005 when the United States hit the North Korean elite with economic sanctions. Washington had been sharpening its coercive toolkit to put pressure on Pyongyang in the diplomatic track. In particular, US officials targeted Banco Delta Asia in Macau because it served as hub for the Kim regime to launder money from illicit activities, notably the sale of weapons, narcotics, and counterfeit goods abroad. On September 15, the US Treasury Department designated Banco Delta Asia as a money-laundering concern, which effectively froze North Korean assets in the bank. The designation had "devastating economic ramifications on North Korea's ability to generate badly needed hard currency," Bruce Bechtol (2010: 85) argues. The financial crackdown posed a serious threat to the Kim regime. Pyongyang relied on the funds earned from illicit trade to sustain elite support and military capabilities. "The United States was taking these more aggressive tactics," Michishita (2009: 170) argues, "in the hope of enhancing its bargaining power." But when the Six-Party Talks resumed, the North Korean team refused to discuss the nuclear issue until the United States lifted the sanctions. After the US delegation rebuffed the request, Pyongyang ordered its diplomats to walk out and boycott the talks indefinitely.

Over the next year, North Korea marched toward the brink of building an atomic weapons arsenal. Pyongyang kept up the tempo of activities at Yongbyon as relations with Beijing deteriorated and Washington crippled the regime's finances. In early July 2006, North Korea fired off the most extensive battery of ballistic missile tests in its history.[18] A statement about the missile launches from the Ministry of Foreign Affairs threatened "to take stronger physical actions of other forms" if the United States or China "put pressure upon it" (KCNA 2006). Washington responded with an effort to expand multilateral sanctions against Pyongyang in the United Nations Security Council, which garnered support from China. North Korea found itself playing a game of chicken with the United States and now China, with each side driving up pressure and daring the other the swerve.

After the plutonium production and missile launch campaigns failed to have much of an impact, Pyongyang played its final mobilization card. North Korea conducted an underground test of a nuclear weapon on October 9, 2006. The small explosive yield from the test—estimated to have been less than one kiloton—led to speculation in the press about whether the device was a failed fizzle or a successful low-yield weapon (Bermudez 2006; Sanger 2006). Pyongyang made clear that the nuclear test was designed in part to put pressure on the United States and, to a lesser degree, China. North Korea's Ministry of Foreign Affairs directly attributed the nuclear test to the sanctions and coercive measures being pursued by Washington and Beijing, yet still held out a promise "to denuclearize the peninsula through dialogue and negotiations" (KCNA 2006b, 2006c). Many Chinese leaders believed "the country was using the threat of developing atomic bombs as an economic bargaining chip," and saw the test as an indicator that the Kim regime wanted "a nuclear trump card to intimidate China as much as the United States," according to reports from the *New York Times* (Kahn 2006b). Having reached the end of the latency continuum, Pyongyang could only generate additional bargaining leverage by following through with its proliferation threat.

With the first nuclear test, North Korea demonstrated its resolve to cross the weapons threshold. As Ankit Panda (2020: 115) argues, the weapons test "appeared to have a modest, but critical objective: to demonstrate North Korea's seriousness about becoming a nuclear power." But North Korea could no longer be considered a purely latent nuclear power after the test. To wrest concessions from Washington and Beijing, Pyongyang would now need to grapple with the prospect of giving up an operational atomic weapons enterprise.

Breakthrough and Breakdown

The crisis moved into its final phase in late October 2006. North Korea used the nuclear test to reset the diplomatic stage in two ways. First, Washington came under immediate pressure to jump-start negotiations with Pyongyang again. "In the aftermath of the detonation," Jonathan Pollack (2011: 151) notes, "US officials expressed renewed awareness of the need to cap the DPRK's plutonium programme." On October 31, the United States agreed to attend a trilateral meeting with North Korea in Beijing. The lead US diplomat, Christopher Hill, exhibited greater flexibility in discussing the issue of financial sanctions, even going so far as to signal "a willingness to explore ways to bring the episode to a close," according to Chinoy (2009: 307). With this key change in the US position on the table, the North Koreans agreed to return to the Six-Party Talks in November. "To Pyongyang," Pollack (2011: 151) argues, "the US willingness to undertake direct negotiations vindicated its decision to test." Although Washington was open to diplomacy, it soon became apparent that North Korea would have to roll back its entire nuclear enterprise to cut a deal.

Second, North Korea's nuclear test exposed the degree to which China would intervene over the nuclear issue. On the one hand, Beijing took modest steps to punish Pyongyang in the aftermath of the denotation (Feng 2006: 46). China reconfigured its armed forces along the northeast border with North Korea to signal that the PLA would not provide a military rescue for Pyongyang (Twomey 2008: 416). Beijing joined with Washington to increase economic pressure at the United Nations (S. Snyder 2007). Chinese diplomats backed another Security Council resolution against North Korea, this time with biting sanctions under Chapter VII of the UN Charter (Twomey 2008: 414). Beijing also ordered a steep reduction in its supply of oil to North Korea (Kahn 2006a). On the other hand, however, China calibrated this coercive campaign to avoid actions that might imperil the Kim regime's survival. Lee (2009: 62) argues that "a large-scale, intensive disruption of energy supply could result in catastrophe in North Korea, creating a political vacuum with refugees fleeing across its borders in their thousands." Beijing was therefore quick to turn the oil spigot back on in November 2006. As a result, China revealed the maximum amount of pressure it would dole out against North Korea.

When diplomacy resumed in November 2006, the United States floated an offer to North Korea. Washington demanded a freeze on operations at Yongbyon, the return of IAEA inspectors, a complete declaration of all nuclear facilities, and an end to nuclear testing. North Korea would receive food and energy aid if it fulfilled these requirements, along with discussions to end the economic sanctions, normalize diplomatic relations, and conclude a peace treaty (Michishita 2009: 173). As Chinoy (2009: 310) underscores, this proposal spelled out "in greater specificity than any previous U.S. envoy, what Washington was prepared to offer" if North Korea gave up its nuclear weapons program. But the North Korean delegation refused to budge until

Washington relaxed its financial stranglehold over Pyongyang. As the Six-Party Talks recessed in December without progress, North Korea began preparations to test another nuclear device.

In response, Washington fell back on exploring whether Pyongyang might be persuaded to limit its plutonium program. During the next round of negotiations in February 2007, the US delegation put various political assurances and energy concessions on the table in exchange for the phased rollback of North Korea's fissile material production capabilities (Pollack 2011: 151). Specifically, Washington offered to lift some of the financial sanctions if Pyongyang shuttered the plutonium reactor, reprocessing plant, and fuel fabrication plant at Yongbyon. Once the facilities were shut down, North Korea would receive a one-time shipment of 50,000 tons of heavy fuel oil—an additional 950,000 tons would be provided after the entire nuclear infrastructure had been declared and then disabled (Pritchard 2007: 159). By sequencing the provision of energy concessions, US officials hoped to hold back the most lucrative rewards until Pyongyang took tangible demobilization steps (Chinoy 2009: 325). North Korea accepted the offer and hashed out terms. The Six-Party Talks had finally produced a tentative nuclear deal.

During the summer of 2007, Pyongyang started to shutter nuclear facilities after Washington unfroze Banco Delta Asia funds (Cha 2012: 294). In July, inspectors from the IAEA returned to verify the shutdown and institute a daily presence at Yongbyon. North Korea also invited official and unofficial US delegations to visit the shuttered reactor and attendant facilities. The United States soon thereafter delivered the first 50,000-ton shipment of heavy fuel oil. Subsequent discussions in October detailed the precise disablement steps North Korea would need to take at each facility in the Yongbyon complex. Pyongyang also had to provide the IAEA with an accurate declaration of its entire nuclear program. Additional energy assistance from Washington depended on these final disablement and verification measures. Over the next year, North Korea fulfilled select obligations from the 2007 accords, such as providing an estimate of the plutonium inventory along with reactor operation records from Yongbyon. In the summer of 2008, North Korea even invited international media to film the destruction of reactor's cooling tower—a largely symbolic but vivid demobilization effort.

But these steps to cease plutonium production masked a much bigger issue with North Korea's nonproliferation assurances. It soon became apparent that Pyongyang wanted to retain the capacity to produce fissile material, along with the plutonium stockpile and small atomic arsenal. North

Korea's nuclear declaration seemed to dramatically understate the quantity of plutonium it possessed and made no mention of enrichment activities at all. Pyongyang refused to allow intrusive inspections of its facilities to verify the accuracy of the information it provided Washington and Vienna. The final session of the Six-Party Talks in December 2008 "proved fruitless, with the DPRK balking at any commitment to written, binding pledges on verification," according to Pollack (2011: 153). Even more problematic, North Korea refused to render the reprocessing plant inoperative at Yongbyon. As a senior North Korea diplomat told an unofficial US delegation in Pyongyang, "Disablement does not imply dismantlement. . . . We are maintaining our deterrent" (Pollack 2011: 153). The United States refused to deliver the rest of the heavy fuel oil as negotiations over nuclear rollback deadlocked.

The 2007 nuclear accords quickly fell apart after North Korea declined to curb its plutonium production capabilities. From the outside, Pyongyang appeared to decide that previously sufficient concessions were no longer good enough to trade away the nuclear program. As the nuclear program crossed the atomic weapons threshold, the Kim regime seemed increasingly reluctant to roll back these capabilities or divest from the underlying production infrastructure.

Bargaining before and after the Bomb

North Korea's checkered diplomatic track record lends strong support for my argument that leveraging latency is most effective in the fissile material sweet spot. Table 5.2 summarizes the outcomes of compellence for each episode I analyzed in the chapter. When Pyongyang acquired plutonium production capabilities in the early 1990s, it employed various mobilization tactics to put pressure on Washington—from the NPT withdrawal countdown clock to the plutonium brinkmanship campaigns. Yet North Korea was also in a prime position to offer promises of nuclear restraint because it could simply freeze the plutonium program. In line with the sweet spot hypothesis (H3), Pyongyang wrested concessions from Washington by making both proliferation threats and nonproliferation assurances credible. Contrary to skepticism about nuclear latency (A1), the first nuclear crisis demonstrates that the weak can compel the strong well before the bomb.

North Korea failed to resolve the threat-assurance trade-off after it marched across the atomic weapons threshold in October 2006. The initial mobilization effort to demonstrate resolve by producing plutonium pushed

Table 5.2 Compellence Outcomes for North Korea

Episode (dates)	Latency	Outcome	Details	Theory support
First nuclear crisis (1991–1994)	Medium	Success	North Korea agreed to freeze Yongbyon operations, seal the reprocessing facility, store and ship its spent fuel out of the country, halt construction of two large reactors, and remain party to the NPT. In return, the United States agreed to the phased delivery of $50 million in heavy fuel oil each year, $4 billion in modern proliferation-resistance nuclear reactor technology, relaxation of economic and political barriers, and a formal assurance against the threat or use of nuclear weapons.	Strong (H3)
Second nuclear crisis (2002–2008)	High; nuclear test in 2006	Failure	The United States offered a phased package of economic, energy, and diplomatic concessions in return for North Korea demobilizing and disabling its entire nuclear weapons program. Pyongyang shuttered some nuclear facilities but rebuffed intrusive inspections to very compliance. North Korea also refused to render the reprocessing plant inoperative at Yongbyon or give up its uranium enrichment capabilities.	Strong (H2)

Pyongyang past the fissile material sweet spot into a high level of latency. Once North Korea went even further with the weapons test, the burden fell on the United States to relax its bargaining position. Yet this episode offers little support for the maximalist school of thought (A2). Pyongyang needed to back this threat with a promise of nuclear restraint to wrest concessions from Washington. As expected by the too much hypothesis (H2), North Korea faced higher barriers to making such an assurance credible. Washington structured the 2007 accords around major demobilization steps. North Korea could no longer just freeze activities at Yongbyon—it had to give up valuable nuclear assets and accept intrusive verification measures. But the costs and risks associated with these rollback steps increased after North Korea built the bomb, for two reasons.

First, the United States needed greater amounts of information to verify North Korea's nonproliferation promises as the nuclear program matured into a military capability. But Panda (2020: 60) underscores that "the North Koreans were allergic to discussions of a verification protocol with their negotiating partners." Perhaps Pyongyang opposed transparency efforts because it wanted to keep nuclear capabilities hidden after cutting a deal—what one US official described as an attempt by the North Koreans to "have their yellowcake and eat it too."[19] North Korea may have also worried about the security risks associated with monitoring nuclear rollback. Pyongyang often charged Washington with using inspections to gather intelligence beyond the nuclear program. To justify the NPT withdrawal in 2003, for example, North Korea claimed that "the United States abused the [IAEA] inspections . . . as a way to spy on our interior and crush our socialist system" (KCNA 2003). The intrusive verification measures under consideration in the Six-Party Talks ran some risk of exposing broader military vulnerabilities or sensitive information about the Kim regime. Pyongyang may have been reluctant to shine light on the nuclear program, lest it illuminate opportunities for foreign espionage and attack.

Second, the domestic survival of the Kim regime appears to have become intertwined with the nuclear weapons program over time. During the Six-Party Talks, the core leadership in Pyongyang relied on a narrow ruling coalition with elites who ran the military, the security services, and the military-industrial complex (Haggard and Noland 2017: 22, 29–30). This small group reaped benefits from managing the nuclear program, especially as it grew into one of the only successful large-scale technological projects in the country. Each step forward with mobilization and then weaponization campaigns likely made it more difficult for Pyongyang to reverse course as military elites became increasingly vested in the program. As Nicholas Eberstadt argues, "Submitting to foreign demands to denuclearize could mean delegitimization and destabilization for the regime."[20] The path-dependent nature of nuclear technology may help explain why the North Koreans agreed to the 2007 accords but eventually abandoned efforts to assure the United States with rollback measures.

The barriers to nuclear demobilization have only become more entrenched since the collapse of the Six-Party Talks. Upon assuming power, Kim Jong-un further consolidated support, winnowing the elite coalition through a series of purges. But the nuclear program appeared to be largely protected from this process. Kim may have even delegated additional autonomy to the scientists and engineers in charge of developing North Korea's nuclear arsenal (Saunders 2019: 181). After several abortive attempts at negotiations with the Obama administration, Kim declared his *byungjin* policy of "making military-technical nuclear progress the regime's top priority in 2013, alongside economic development," Van Jackson (2018: 7) notes.[21] This public announcement effectively locked in Pyongyang to retaining nuclear weapons for the foreseeable future.

The forecast for the future of nonproliferation on the Korean Peninsula is bleak. Pyongyang may agree to partial freezes or caps on weapons and launchers in the future—the classic stuff of arms control. But it is unlikely to trade away nuclear capabilities that are central to managing external threats and maintaining internal elite support. Given the model of regime survival in North Korea, Kim Jong-un will likely find it too risky to consider giving up this invaluable investment, even if the security situation on the Korean Peninsula improves.

6

Iran

Some countries leverage latency after they are caught marching toward the bomb in secret. Iran provides a prime illustration. Compellence was a second-choice strategy for Tehran. The first part of this chapter explores how Iran developed its nuclear program from 1953 to 2002. I find that Iranian leaders focused on hiding nuclear fuel cycle and weaponization activities throughout the 1980s and 1990s. The chapter then investigates a critical juncture in the evolution of Iran's nuclear program: the revelation of clandestine enrichment and heavy-water facilities in August 2002. Over the next year, Iran botched a deception campaign before reconfiguring the nuclear program around a safer hedge posture. Iranian leaders also decided to leverage latency against Washington and its nonproliferation partners in Europe. However, this strategy was circular in nature—Tehran used the threat of proliferation to compel acceptance of its latent nuclear capabilities.

Iran pursued three distinct diplomatic campaigns from 2003 to 2015. In the first episode (2003–2005), Iran mobilized its enrichment assets in the fissile material sweet spot to cut a series of temporary deals with the Europeans. This initial effort helped to shield Tehran from multilateral sanctions and military attack. But it was not enough to wrest deeper concessions from the West over accepting the enrichment program itself. In the second episode (2009–2010), Tehran accepted an offer from Washington to swap out most of Iran's enriched uranium in exchange for research reactor fuel plates and an easing of diplomatic tensions. Yet this deal quickly fell apart because Iranian leaders found themselves unable to curb the nuclear program at a high level of latency. Iran moved to the cusp of the bomb during the third episode (2013–2015). In contrast to my theoretical expectations, Tehran successfully cut a nuclear deal and extracted concessions from the United States, notably over retaining lower levels of enrichment under intensive inspections. But achieving this goal came at tremendous cost for the regime. Table 6.1 summarizes each episode along with the outcomes expected by the book's theory.

Leveraging Latency. Tristan A. Volpe, Oxford University Press. © Oxford University Press 2023.
DOI: 10.1093/oso/9780197669532.003.0006

Table 6.1 Compellence Cases by Iran

Episode (dates)	Latency	Target	Demands	Expected outcome
First diplomatic dance (2003–2005)	Medium	France, Britain, Germany as surrogates for the United States (adversaries)	Tehran pursued a circular compellence strategy—it leveraged latency to demand that the West accept Iran as a latent nuclear power. Iranian negotiators wanted the Europeans to support closing the IAEA nuclear file and block referral to the UNSC. Tehran also demanded Washington change its "zero enrichment" policy by accepting Iran's plan to enrich uranium for purportedly peaceful purposes.	Success
Fuel swap proposal (2009–2010)	High	United States (adversary)	Iran requested IAEA assistance with finding a foreign supplier of fuel for the Tehran Research Reactor, which had exhausted its supply of enriched uranium fuel plates. The United States stepped in with an offer to secure a fuel contract for Tehran with Russian vendors in exchange for Iran exporting most of its enriched uranium.	Failure
Joint Comprehensive Plan of Action (2013–2015)	Ultra-high	United States (adversary)	Iran again pursued a circular approach whereby it increased nuclear latency to underwrite demands for sanctions relief over the nuclear program. Iranian negotiators also made it clear that their central goal was to maintain the enrichment program along with other key nuclear assets.	Failure

Iran offers several key insights into how nuclear latency shapes compellence outcomes. Unlike North Korea, the process of foreign policy decision-making in Tehran has been more visible to outside analysts. This allows me to better investigate the internal deliberations around nuclear proliferation strategy that occurred in the aftermath of exposure and continued with each compellence episode. The evidence indicates that Iranian leaders deliberately used latency to compel the acceptance of latency. This circular strategy seems unusual. But it has long guided Tehran's approach to nuclear negotiations. Moreover, Iran exhibits within-case variation in latency that subjects my theory to a hard test. According to the Goldilocks principle, Tehran should have been best positioned to cut a deal when the nuclear program was in the sweet spot in 2003–2005. I expect to find evidence that the threat-assurance trade-off became more severe for Iranian leaders as they ramped up uranium enrichment activities after 2006. A more advanced Iranian nuclear program should have made the threat of proliferation more credible, while also undermining assurances that Iran would refrain from proliferating in future. Yet more latency appeared to be better for Iran, giving it the leverage to cut a major nuclear deal with the United States in July 2015. As a result, I attempt to falsify the book's central hypotheses by analyzing the degree to which compellence worked for Iran at higher levels of latency.

The Road to Revelation, 1953–2002

Iran's nuclear program had its genesis during the halcyon era for atomic energy. In 1957, Shah Mohammed Reza Pahlavi took advantage of the Eisenhower administration's Atoms for Peace program to import civil nuclear technology, starting with a research reactor in Tehran (Krige 2006). As this small reactor came online in 1967, Iran signed the nuclear nonproliferation treaty. The shah then created the Atomic Energy Organization of Iran (AEOI) in 1973—tasking it with training Iranian nuclear engineers and concluding nuclear assistance deals abroad.[1] These efforts culminated in contracts with European vendors to supply nuclear fuel cycle technology and construct two light-water reactors at the Bushehr complex south of Tehran. By the end of the 1970s, the shah had set the foundation to build up the nuclear program in the years ahead.

The Islamic Revolution of 1979 brought Tehran's nuclear quest to a halt. After the shah fled the country, the new regime led by Ayatollah Ruhollah Khomeini seized power with little interest in the nuclear program. As part of an effort to divest from the shah's projects, Khomeini stripped the AEOI of its budget and canceled the construction contracts with European firms (Patrikarakos 2012: 100). A wave of purges led to an exodus of scientists and engineers from Iran, further draining the nuclear program of expertise. In addition, the American Embassy hostage crisis ended all nuclear cooperation between Iran and the United States.[2] Within a few years, the revolution had hallowed out the Iranian nuclear program, leaving behind a few research centers and an unfinished reactor complex at Bushehr.

In the early 1980s, however, the leadership in Tehran restarted the nuclear program amid the Iran-Iraq war. Beyond the significant costs of the conflict, Iran found itself vulnerable to Iraqi chemical weapon attacks on the battlefield and ballistic missile strikes against civilian population centers (Chubin 1994: 21, 2002: 77; Takeyh 2009: 102). Even more worrisome, the Israeli strike on the Osirak nuclear reactor complex in Iraq revealed that Saddam Hussein had been marching toward the bomb. Alarmed by this discovery, Khomenei authorized an aboveboard attempt to finish the Bushehr reactors (Coughlin 2010: 225). But this plan made little progress because it depended on foreign firms who were now reluctant to engage in civil nuclear cooperation with Iran.[3]

Iran soon refocused its efforts around the secret pursuit of nuclear fuel cycle technology. As part of a broader strategy to circumvent export controls and trade embargoes, the Islamic Revolutionary Guard Corps (IRGC) had already spent years building illicit procurement channels throughout Europe.[4] In 1985, Iranian agents came into contact with the German partners of Abdul Qadeer Khan—the father of Pakistan's nuclear bomb who went on to establish an illicit global network for selling sensitive nuclear technology.[5] Over the next year, Kahn and associates put together an offer to provide Iran with a nuclear "starter kit," which would include a complete centrifuge enrichment plant and even the equipment for casting uranium metal into the fissile core of a bomb (Albright 2010: 77–78). After receiving approval from top leaders in February 1987, Iran's nuclear program accepted the Khan package and set out to master centrifuge technology at a constellation of small workshops hidden throughout the country.[6]

The clandestine quest to develop sensitive nuclear technology made halting progress over the next decade. In the summer of 1989, Ayatollah Ali Khamenei became supreme leader after the death of Ayatollah Khomeini, while Akbar Hashemi Rafsanjani took over the presidency with a mandate to rebuild the war-torn country (Arjomand 2009; Takeyh 2007: 34–40; Thaler et al. 2010: 68–70). This change in leadership mattered for two reasons. First, Rafsanjani shifted the focus of the nuclear program back to courting foreign suppliers for atomic assistance again, notably cash-strapped enterprises in Russia and China (Vaez and Sadjadpour 2013: 9). Under pressure from

Washington, however, Beijing cut off nuclear cooperation with Tehran in 1997. Similarly, Moscow agreed in 1995 to limit the scope of its atomic assistance to the completion one light-water reactor at Bushehr.[7] With the bulk of political attention and material resources going into these nuclear supply deals, secret research on enrichment and heavy-water reactor technologies remained relegated to small, poorly managed laboratories.

Second, the elevation of Ayatollah Khamenei proved to be instrumental in empowering elites to develop the front and back end of the nuclear fuel cycle. After reaping only modest returns from foreign nuclear suppliers, Khamenei was growing "sick of the slow pace of nuclear progress and wanted to press on," according to field interviews by David Patrikarakos (2012: 143). In 1997, Khamenei replaced the long-standing head of Iran's nuclear program with Gholam Reza Aghazadeh, who reorganized the AEOI to prioritize mastering enrichment technology as well as building a heavy-water reactor complex.[8] With backing from Khamenei, Tehran then allocated almost $800 million for Aghazadeh to expand the human and infrastructure base of these projects (Coughlin 2010: 300; Patrikarakos 2012: 164). The nuclear program surged forward. Scientists began feeding uranium gas into centrifuges in 1999 (Albright and Hinderstein 2004). Within a few years, they were ready to scale up operations beyond the secret laboratory complex. As construction began on two fuel enrichment plants at Natanz and a heavy-water reactor near Arak, Iran approached the cusp of being able to produce fissile material.

At the same time, Iran also prepared to manufacture and even test nuclear weapons. A trove of documents suborned from Iran's nuclear program by Israel in 2018 show that Tehran authorized a well-resourced weaponization effort—designated Project AMAD—to build a handful of atomic weapons once Iran had enough fissile material.[9] From 1999 until the summer of 2003, the project "made considerable progress on nearly every aspect of developing and manufacturing nuclear weapons, including implosion testing, weapon design, neutron generators, casting and machining (though with surrogate materials, not uranium), and integration of warheads and reentry vehicles," according to an assessment of these documents by analysts at Harvard University's Belfer Center for Science and International Affairs (Arnold et al. 2019: 7). Notably, Iran finished design work on an atomic weapon and excavated a tunnel system at the Parchin military complex where highly enriched uranium could be fabricated into weapons components (Arnold et al. 2019: 7, 11). It remains uncertain whether Tehran would have actually crossed the nuclear Rubicon with a test denotation. As these activities make

clear, though, Iran at least wanted to have the capability on hand to manufacture nuclear weapons in secret. The aim of the nuclear program would soon
change in the aftermath of its premature exposure.

Discovery and Strategy Transition, 2002–2003

In August 2002, Iran's clandestine nuclear program was exposed to the world.
The public revelation came from an Iranian dissident group—the Mujahedin-
e-Khalq—who shed light on hidden facilities in Iran along the front and back
ends of the nuclear fuel cycle (Patrikarakos 2012: 176). Several months later,
the US government released satellite imagery of the fuel enrichment plants
at Natanz and the Arak heavy-water plant (Albright and Hinderstein 2002;
Sanger 2002). This discovery marked the start of a transition period in the
aim of the nuclear program. Instead of pursuing the bomb in secret, Iran now
needed to preserve its blown nuclear assets while avoiding economic or military punishment. Over the next year, Iran slowly reconfigured the nuclear
program into a safer hedge posture before opening a diplomatic channel to
the West.

Iran faced a worrisome security situation upon exposure. Top leaders in
Tehran believed Washington could use the nuclear exposure as the pretext to
impose greater economic sanctions or even launch military strikes (Takeyh
2003: 22–23). Indeed, Director of Central Intelligence George Tenent
claimed in early 2003 that Iran was "continuing to pursue development of
a nuclear fuel cycle for civil and nuclear weapons purposes."[10] The Iranians
became desperate to avoid the fate unfolding for Saddam Hussein in Iraq
(Filkins 2013). As a precondition for direct diplomacy, however, US officials
demanded Iran first abandon its entire enrichment program. Tehran balked
at this zero-enrichment standard. The United States then worked through its
European allies—the so-called EU3 triumvirate of France, Germany, and the
United Kingdom—to ratchet up pressure on Iran.

Tehran soon switched into survival mode. Iranian officials orchestrated
a deception campaign designed to recast the nuclear program as a purely
peaceful endeavor. This involved a botched attempt to cover up past activities
while bringing in inspectors from the International Atomic Energy Agency
(IAEA). After delaying the IAEA access for six months, Tehran allowed a
team led by Director General Mohammed ElBaradei to visit most of Iran's
declared nuclear facilities in February 2003, including the Natanz complex.

When ElBaradei queried how Iran had developed such an advanced centrifuge program, the Iranians claimed to have relied only on open-source information and computer simulations.[11]

But this cover story quickly fell apart. Over the summer of 2003, the IAEA found enriched uranium particles in environmental samples collected from several nuclear sites.[12] This evidence indicated that Iran must have received foreign technical assistance and/or been engaged in centrifuge tests with nuclear material prior to 2002. Iranian officials struggled to revise their story as further evidence and inconsistencies came to light.[13] In September 2003, the IAEA formally called on Iran to freeze all enrichment work while it cleared up these issues about past nuclear activities. The United States threatened to refer Iran to the United Nations Security Council (UNSC) if it did not comply with the resolution.

As international pressure mounted, Iran's core leadership met with elite stakeholders to deliberate response options. From September to October 2003, moderate and hard-line factions advanced two opposing strategies. Although both groups were concerned about punishment from the United States, each offered different ways to manage the threat (Patrikarakos 2012: 188–89). The moderates led by President Mohammad Khatami argued that the safest option was for Iran to freeze the nuclear program and accede to the demands from Vienna and Washington for greater transparency. By contrast, hard-liners favored a competitive buildup of nuclear latency (De Bellaigue 2007: 55). If Iran ignored the IAEA and pressed ahead with its gas centrifuge program, they argued, Tehran might be able present a fait accompli over uranium enrichment. In turn, these elites believed that "the West would quickly fold and, as with North Korea, 'bribe' it to stay in the NPT," according to Patrikarakos (2012: 189). The hard-liners contended that building up Iran's nuclear assets would put Tehran in a stronger position to resist the West.

Ultimately, Khamenei rejected both options in favor of an alternative bargaining strategy. The idea to negotiate for an advantageous end to the nuclear crisis came from Hassan Rouhani (De Bellaigue 2007: 59). As head of the Supreme National Security Council, Rouhani proposed Iran fall back on diplomacy to achieve a new set of goals with the nuclear program (Patrikarakos 2012: 191–93). The main objective was to protect Iran's nuclear assets while ensuring regime survival. Rouhani and his team seemed to recognize that they would have to walk a fine line between giving up the nuclear program on one side and economic sanctions on the other. The second goal was to improve Iran's legal position with the IAEA, thereby providing some cover to expand nuclear assets in the future without triggering war. Finally, Rouhani wanted to use the nuclear program itself as a means to extract concessions from the West. In particular, Iran expected to be compensated for its cooperation with the IAEA (Mousavian 2012: 74). Tehran was willing to accept greater transparency measures, but only for the right price.

The notion of leveraging Iran's blown nuclear facilities set Rouhani's strategy apart from the other options on the table. He received authorization from Tehran to lead Iran's nuclear negotiation team in pursuit of these goals. As Seyed Hossein Mousavian (2012: 100) recounts in his memoir of this effort, "The most important objective of Iran's negotiators was to obtain maximum concessions from their foreign counterparts in return for cooperation." In the short term, Iran needed to compel the Europeans to underwrite Iran's security. This meant striking a deal whereby Europe promised to restrain the United States and delay referral of Iran's case to the Security Council. "From the European point of view," Mousavian (2012: 74) pointed out, "not referring Iran to the UN Security Council was a concession, as Article XII of the IAEA Statue calls for such a referral." A closed IAEA nuclear file would be a significant step in this direction. Beyond warding off punishment, Mousavian (2012: 99) claims that the nuclear negotiations were also part of a broader effort to "pursue a long-term strategy of 'turning threats into opportunities.'" In particular, Tehran wanted the United States to change its zero-enrichment standard by accepting Iran's plans to enrich uranium, ostensibly to fuel future civilian nuclear power plants.

In the lead-up to this major strategy shift, Iran reconfigured its nuclear program around a safer hedge posture.[14] Foremost, Khamenei issued a secret "halt order" to stop the main thrust of weaponization work in the nuclear portfolio.[15] The documents in the Iran archive illustrate that scientists were instructed to abandon most research that could not be excused as part of a civilian nuclear energy program (Arnold et al. 2019; Bergman 2018a). One notable exchange among Project AMAD leadership made clear the strategic logic behind the stop work order being implemented in August and September 2003. "We should make a distinction between 'overt' and 'covert' activities," one project leader argued. "Overt activities are those that can be explained as part of something else," the leader underscored, "and not as part of the [weapons] project itself, so we have an excuse to do them." The memo emphasized that a weaponization activity such as "neutron research could not be considered 'overt' and needs to be concealed. We cannot excuse such activities as defensive. Neutron operations are sensitive and we have no explanation for them."[16] Instead of trying to hide activities with clear military dimensions, Iran would now claim to be pursuing dual-use nuclear technology for peaceful purposes. Tehran began crafting a nationalist narrative about Iran's need to gain self-sufficiency in the production of nuclear fuel and atomic energy (Tabatabai 2014). Rouhani and his team could generate further plausible deniability by pointing to Khamenei's October 2003 public fatwa on the prohibition of nuclear weapons in Iran under Islamic law.

Shuttering weaponization projects over the summer of 2003 set the stage for Iran to begin nuclear negotiations in the fall. But this neat coincidence belies the messy nature of policymaking in Tehran. After Iran was caught in August 2002, leaders muddled through several responses over a long fifteen-month period. The growing fear of preventive military attack, the botched deception campaign with the IAEA, and the opportunity to bargain with the West all likely contributed to the final shift in strategy during the fall of 2003. Tehran was ready to leverage latency as a bargaining instrument, albeit in a circular fashion to demand that the West accept Iran as a latent nuclear power.

The First Diplomatic Dance, 2003–2005: Medium Latency

In the middle of October 2003, Rouhani courted diplomats from France, Britain, and Germany (the EU3) to begin nuclear negotiations at the Sa'dabad palace in Tehran. The European triumvirate acted as a diplomatic surrogate for the United States—pushing Iran to clarify suspicious nuclear activities and abandon its enrichment program altogether (Miller 2006: 568–69). But Rouhani and his team underscored that Iran was committed to mastering the front and back ends of the nuclear fuel cycle for civilian purposes. Diplomacy deadlocked over the zero-enrichment standard. On October 21, the Iranian negotiators broke the impasse by agreeing to suspend uranium enrichment while diplomacy over the fate of the nuclear program continued in months ahead. In exchange, the Europeans agreed to keep Iran's nuclear case out of the UNSC, so long as Tehran continued to cooperate with the IAEA.[17]

Domestic politics within Iran came into play as the negotiators wrapped up the agreement. Rouhani only put the enrichment pause on the table after seeking top-level approval from the core leadership in Tehran—presumably Khamenei. He reportedly told diplomats that even this temporary freeze required him to take "a huge, personal risk," according to Patrikarakos (2012: 198). Hard-line elites were incensed with Rouhani for accepting any constraints over the nuclear program. They sent Basij paramilitary protesters to surround Sa'dabad and briefly block the European delegates from leaving the palace grounds. At the official announcement for the accord, Rouhani championed his diplomatic labors as an effort to resist pressure from the West and assert Iran's sovereignty (Patrikarakos 2012: 199).

The Tehran agreement created space for Iran to improve its position. In November 2003, Rouhani mobilized the nuclear program by interpreting enrichment suspension in the narrowest possible terms. He claimed the freeze only applied to the actual enrichment of uranium gas in operational centrifuges—all other activities were fair game (De Bellaigue 2007: 60). Under Rouhani's direction, the nuclear program churned out scores of centrifuges and accelerated construction efforts at the Isfahan uranium conversion facility and the Arak heavy-water plant.[18] In an interview with an Iranian journalist, Rouhani (2005) later admitted that this effort was part of a deliberate plan: "The matter that we constantly had in mind was that when it came to suspension, we should suffice to the minimum extent, in order to suspend as little of our activities as possible. More importantly, when a certain activity was suspended, during that period we would concentrate all of our effort and energy on other activities." He illustrated this tactic by pointing to the shift toward work on uranium conversion, emphasizing that "the day when Natanz was suspended, we put all of our effort into Esfahan" (Rouhani 2005: 7). European diplomats balked at this buildup but still met with the Iranians for a second round of negotiations in Brussels in February 2004. Rouhani rejected an offer to give up the enrichment program in exchange for minor concessions from Europe. However, Iran agreed to suspend the centrifuge production campaign by April 2004 to keep hope alive for diplomacy (Patrikarakos 2012: 204).

Over the next few months, the nuclear program raced to produce as many centrifuges as possible before the April suspension deadline came into effect. In May 2004, Iran allowed the IAEA into its centrifuge workshops to establish a baseline for the enrichment freeze.[19] Yet the director general of the IAEA reported that Iran continued to delay inspections, cover up past nuclear activities, and evade technical verification measures.[20] The breaking point came when the IAEA board of governors adopted a resolution in June deploring Iran's failure to cooperate adequately with inspectors.[21] In response, Iran resumed work on the enrichment program, bringing the Isfahan conversion facility online to produce uranium hexafluoride gas feedstock for the centrifuge plants. By the fall of 2004, the IAEA adopted another resolution condemning Iran, this time reviving the threat of referral to the UNSC.[22] This mix of mobilization and concealment tactics eroded the credibility of Iran's assurances, which made it increasingly difficult for the West to back down.

In November 2004, Tehran resumed negotiations with the Europeans in Paris to manage the pressure mounting from Vienna and Washington. At first, it seemed as though Rouhani's mobilization campaign had moved the goalpost for diplomacy. European negotiators initially focused on persuading Iran to live up to the terms of the original Tehran agreement from October 2003. The Iranians agreed to once again suspend enrichment for three months while diplomats worked toward a comprehensive deal (Mousavian 2012: 150). Yet the gap between the two sides proved to be insurmountable. Iran floated a range of nonproliferation assurances but ultimately would not give up the enrichment program. As Rouhani (2005: 3) later underscored, his team had firmly decided that "the nuclear fuel cycle was our red line and under no circumstances would we waive it." As a result, the Europeans could neither bring the Americans to the table nor offer more substantial concessions. Diplomacy reached an impasse by the summer of 2005. Eighteen months of negotiations in Tehran, Brussels, and Paris came to end without resolving the nuclear crisis.

Iran's initial foray into the diplomatic arena generated mixed results. On the one hand, Rouhani accomplished his main goal of preserving the nuclear program while warding off economic or military punishment. "You remember the conditions of two years ago . . . when everything in the country had been frozen," he argued in a speech from August 2005, "[but] we were able to emerge from that dangerous phase with prudent management . . . [and] a proper plan. With the help of our valued diplomats and the negotiation team . . . we were able to get through one of the most difficult national challenges."[23] Rouhani credited his strategy with getting the country out of the postrevelation danger zone. He persuaded the Europeans to keep Iran out of the UNSC docket despite the exposure of hidden nuclear facilities and ongoing efforts to master sensitive technology. His nuclear buildup even left Iran with more latency as negotiations came to an end. On the other hand, however, Rouhani and his team could not bring home bigger concessions. Iran's nuclear file with the IAEA became more problematic. The West refused to abandon the zero-enrichment standard with Tehran. These issues would continue to haunt Iran as new leaders took control of the nuclear file in June 2005.

At a modest level of latency, Rouhani's compellence strategy yielded partial success. In line with the Goldilocks hypothesis (H3), Iran had enough latent power on hand to persuade the Europeans to conclude a series of temporary deals. The nuclear program had just made its first achievements in enrichment. Even though these capabilities were developed in secret, Rouhani was able to get away with offering minimal nonproliferation assurances. For over two years, this diplomatic campaign shielded Tehran from multilateral sanctions and military attack—an important accomplishment in the wake of the Natanz and Arak revelation. As a result, this episode lends some support for the sweet spot hypothesis (H3).

Despite being in the sweet spot at the time, Iran lacked the leverage to wrest deeper concessions from the West over the enrichment program itself. Rouhani applied pressure by maintaining operations along the nuclear fuel cycle. But this mobilization campaign proved insufficient to alter the US goal of "stopping Iranian enrichment," as former president George W. Bush (2011: 416) later recounted. Tehran needed more time and space to bring the fuel enrichment plants at Natanz online. At the time, Washington had limited options for changing Tehran's calculus beyond the threat of UNSC referral.[24] After diplomacy broke down, both sides set out to acquire greater leverage. The United States imposed economic pain and prepared the field for military action. "Iran continuously expanded its nuclear program," Richard Nephew (2017: 118) argues, "creating new leverage and new cards to trade in a future negotiated solution." The case suggests a key qualification to the Goldilocks principle. When it comes to bargaining over changes in nonproliferation policy, the nuclear aspirant may need greater amounts of bomb-making potential on hand to present the sheriff with a fait accompli.

The Fuel Swap Proposal, 2009–2010: High Latency

From 2005 until 2009, Iran shifted away from diplomacy to focus on building up its nuclear program. In June 2005, Mahmoud Ahmadinejad and his hardline faction assumed power in Tehran. In a rejection of the Paris accord, they ordered work to resume along the front and back ends of the nuclear fuel cycle. By the spring of 2006, Iran reached a milestone. The fuel enrichment plants at Natanz started to produce low-enriched uranium (LEU—between

3.5% and 5.0% U-235). In a large televised celebration of this technological breakthrough, President Ahmadinejad declared, "Iran has joined the nuclear countries of the world" (Fathi and Sanger 2006). Tehran poured resources into the program, enabling the rapid installation of several thousand centrifuges and accumulation of LEU.[25] Iranian diplomats remained active in an attempt to delay and dilute international pressure, but rebuffed substantive offers from the P5 + 1 coalition—the five permanent members of the UNSC plus Germany.[26] After one such meeting with the Iranians in July 2008, Under Secretary of State William Burns reported back to Washington that Tehran's "tactical goal seems clearly to be to start negotiations without giving away anything up front, and dragging things out as long as possible."[27] In lieu of diplomacy, Iran expanded its capacity to produce fissile material. Tehran steadily marched toward a high level of nuclear latency, even as the UNSC levied sanctions during this period.

In June 2009, Iran's enrichment program crossed another major threshold. It had produced enough LEU for a single atomic weapon.[28] With further enrichment, the 1,400-kilogram stockpile at Natanz could be distilled down into a bomb's worth of material—about 25 kilograms of highly enriched uranium.[29] The international community was able to track this growth in Iran's nuclear latency because Tehran continued its cooperation with the IAEA. Inspectors collected data on the quantity and disposition of enriched uranium at Natanz, as well as other activities along the nuclear fuel cycle.[30] By allowing the IAEA to shine a steady light into declared nuclear facilities, Tehran kept the main elements of its fissile material production campaign out in clear view.

An opportunity to renew nuclear negotiations emerged over the summer of 2009. By this point, officials in the new Obama administration wanted to find a way to freeze and roll back the clock on Iran's enrichment capability.[31] IAEA director ElBaradei came across a novel idea. The Iranians had requested the IAEA help them to find a foreign supplier of fuel for the Tehran Research Reactor, which had exhausted its supply of enriched uranium fuel plates. "If Iran were denied a fuel core from abroad," ElBaradei (2011: 294) underscored, "it would have every justification to proceed with higher-level enrichment at home to satisfy its own fuel needs." ElBaradei suggested that Washington help line up a foreign supplier to take this cover story off the table while sending Tehran a cooperative signal.

American officials turned ElBaradei's idea into what came to be known as the fuel swap proposal. Washington would secure a fuel contract for

Tehran with Russian vendors, "but insist in return that the Iranians 'pay' with about twelve hundred kilograms of 5 percent enriched uranium, roughly the amount that it would take to produce a batch of 20 percent fuel plates," Ambassador Burns (2019: 349–50) recounted in his memoir. "From the US perspective, this trade made good sense," Nephew (2017: 72) underscored, "as Iran would receive nuclear fuel that could not be easily used in nuclear weapons, while its creeping stock of more easily diverted material left the country." As a nonproliferation measure, ElBaradei (2011: 294) emphasized, "It was ingenious. . . . The international community would receive reassurance that Iran's LEU stockpile was not being reserved for or channeled toward nuclear weapons." If the Iranians exported most of their enriched uranium out of the country, one former official involved with the offer noted, "it would take them more time to get back up to a bomb's worth of material," thereby opening up space for more serious diplomacy.[32]

Tehran agreed in early September 2009 to engage with Washington over the fuel swap proposal. American officials tapped their counterparts in the P5 + 1 coalition to schedule the first round of talks in Geneva for early October. Domestic politics appeared to play a major role in driving Iran back to the bargaining table. Disputes over the presidential elections in June sparked public opposition (Ansari 2010; Worth and Fathi 2009). In the aftermath of the violent crackdown on protesters, Ahmadinejad apparently wanted to shore up his legitimacy at home by touting a diplomatic victory over the West (Abulof 2013; Davies 2012). Given Iran's advanced level of latency, engaging with the United States and its partners over the fuel swap could bear such fruit at marginal cost, as Tehran could still reconstitute its enriched uranium stockpile.

In the runup to negotiations, however, Iran revealed another hidden nuclear site—the Fordow fuel enrichment plant buried underneath a mountain near Qom. Unlike the large centrifuge cascade halls at Natanz, the small size of the hardened facility made it suboptimal for producing fuel for civilian reactors. But Fordow could house just enough centrifuges to enrich at least a bomb's worth of fissile material every year.[33] The United States and several close allies already knew about the site, though the Iranians had managed to hide it from the IAEA and most of the world (Burns 2019: 350; Parsi 2012: 123). By the middle of September, officials in Tehran apparently became concerned that Washington might expose the clandestine facility during the talks in Geneva (ElBaradei 2011: 299; Parsi 2012: 123–25). Indeed, one former White House official recounted that they were waiting to play the Fordow card until it "would be most damaging and embarrassing to the Iranians."[34] Tehran attempted to preempt this move by coming clean. Taking a page out of the Natanz postrevelation playbook, the Iranians penned an informal letter to ElBaradei, notifying him of construction work on an undeclared nuclear facility near Qom (ElBaradei 2011: 298–300; Patrikarakos 2012: 253).

The Fordow disclosure backfired against Iran. ElBaradei showed the letter to a small delegation of US officials at a United Nations meeting in New York on September 20. The Americans realized that the Iranians were trying to claim they had declared the secret Fordow fuel enrichment plant to the IAEA. In response, the Obama administration moved "to beat them to the punch and just expose it," as one former US official recounted.[35] Before going public, the Americans shared the evidence on Fordow with their Russian counterparts in New York, who were reportedly furious with the Iranians for deceiving them (Burns 2019: 351; Stent 2014: 232–33). At a high-level summit, American, British, and French leaders ratcheted up the pressure on Iran, presenting their declassified intelligence on the fuel enrichment plant at Fordow (Sanger and Broad 2009). The revelation gave Washington "a fair amount of leverage with the Iranians," Burns (2019: 351) recalled, because "it deepened the resolve of the P5+1 to push the Iranians hard at the meeting that had already been scheduled in Geneva on October 1, and left Tehran backpedaling."

Facing domestic and now international incentives to reach a deal, the Iranian negotiation team agreed to the fuel swap proposal on the first day of discussions in Geneva.[36] After making little headway in the morning with all the P5 + 1 partners at the table, the lead US diplomat—Under Secretary Burns—offered to speak with the Iranians in private. Ambassador Saeed Jalili agreed, and small teams from each side broke off from the main group. Ambassador Burns presented the main contours of fuel swap proposal. Jalili accepted the deal in unequivocal terms. Iran would export twelve hundred kilograms of enriched uranium in exchange for the fuel plates (Parsi 2012: 129–31). As Burns (2019: 352) recounts, Jalili seemed "to appreciate how Iran would benefit from such a reciprocal arrangement." Robert Einhorn—a leading nuclear expert from the State Department—went over each step in the swap to make sure the Iranians understood it. Jalili's deputy, Ali Bagheri, agreed to the entire package. His sole condition, according to one US official, was that the details not be made public yet, "because they needed first to explain this in Tehran."[37] After the diplomats departed Geneva, Jalili and Bagheri set out to sell the deal back home.

Unfortunately, when implementation talks began several weeks later in Vienna, it became apparent that Jalili had been instructed to kill the agreement. "Right from the start, the Iranians walked it back," a senior US official at the meeting recalled. "It was clear they had run into a political buzzsaw at home, and just could not do the deal."[38] The chief compliant from Jalili and his team concerned the phased nature of the swap. Tehran would only export the enriched uranium if Iran received the new fuel plates at the exact same time. Desperate to save the deal, ElBaradei drafted up a legal IAEA contract that committed Washington to support the effective implementation of the swap (ElBaradei 2011: 307–10). The Iranians returned to Tehran with the contract. But the proposal was dead on arrival in Iran.

Domestic politics seems to have driven Iran's sudden diplomatic reversal in two ways. First, Ahmadinejad had staked his reputation on working toward a diplomatic triumph over the West. In the turbulent wake of the electoral crackdown, however, other elites in the regime were eager to deny him any semblance of a win on the world stage (Crist 2012: 549; Hurst 2016: 548–49; Mousavian 2012: 359). Second, at this advanced stage of latency, the nuclear program had strong stakeholders and support among the mass public (Kaussler 2014: 83; Tabatabai 2014). Elite opposition groups could influence foreign policy by turning Ahmadinejad's long-running campaign to activate public support for the nuclear program against him. "Any Iranian policymaker signing an agreement perceived as surrendering Iran's 'rights' can expect to face a strong domestic backlash," Steven Hurst (2016: 548) points out, emphasizing that "many Iranians seemingly regarded the transferring out of the country of a significant proportion of Iran's LEU as the surrender of a key bargaining chip."

After the deal died in Tehran, the United States worked with its partners to build a more robust international sanctions regime. In response, Ahmadinejad mobilized the nuclear program in brazen fashion— announcing plans to build ten new fuel enrichment plants and enriching fuel up to 20% U-235 at Natanz.[39] Brazil and Turkey attempted to resurrect diplomacy as tensions mounted.[40] In May 2010, they convinced the Iranians to accept the old fuel swap proposal again. However, the deal had been overcome by events on the ground—notably the steady increase in Iran's bomb-making capacity at Natanz.[41] The effort was "too little, too late," Burns (2019: 353–54) underscored, because "the Iranians now had accumulated enough low-enriched uranium for two bombs, [so] exporting half would still leave them with enough for a bomb." As Iran inched closer to the bomb, Russia and China came around to supporting tougher sanctions. UNSC Resolution 1929 set the foundation for American officials to turn up the heat. As Nephew (2017: 78), a key architect of the sanctions regime for the US government recalled, "Three levels of sanctions—UN, multinational, and corporate (enforced by U.S. coercion)—hammered Iran from a variety of different angles starting in June 2010 with UNSCR 1929's adoption." Ahmadinejad had failed to achieve a diplomatic breakthrough or protect Tehran from serious economic punishment.

Iran's second stab at diplomacy in 2009 illustrates the sharp trade-off leaders face between making threats and assurances credible with high levels of latency (H2). By acquiring a bomb's worth of LEU, Tehran put pressure on Washington to explore diplomatic options again. The Iranians had so far managed the consequences of their nuclear buildup, framing enrichment as a peaceful activity. Yet the exposure of the hardened enrichment plant at Fordow undercut this narrative—turning up Iran's proliferation threat and alienating partners in Moscow and Beijing. In response, Ahmadinejad apparently authorized his negotiators to accept the fuel swap proposal, which would have demobilized the most worrisome capability in the nuclear program. But it became impossible to sell this assurance back in Iran. The modest confidence-building measure crossed too many red lines that Ahmadinejad himself had established as he helped make the nuclear program a popular nationalist symbol and valuable asset for elites. This case supports my claim that it becomes difficult for leaders to curb mature nuclear programs.

The Iran Nuclear Deal, 2013–2015: Ultra-high Latency

From 2010 until 2013, the United States led a broad effort to impose greater pressure on Iran. Economic sanctions against Iran's state-owned banks and enterprises had a substantial impact, further cutting off Tehran from the international marketplace (Crist 2012: 569; Katzman 2014; Nephew 2017: 7). The drumbeat for military action also grew louder in Washington. Israel seemed to be on the verge of launching preventive strikes against key facilities in Iran (Bergman 2018b: 627–28). The Pentagon accelerated work on a huge "bunker buster" bomb capable of destroying hard and deeply buried targets, such as the Fordow facility (Karl 2009). Beyond these acknowledged activities, reports of possible sabotage surfaced in the press—such as the infamous Stuxnet computer worm that allegedly destroyed scores of centrifuges at Natanz.[42] Tehran was incurring high costs and running dangerous risks to enrich uranium.

In the face of growing pressure, however, Iran steadily built up its nuclear program. Tehran focused on developing an ultra-high level of latency along the front end of the fuel cycle. The Iranians more than doubled the number and performance output of centrifuges spinning at Natanz and Fordow. By the summer of 2013, Iran's stockpile of LEU had grown to almost ten thousand kilograms—enough material to enrich further into a handful of weapons.[43] Tehran also expanded construction efforts on the Arak heavy-water site, keeping open another route to the bomb along the back end of the fuel cycle. In Washington, Nephew (2017: 118) recalled, it seemed that Tehran was "creating pressure on the United States to seek a deal rather than face an Iran with a latent nuclear weapons capability." By expanding fissile material production at observable nuclear facilities, the Iranians were brandishing their resolve to continue marching toward the bomb, albeit in a calibrated manner.

In July 2012, Iranian and American officials started probing the prospects for diplomacy through a back-channel exchange in Oman.[44] Still smarting from the Geneva about-face, both sides kept the talks secret to insulate themselves from domestic politics and outside spoilers (Burns 2019: 360; Rozen 2013). The delegation from Tehran signaled their desire to ease tensions. From the outset, though, the Iranians also made it clear that they would not give up the enrichment program—claiming the NPT enshrined their "right" to develop nuclear technology for peaceful purposes.[45] This long-standing position had changed little from the first round of nuclear negotiations in 2003. But now the Americans were apparently under no illusions about their ability to achieve the zero-enrichment standard, even with sanctions bearing down on Tehran (Parsi 2017: 217–18). When talks resumed in March 2013, the US team, led by Deputy Secretary of State Burns, floated a new offer (Rozen 2014). If the Iranians took tangible steps to resolve the "gaping credibility problem" with their nonproliferation assurances, Burns (2019: 366, 364) recounted, Washington "would be willing to explore whether and how a domestic enrichment program could be pursued in Iran, as part of a comprehensive settlement of the nuclear issue." Offering enrichment—even with stringent conditions and caveats—represented a watershed moment for nuclear diplomacy (Parsi 2017: 10; Sherman 2018: 43; Solomon 2016: 264).

Iran's dramatic increase in nuclear latency appears to have been primarily responsible for persuading American officials to abandon their zero-enrichment standard. In his memoir, Burns (2019: 362) details how Iranian mastery of enrichment shaped strategic thinking at the White House in the winter of 2013: "The president was convinced that we'd never get an agreement with the Iranians without some limited form of domestic enrichment. They had the knowledge to enrich, and there was no way you could bomb, sanction, or wish that away." Even under harsh sanctions, Iran could continue to expand its enriched uranium stockpile, making war more likely with each increase in bomb-making capacity.[46] The goal of diplomacy shifted toward convincing Iran to accept serious constraints and intrusive verification measures over its enrichment program. "Maybe we would have gotten to a zero enrichment outcome a decade earlier," Burns (2019: 362) goes on to lament, "when they were spinning a few dozen centrifuges. That was extremely unlikely to happen in 2013, with the Iranians operating some nineteen thousand centrifuges, and with broad popular support across the country for enrichment as part of a civilian program." Leaders in Tehran had committed themselves to enrichment in front of multiple audiences. From the US perspective, it appeared unlikely that Iranian negotiators would trade away this crown jewel.[47]

Leadership changes in Tehran over the summer of 2013 gave diplomacy an additional boost. Hassan Rouhani—the architect of Iran's original bargaining strategy after the Natanz exposure—triumphed in the presidential elections. He campaigned on resolving the nuclear issue to alleviate economic pain from sanctions (Peterson 2013; Rezaian 2013). Upon assuming office, Rouhani cultivated a broad coalition of elites, including conservatives with vested interests in the nuclear program (Harris 2013). He elevated nuclear negotiations by moving the file to the Foreign Ministry, now headed by veteran diplomat Javad Zarif (Wright 2014). Unlike his diplomatic labors in the early 2000s, Rouhani did not need to push Khamenei and other conservatives to engage with the West. The direct link to Washington was already up and running.

After several months of secret negotiations, Iran and the United States coalesced around an initial confidence-building measure in October 2013. The United States would provide temporary sanctions relief while Iran froze its nuclear program and even rolled back some of the enriched uranium stockpile. With this quid pro quo in place, American diplomats carefully revealed the back channel and merged it into overt diplomacy with the rest of the P5 + 1 coalition.[48] A series of intense multilateral negotiations produced a formal agreement in late November 2013—the Joint Plan of Action.[49] Under the temporary accord, Iran paused its entire enrichment program, halted construction at the Arak complex, diluted its stockpile of 20% enriched uranium, and accepted daily inspections of facilities and supply chain activities by the IAEA. In exchange, the United States provided modest sanctions relief while discussions continued over a more comprehensive deal (Saikal 2019: 216). The accord came into effect on January 20, 2014. It set the stage for negotiators to work toward a more comprehensive resolution over the ensuing six months.

As the pace of public diplomacy intensified, leaders in Washington and Tehran established red lines for their respective negotiation teams. President Obama made it clear to the American delegation—now led by Secretary of State John Kerry—that the core goal was to keep Iran at least one year away from accumulating a bomb's worth of fissile material (Lakshmanan 2015).[50] This meant foreclosing all rapid and covert pathways to highly enriched uranium or plutonium. By this point, though, the Iranians had paused their nuclear program on the cusp of the bomb—it would only take them a few months to enrich enough uranium for a single weapon. From the American perspective, Iran would need to move back down the latency continuum by giving up some of its enrichment capability. In addition, the president could only accept a deal if Iran promised to stay at a modest level of latency for at least a decade, with intrusive monitoring measures in place to verify compliance.[51]

Ayatollah Khamenei also drew red lines around Iran's nuclear program. He supported Rouhani's objective of wresting sanctions relief from the West. But in a series of public and private directives, Khamenei set limits on what Zarif and his team could offer up to the Americans.[52] Specifically, he prohibited the negotiators from agreeing to close any nuclear facility, halt research and development (R&D) work on centrifuges, or accept novel safeguards over the nuclear program.[53] The red lines took some core capabilities off the bargaining table while still providing "the negotiators with room to maneuver," according to field research by Ariane Tabatabai (2017: 237). Converting the Fordow enrichment plant to produce medical isotopes, for instance, technically adhered to Khamenei's guidance. "This served a domestic political purpose," Tabatabai (2017: 237) notes, because "the [negotiation] team could tell its constituency that Fordow was kept open and operational despite the West's insistence that it would have to be closed." In essence, the Iranians needed to bring home a deal that could be sold to other elites as well as the general public (Tabatabai 2019: 4). Khamenei's red lines helped them avoid running into a political buzzsaw at home again.

Although the basic parameters for a deal were coming into alignment, it took diplomats over eighteen months to nail down the details. Several sticking points emerged in the negotiations.[54] The most contentious concerned the curbs on Iran's enrichment program. To no one's surprise, Zarif and his team fought to keep as much enrichment capacity as possible (Solomon 2016: 268). They eventually came around to accepting constraints over centrifuge capacity and the enriched uranium stockpile. To make these rollback steps palatable to constituents back home, however, the Iranians pushed hard against limitations on centrifuge R&D and long-term enrichment capability. Scientists needed to continue working on peaceful projects, they claimed, lest their knowledge base atrophy (Tabatabai 2017: 237). Khamenei also demanded that Iran be permitted to multiply its enrichment capacity nearly eightfold in the future, ostensibly to provide fuel for the Bushehr nuclear power plant.[55] "It was an outrageous and unexpected assertion," former secretary of state John Kerry (2018: 501) noted in his memoir. But the aspirational nature of Khamenei's announcement may have been designed to generate bargaining leverage, Tabatabai (2017: 238) argues, because "it provided the negotiators with some room to reach a zone of possible agreement with the P5+1."[56] Finally, the modalities of sanctions relief bogged down diplomacy.[57] Iran was enmeshed in a sticky web of policies. It was difficult for the Americans to promise instant relief or guard against electoral shifts in Washington.

The final deal emerged on July 14, 2015. In Vienna, Zarif and Kerry headlined the announcement of the Joint Comprehensive Plan of Action (JCPOA), along with the other P5 + 1 diplomats (Lakshmanan 2015). Under the terms of the agreement, Iran would receive phased sanctions relief as it hit milestones over the coming months.[58] In exchange, Tehran committed never to build nuclear weapons and curtailed its latent capacity to do so. On the front end of the fuel cycle, the Iranians moved from a few months to about one year away from being able to produce enough highly enriched uranium for a bomb. They promised to cull almost two-thirds of all operational centrifuges, as well as reduce the fissile material stockpile by 98%, capping it off at three hundred kilograms of LEU (up to 3.67% U-235). The hardened Fordow facility would be converted to produce medical isotopes and house centrifuge R&D work under limits (Stone 2015). Along the back end of the fuel cycle, Iran pledged to foreclose the plutonium option, agreeing to pour concrete into the Arak heavy-water reactor core. In an apparent violation of Khamenei's red lines, the Iranians also accepted one of the most intrusive monitoring and verification regimes ever devised (Nephew 2015). Some of the provisions were set to expire over the next ten to fifteen years, notably the physical constraints over uranium enrichment. Other conditions—such as exporting any spent fuel from Arak and adhering to the Additional Protocol—would remain in place permanently (Davenport 2020; Samore 2017).

Managing the Threat-Assurance Trade-off

Iran's pursuit of compellence suggests that leaders face an increasingly severe trade-off between making proliferation threats and nonproliferation assurances at high levels of latency. However, the track record of diplomatic outcomes lends mixed support for my theory. Table 6.2 summarizes the results from the three compellence episodes I analyzed in the chapter. The failed fuel swap proposal in 2009–2010 offers the strongest support for the theory. Acquiring a bomb's worth of LEU made the threat of proliferation more credible, but it also created domestic constraints on demobilization that ultimately killed the deal. I find more modest support for the theory in the other two episodes. The circular nature of Iran's compellence strategy—using latency to compel acceptance of latency—may be responsible for undercutting the theoretical expectations. In the first episode, for example, Iranian negotiators had enough latent power on hand to pressure the Europeans by maintaining operations along the nuclear fuel cycle. But the nuclear program was not advanced enough to persuade US officials to abandon the zero-enrichment formula for Iran. Rouhani's gambit may have yielded only partial success because he was bargaining with latency to maintain latency, rather than pushing for material concessions beyond the four corners of the nuclear program.

The main challenge to book's argument comes from the apparent success of compellence at an ultra-high level of latency. In 2015, Tehran accomplished its long-standing goal of getting Washington to accept an Iranian enrichment program. This achievement casts doubt on the alternative argument advanced by skeptics who claim that states cannot reap coercive advantages from nuclear latency until they build the bomb (A1). But the terms of the JCPOA seem to

Table 6.2 Compellence Outcomes for Iran

Episode (dates)	Latency	Outcome	Details	Theory support
First diplomatic dance (2003–2005)	Medium	Partial success	Iran successfully persuaded the Europeans to conclude a series of temporary deals that shielded the nuclear program and regime from multilateral sanctions and military attack. Diplomacy also opened space for Iran to accelerate its nuclear efforts beyond the four corners of the suspension deals. However, Tehran failed to pressure the West into abandoning the zero-enrichment standard or offering more substantial concessions.	Modest (H3)
Fuel swap proposal (2009–2010)	High	Failure	Iran's buildup of nuclear latency put pressure on the United States to explore diplomatic options, culminating in the fuel swap proposal. Iranian negotiators initially accepted the reciprocal arrangement to export most of Iran's LEU in exchange for fuel plates for the Tehran Research Reactor. But domestic politics within Iran subsequently forced the Iranians to scuttle the deal in the face of strong elite and public opposition.	Strong (H2)
Joint Comprehensive Plan of Action (2013–2015)	Ultra-high	Success	Tehran persuaded Washington to abandon the zero-enrichment standard and accept a lower level of nuclear latency in Iran, albeit within narrow parameters and under intrusive inspections. The United States also agreed to provide phased sanctions relief as Iran rolled back its nuclear program. But Iranian leaders still faced a severe threat-assurance trade-off during the negotiations, which made it costly and difficult to curtail the nuclear program.	Modest (H3)

undermine my core claim—the notion that more nuclear latency does not always translate into greater bargaining advantages (H2). Even on the cusp of the bomb, Rouhani and Zarif managed to trade away some valuable nuclear assets and make credible nonproliferation assurances in exchange for concessions on enrichment and sanctions relief. In line with the maximalist school of thought (A2), perhaps more latency was better for Iran, giving negotiators enough leverage to wrest policy changes from the United States.

Upon deeper examination, however, the episode reveals that leaders in Tehran still confronted an acute threat-assurance trade-off. In line with the book's theory, the threat of proliferation became quite credible as Iran added more centrifuges and enriched uranium. Tehran signaled resolve via mobilization and brinkmanship, taking steps toward the bomb that risked pulling the United States or Israel into war. Washington came under pressure to consider diplomacy before it faced an even worse situation. "The nuclear clock was ticking much faster than the economic clock," a former Obama administration official recounted. "Iran would have passed the nuclear finish line before its economy would have collapsed."[59] Within the domestic political arena, moreover, Iranian leaders had committed themselves to maintaining the core elements of the nuclear program. "The further Iran progresses with its nuclear programme," Wyn Bowen and Matthew Moran (2014: 42) observed at the time, "the less likely Tehran is to give up its capabilities." These factors all likely led American officials to put the enrichment concession on the table early in negotiations. "If we could create an option in which Iran eliminated every single nut and bolt of their nuclear program," President Obama (2013) rued in July 2013, "I would take it. But that particular option is not available."

Rouhani and the nuclear negotiation team faced formidable barriers when it came time to offer constraints over the Iran's bomb-making capacity. As stipulated by the too much hypothesis (H2), the tactics Tehran employed to gain leverage made it harder to offer credible assurances. Given its pattern of hiding sensitive facilities, Iran had to go to great lengths to illuminate the nuclear program, accepting the additional security risks that come from letting other countries closely monitor a wide range of activities (Long 2015). The Iranians also had to move away from the cusp of the bomb. But many opponents of the JCPOA in the United States and Israel argued that the Iranians were not giving up enough nuclear latency to make their assurances credible (Hurst 2016: 554–58). Within Iran, Rouhani and Zarif ran into domestic opposition as they probed these roll-back steps. After negotiating the JCPOA, for instance, a top Iranian military commander warned that Iran had "given the maximum and received the minimum."[60] Once again, elite empowerment and public activation made it difficult for Iranian leaders to curtail the nuclear program.

Perhaps the pushback from regime hard-liners was part of a plan to improve Iran's bargaining position, using domestic politics to tie one's hands on the international stage.[61] But Khamenei had to play an active role in lowering the domestic costs for Rouhani, advocating "heroic flexibility" in the negotiations while drawing red lines around acceptable constraints.[62] "As the constraining effects of Iran's nuclear nationalism have gained momentum," Bowen and Moran (2014: 42) underscored, "it has become increasingly difficult for the regime to reverse its diplomatic trajectory." When negotiations stretched out, infighting among elites intensified, "leading [Khamenei] to take a clear and public stance and, on several occasions, even cautiously come out in support of the negotiators to shield them from opponents," Tabatabai (2019: 4) observed. These interventions appear to have been instrumental in enabling the Iranian negotiators to offer credible nonproliferation assurances.

Iran also paid a steep price to develop its nuclear program, leading some to argue that the apparent success of the July 2015 deal masked a costly Pyrrhic victory for Tehran. It is difficult to tabulate the costs and benefits of Iran's nuclear program in an objective manner, especially since sanctions had differential effects on elite actors within the country.[63] With this caveat in mind, several net assessments offer evidence that supports both the too much hypothesis (H2) and the pessimist school of thought (A3). According to Thomas Juneau and Sam Razavi (2018: 85), "the massive economic and financial costs of sanctions" far outweighed any tangible benefits Iran reaped from the nuclear program.[64] A decade of defiant enrichment campaigns primed the international community to impose increasingly harsh sanctions. Cutting a deal that included relief from these same sanctions can hardly be chalked up as an unalloyed win for Iran. Moreover, Tehran had to curb its nuclear program while Washington preserved its ability to reimpose sanctions down the road. Beyond the economic costs, Iran appears to have made itself less secure over the long term, exacerbating its security dilemma with Israel and sparking a latent nuclear arms race with Saudi Arabia (Miller and Volpe 2018a; Russell 2012).

The Iran nuclear deal demonstrates that it is possible to offer credible assurances, even on the cusp of the bomb. But the costs and difficulties involved with restraining oneself from crossing the weapons threshold suggest that such outcomes should be quite rare.

7

Conclusion

This book assesses how nations wield the capacity to build atomic weapons against the strongest states in the international system. From Japan's quiet campaign over Okinawa to North Korea's more blatant plutonium brinkmanship, allies and adversaries have long leveraged latency to compel concessions from great powers. The conventional wisdom is that the strategy is most likely to work when states are close to the bomb. But this intuitive notion is wrong. My theory reveals that compellence creates a trade-off between making threats and assurances credible. States need just enough bomb-making capacity to threaten proliferation, but not so much that it becomes too difficult to promise nuclear restraint. I find that the boundaries of this sweet spot align with the capacity to produce the fissile material at the heart of an atomic weapon.

The empirical chapters test this argument with comparative case studies of four countries that leveraged latency against great powers over time. In Chapters 3 and 4, I examine how Japan and West Germany used atomic energy programs built in plain sight to put pressure on officials in Washington (and Moscow). Chapters 5 and 6 assess attempts by North Korea and Iran to flip exposed nuclear programs into assets for extracting concessions from the United States and its allies. Utilizing historical accounts of negotiations, I trace out how variation in nuclear latency shaped ten distinct bargaining outcomes for these challengers across the atomic age. Overall, the results demonstrate that more latency does not always translate into greater leverage. Instead, all four challengers were most able to wrest concessions from the United States (and the Soviet Union in the West German case) once they entered the fissile material sweet spot.

As nuclear latency continues to cast a shadow over the global landscape, the book provides scholars and policy practitioners with a systematic assessment of its coercive utility. For international relations theorists, my compellence framework advances the study of coercion in world politics. I identify a generalizable mechanism—the threat-assurance trade-off—that helps us understand why more power often makes compellence less

Leveraging Latency. Tristan A. Volpe, Oxford University Press. © Oxford University Press 2023.
DOI: 10.1093/oso/9780197669532.003.0007

likely to work. The book also contributes to a growing research program on asymmetrical relationships between strong and weak states. I demonstrate how weaker states can overcome structural disadvantages to influence the behavior of great powers. Finally, the book improves the study and practice of nonproliferation. I illuminate one key set of choices states make with potential power in lieu of building weapons. This sets the foundation to re-fine policy options for inhibiting the spread of nuclear and other dual-use technologies.

The first part of this chapter summarizes the book's results in greater detail. I specify the degree to which the case studies support the core theory relative to alternative arguments. In addition, I unpack the surprising result that the fissile material sweet spot remained remarkably stable over the last seven decades. The second part considers the implications of my research for studying coercion, proliferation, and technology in international relations. The final part derives policy implications from the book's theory and empirical results. I assess contemporary factors that may lead US allies and partners to leverage latency again. This forecast points toward the need for the United States—and perhaps China—to bargain with the next generation of potential challengers at an early stage of latency.

Summary of Findings

The general theme of this book is that potential power can provide states with an effective coercive instrument. The bargaining advantages of latency are pronounced in the nuclear realm, where actual atomic weapons tend to be ill-suited for compellence (Sechser and Fuhrmann 2013).[1] By contrast, the mere capacity to build the bomb can yield significant diplomatic dividends. By marching up the latency continuum, allies and adversaries alike have been able to wrest concessions from great powers who oppose the spread of nuclear weapons. North Korea's blatant blackmail demands and Iran's explicit bargaining tactics are but the most vivid manifestations of this strategy. Even countries such as Japan and West Germany with civil nuclear energy enterprises were able to allay concerns about proliferation for the right price. Yet this strategy does not always work. I present a new theory to explain when compellence with nuclear latency is most likely to succeed or fail. My framework and core hypotheses receive substantial support from the three main findings in the book.

Hedgers and Hiders Leverage Latency against Great Powers

Who leverages latency? The first finding is that a diverse but small number of states made deliberate decisions to leverage latency against great powers. As expected, I find no signs of governments investing in military or civil nuclear programs just to gain bargaining chips. From Japan to Iran, more fundamental security and economic factors always drove states to the march up the latency continuum. But many leaders still ended up leveraging latency at various stages of nuclear development. On this point, a country's proliferation strategy appears to shape the relative allure of compellence.[2] In line with my assumptions from Chapter 1, ally hedgers and adversarial hiders sometimes found it useful to leverage latency for different reasons. Japan and West Germany demonstrate that hedgers with transparent civil nuclear programs tend to pursue a subtle quid pro quo form of compellence with implicit proliferation threats. North Korea and Iran show how the exposure of covert nuclear facilities can drive leaders to fall back on compellence, even if the transition process is often messy. Despite major differences among these countries, they all hewed close to the core logic of compellence in negotiations with the United States (and Soviet Union).

The book also shows how growing great power opposition to proliferation created an opportunity for allies and adversaries to bargain with their nuclear programs. Soviet fear of the German nuclear energy program offers a prime illustration early in the atomic age. Leaders in Bonn and Washington both recognized that they could manipulate these concerns as a diplomatic lever over Berlin and reunification. But the subsequent adoption of stronger US nonproliferation policies toward allies set the stage for West Germany, as well as Japan, to play the nuclear card against the Americans.

In the ensuing years, the United States sharpened its coercive tools for pressuring countries to abandon their nuclear weapons programs (Ellis 2003; Lissner 2017; Miller 2018; Gibbons 2022). I find that there is another side to this story. Even adversaries who were caught with secret nuclear weapons programs still attempted to exploit US nonproliferation preferences as a way of gaining otherwise unattainable bargaining advantages. By opposing the spread of nuclear weapons, the United States made itself the main target of compellence with nuclear latency. Washington cut deals with latent nuclear powers precisely because it wanted to keep them from actualizing their weapons potential.

But this finding about the willingness of sheriffs to bargain over nuclear programs raises another puzzle. Compellence with nuclear latency is rare. Why have not more states pursued this strategy? My study suggests that states faced fewer opportunities to leverage latency after the halcyon era for nuclear energy came to an end in the early-1970s. One reason is that it became harder to develop fissile material production capabilities under the guise of nuclear energy enterprises over time. Sheriffs adopted more stringent supply-side controls that cut off new nuclear aspirants from the aboveboard market for sensitive nuclear technology. This forced many states to either give up the fissile material quest or pursue indigenous enrichment and reprocessing (ENR) capabilities in secret (Koch 2022). The overall pool of potential candidates for compellence with nuclear latency shrank, leaving a smaller number of states who had to consider the strategy as a last resort in the aftermath of exposure. Other states may have shifted toward alternative forms of potential power with lower political barriers to entry, such as rocket and space technologies.[3] Future research should examine whether states were more likely to pursue compellence with nonnuclear forms of latency as they faced greater difficulties acquiring fissile material production plants.

Nuclear aspirants may have also drawn the attention of sheriffs at early stages of developing enrichment or reprocessing technology. The United States often preemptively extended various packages of technical and military assistance to keep allies and partners out of the fissile material sweet spot. In the 1970s, for instance, the US officials started to condition valuable nuclear trade agreements on the recipient giving up partial or total control over ENR decisions (Gibbons 2020; Miller 2017). This would help account for some states with lower levels of latency that avoided compellence altogether. But additional research is needed to systematically explore the degree to which early nuclear "buyouts" generated noncoercive benefits for such states.

Leveraging Latency Is Most Successful in the Sweet Spot

When does this strategy work? The second key finding is that compellence is likely to succeed when nuclear programs are in the sweet spot. Table 7.1 summarizes the strength of support each case lends to my hypotheses. I find evidence that great powers brush off proliferation threats as infeasible when a challenger's nuclear program is in its infancy (H1). In the West Germany case,

Table 7.1 Summary of Empirical Findings

Country	Episode	Dates	Latency	Outcome	Theory support
Japan	Security pact crisis	1957–1960	Low	Failure	Strong (H1)
	Satō's Okinawa gambit	1964–1970	Medium	Success	Strong (H3)
West Germany	Adenauer's LTBT gambit	1961–1963	Low	Failure	Strong (H1)
	Erhard's NATO push	1963–1966	Medium	Partial success	Modest (H3)
	Kiesinger's NPT campaign	1966–1969	Medium	Success	Strong (H3)
North Korea	First nuclear crisis	1991–1994	Medium	Success	Strong (H3)
	Second nuclear crisis	2002–2008	High to acquisition	Failure	Strong (H2)
Iran	First diplomatic dance	2003–2005	Medium	Partial success	Modest (H3)
	Fuel swap proposal	2009–2010	High	Failure	Strong (H2)
	Iran nuclear deal (JCPOA)	2013–2015	Ultra-high	Success	Modest (H2)

for example, Adenauer's warning shots rang hollow because the Kennedy administration knew the country was still years away from producing large amounts of fissile material. Marching to the cusp of the bomb solves this threat credibility problem, as evident in the tactics employed by the North Koreans and the Iranians at high levels of latency. Yet it also becomes harder to make nonproliferation assurances that involve trading away or limiting mature nuclear programs (H2). The North Korean nuclear crisis in 2002–2008 and the 2009–2010 Iranian fuel swap proposal lend strong support for this hypothesis. In both episodes, leaders faced a sharp trade-off between making threats and assurances credible with high levels of latency. The 2015 Iran nuclear deal offers less support because Tehran managed to extract concessions from the West in exchange for curbing the nuclear program. But leaders in Tehran still faced a sharp threat-assurance trade-off. As expected by the theory, the same tactics that proved useful in putting pressure on the West increased the costs of nuclear restraint during the diplomatic endgame in 2013–2015.

All four countries support the sweet spot hypotheses to varying degrees (H3). Admittedly, several episodes from the West Germany and Iran studies provide the least amount of support. Despite wielding medium levels of latency, neither country accomplished a total diplomatic victory. Bonn failed to save the Multilateral Force or reverse the nuclear nonproliferation treaty (NPT) fait accompli, even though Erhard and especially Kiesinger succeeded in extracting other valuable concessions from the superpowers. In 2003–2005, Rouhani's diplomatic campaign protected the Iranian nuclear program—and the regime—from punishment in the wake of the Natanz exposure. But he was unable to wrest deeper concessions from the West over the enrichment program itself—a feat that only became possible at higher stages of latency. Both countries point to the limits of leveraging latency to compel nuclear policy concessions from great powers. However, Japan and North Korea offer strong evidence in support of the sweet spot hypothesis. Tokyo gained significant leverage in negotiations over Okinawa after the Japanese civil nuclear program marched into the sweet spot during the mid-1960s. Decades later, Pyongyang pursued an effective proliferation blackmail strategy after its plutonium program was exposed. In both cases, I find evidence that the medium level of latency enabled leaders to surmount the threat-assurance trade-off and wrest concessions from the United States.

The results also provide little support for the notion that sheriffs let some countries attain higher levels of latency instead of making concessions earlier. This selection bias issue emerged in the research design phase, where it became apparent that compellence may have failed because sheriffs refused to provide concessions to challengers at earlier stages of nuclear development. On initial consideration, the case of Iran seems to offer some support for this claim, as the United States balked at offering the adversarial regime major concessions in the sweet spot. By contrast, US officials may have been relatively more comfortable with acceding to demands from Japan and West Germany when these allies were in the sweet spot. Upon deeper consideration, however, the case studies offer limited support for this notion. The United States provided North Korea with concessions under the Agreed Framework when it was in the sweet spot. Although the Bush administration was loath to "reward" Pyongyang after 2002, Washington ultimately put a serious package of phased concessions on the table during later rounds of the Six-Party Talks. The Obama administration also tabled concessions to Tehran as part of the failed fuel swap proposal and successful JCPOA.

Support for the theory matters because it helps to resolve a sharp disagreement among scholars and analysts about the coercive utility of nuclear latency. As discussed in Chapter 2, some skeptics claim that nuclear programs are only useful for acquiring atomic weapons (A1). Many others argue that sitting on the cusp of the bomb gives states additional bargaining power (A2). The evidence to support these alternative arguments is weak. The six successful compellence episodes demonstrate that states can wield nuclear latency to accomplish some of their strategic goals. Contrary to Kenneth Waltz's (1997) skepticism, I find that being a few steps removed from an actual atomic weapon often enables nuclear aspirants to gain bargaining advantages over nuclear-armed great powers. When compellence failed, the challenger always had too little or too much latency to surmount the threat-assurance dilemma. This track record of failure at the high end of the latency continuum also undermines the maximalist argument. Even in the one Iranian episode where more latency may have better for ratcheting up pressure on the West, the high costs associated with making nonproliferation assurances credible indicate that such diplomatic outcomes are likely to be infrequent.

My results suggest that some degree of pessimism about bargaining with nuclear latency is warranted under specific conditions (A3). The benefits at stake in almost every episode appeared to be lower than the costs of building the bomb (Fuhrmann 2019; Sechser and Fuhrmann 2017). In some instances, notably the West Germany case, the small stakes of compellence may have set upper limits on what challengers could achieve. But many other leaders were able to overcome this issue by employing various bargaining tactics, especially in the fissile material sweet spot. My theory also refines the claim from some pessimists that leveraging latency generates onerous costs for marginal rewards (Mehta and Whitlark 2017; Narang 2014). I specify when and how challengers are likely to end up in this type of situation. At low levels of latency, proliferation threats are not credible. Great powers face few incentives to comply with the challenger's demands, as Japan and West Germany discovered. Challengers with high levels of latency often suffer more serious blowback as the threat of proliferation becomes increasingly credible. As evident in the North Korea and Iran cases, moving to the cusp of the bomb can also make diplomatic goals more costly and difficult to achieve. In contrast to pessimists, I identify a Goldilocks zone along the latency continuum where challengers can manage these consequences.

The Fissile Material Sweet Spot Remains Stable

Where is the sweet spot? How much latency is "just enough" for challengers to make threats and assurances credible? The book's third finding is that the boundaries of the sweet spot align with the capacity to produce fissile material. I discover that the lower and upper borders of this Goldilocks zone along the latency continuum underwent little change over time. All four challengers entered the sweet spot when they reached the cusp of being able to enrich uranium or reprocess plutonium. Japan, West Germany, and North Korea edged toward producing large amounts of plutonium as they mastered the underlying technology and started to bring various reprocessing facilities online. Iran mastered enrichment at an experimental level before installing gas centrifuge cascades at Natanz. Subsequent fissile material production campaigns—either for peaceful or for military purposes—pushed each country to higher levels of latency. Most important, all four challengers faced a mild threat-assurance trade-off in this middle Goldilocks zone, especially compared to lower and higher latent nuclear capabilities. The fissile material sweet spot remained remarkably stable across the atomic age.

On initial consideration, this result seems surprising given the pace of innovation over the last seven decades. Iran and North Korea faced a different technological environment compared to Japan and West Germany. The menu of options for mastering the nuclear fuel cycle expanded and arguably became easier to execute from a purely technical standpoint.[4] Many methods are old and well understood by scientists. The PUREX reprocessing technique, for example, dates to the Manhattan Project. Uranium gas centrifuges reached commercial maturity during the 1970s. Steady advances in industrial production seemed to further erode the barriers to acquisition. We might expect the sweet spot parameters to shift as ENR capabilities became easier to develop over time.

Upon deeper examination, the book suggests that technological progress has yet to reshape the boundaries of the sweet spot for two reasons. First, nuclear fuel cycle innovations only resulted in marginal cost improvements for building ENR plants. These large projects always required significant resources, even when new options emerged with lower barriers to entry. For instance, the jump from gaseous diffusion plants to gas centrifuges made it relatively cheaper and easier to enrich uranium (Kemp 2012). Yet building centrifuge enrichment plants remained a resource-intensive endeavor, as evidenced by the costs Iran paid to move into the sweet spot. Second, great powers made it harder for states to develop ENR capabilities over time. The genesis of the Nuclear Suppliers Group in 1974 cut off many countries from being able to import ENR plants from aboveboard suppliers (Anstey 2018; Koch 2019). The United States then erected additional barriers to keep states out of the fissile material sweet spot, from reactor fuel supply assurances to ENR restrictions baked into bilateral nuclear cooperation agreements.[5] In turn, later generations of ENR aspirants were forced down more costly and suboptimal development routes (Montgomery 2013; Kemp 2014; Koch 2022).

These twin factors help to explain why states consistently paid high costs to master the nuclear fuel cycle over the last seven decades. Despite major innovations in nuclear technology, atomic weapons potential always boiled down to the capacity to enrich uranium or reprocess plutonium. No viable shortcuts emerged for states to get around this laborious process. The tactics for making threats and assurances credible continued to depend heavily on fissile material production capabilities. As a result, the parameters of the sweet spot remained stable during periods of considerable technological flux.

Implications for Scholarship

The book's theory and empirics have implications for how scholars study coercion, proliferation, and technology in world politics.

Studying Coercion

The results in this book undermine a long-standing tenet in coercion theory—the notion that more power is better for making effective compellent demands. I show that the axiom is wrong on both theoretical and empirical grounds. States need enough power to underwrite threats, but not so much that it impedes their ability to make believable assurances. Although the fissile material sweet spot is unique to nuclear technology, the underlying mechanism is generalizable. The threat-assurance trade-off can help to explain how a nation's military potential shapes the viability of compellence in other situations.[6] Robert Art and Kelly Greenhill (2018a: 18–19) identify a similar "capability-intention dilemma" at play when powerful states fail to back their compellent threats with credible commitments not to use military force in the future. The book reveals that weaker states also grapple with an acute version of this trade-off as they accumulate potential power. The severity of this trade-off can account for the surprising failure of coercive demands at high levels of latent power.

My framework suggests that scholars pay close attention to how the means of coercion shape the threat-assurance trade-off beyond the nuclear realm. In line with comparative studies of coercive capabilities, I find that the nature of the technology being employed in a compellence campaign matters—it directly affects the bargaining tactics and likelihood of success (Lindsay and Gartzke 2019: 3–4). The trade-off should be especially severe for other forms of potential power that require governments to make large, sticky investments. For instance, states have long attempted to gain leverage by threatening to build up their military capabilities (Knorr 1956; Slantchev 2011; Trager 2017). Leaders who empower elites to mobilize armament factories or activate public support for new weapons programs can certainly make compellent threats more credible. Yet the domestic politics of developing such projects may make it more difficult for both democratic and autocratic leaders to offer credible assurances by liquidating such investments. In the book, this feature cuts across regime type (Hyde and Saunders 2020; Saunders 2019). Additional research should explore whether democratic or autocratic leaders enjoy coercive advantages when it comes to leveraging other types of potential power.

The book also contributes to several strands of scholarship on coercion in asymmetrical relationships between strong and weak states. The first challenges the notion espoused by the Athenians that the strong do what they can in world politics, as Paul Musgrave (2019) notes. In contrast to this old adage, studies from Todd Sechser (2010), Phil Haun (2015), and Dianne Chamberlain (2016) show that compellence is more difficult for great powers because they often make incredible assurances, demand too much, or employ relatively "cheap" standoff capabilities.[7] When it comes to putting pressure on weaker states to forgo atomic weapons, the book finds that *when* the great power engages in diplomacy matters a great deal to the ultimate outcome. The United States was best able to wield influence over states at early stages of nuclear development. This leverage declined after states started to master ENR technology. Additional research is needed to determine if this result holds across development timelines for other strategic capabilities, notably chemical weapons (Bowen, Knopf, and Moran 2020) or missile systems (Bowers and Hiim 2021; Hiim 2022).

The second strand investigates whether the weak must always suffer what they must under the yoke of the strong. In line with this scholarship (Arreguín-Toft 2005; Walt 2006; Greenhill 2010; Long 2017; Castillo and Downes 2020), the book argues that weaker nations can surmount formidable disadvantages to compel concessions from great powers. I find that power asymmetries—such as the gulf between the nuclear weapon "haves" and "have-nots"—can be exploited as a diplomatic lever. Weaker states that figure out how to equalize the relationship can put tremendous pressure on the strong to halt such an adverse power transition. So long as preventive war motivations can be held at bay, threatening to erode the advantages enjoyed by great powers can be a powerful means of coercion. Weaker states may increasingly be able to avail themselves of this unique opportunity if emerging technologies provide them with new "strategic equalizers" (Chyba 2020; Horowitz 2020; Schneider 2019). The structure of the international system privileges great powers, but also makes them sensitive to such threats from the weak.

Studying Proliferation and Technology

Beyond coercion, the book offers two final considerations for explaining the consequences of nuclear latency and technology on conflict and peace outcomes.

First, the book joins an ongoing effort to better understand latent nuclear statecraft. Policy analysts and government officials have long grappled with the consequences of choices states make along the nuclear timeline before the bomb (Einhorn 2006; Meyer 1986; Quester 1972; Wohlstetter 1979). Yet nuclear latency received relatively little attention from political scientists compared to the dominant focus on actual atomic weapons. Over the last fifteen years, however, the field of international relations has started to catch up.[8] Studies on the spread of nuclear latency set the empirical foundation for scholars to explain how it affects a variety of outcomes, from proliferation strategies such as hedging to security dilemmas and preventive war risks.[9] Working in this vein, the book develops and tests a novel theory of compellence to strengthen a key analytic pillar in this research program.

But it is important to be clear about the scope of my study. The book does not attempt to explain the other face of coercion: deterrence with nuclear latency. Instead of extracting concessions, states may be able to use their nuclear

programs to deter arms races or even conflict. This idea enjoys a long intellectual lineage (Acheson-Lilienthal 1946; Acton 2015a; Ford 2011; Perkovich
1993; Schell 1984). Several major studies are underway to explain whether
latent or "virtual" nuclear deterrence works.[10] But we should be careful about
stretching the concepts and results from the book to account for these distinct deterrent outcomes. Matthew Fuhrmann (2019) finds that the fundamental logic of deterrence with nuclear latency differs from compellence in
several ways, even though both strategies use the same means of coercion.
The biggest difference is that the latent nuclear power must position itself to
build the bomb if and only if the attacker initiates conflict. When deterrence
is the goal, it may be useful for such defenders to develop postures around
advanced nuclear programs so they can quickly follow through on the proliferation threat in the wake of an attack. The threat-assurance trade-off may
still bedevil latent nuclear deterrence, however. If the defender appears to be
on an inexorable march to the bomb, nuclear latency could encourage rather
than dissuade an attack. But additional research is needed to determine
whether defenders struggle to make nonproliferation assurances credible at
high levels of latency for the same reasons identified in this book.

Second, the book sets the stage for future research on how technology
shapes broader bargaining dynamics in international relations. Almost every
method for producing fissile material is "dual use" because enriched uranium
and reprocessed plutonium have both military and civil uses (Acton 2016).
This central attribute of nuclear technology appears to make compellence an
attractive choice for state leaders. On the military side of the coin, they can
cultivate concerns about the weapons potential lurking within atomic energy
programs. On the civil side, however, leaders protect themselves from blowback by emphasizing the peaceful pursuit of nuclear fuel cycle technology.
The United States often struggled to draw clear distinctions between civil and
military ENR programs, even when the revelation of hidden facilities indicated a strong proclivity for the bomb. The relative indistinguishability of nuclear technology may make compellence a more viable strategy for the weak
to pursue in the shadow of great powers.

Yet almost every modern technology is dual use in nature to some degree.
The core military capabilities for projecting power across air, land, sea, space,
and now cyber domains all have peaceful analogues.[11] For instance, aircraft,
motor vehicles, naval vessels, rockets, and computer networks constitute the
technological backbone of advanced economies and militaries today. Much
like nuclear programs, states can reap commercial and security dividends

from these technologies. But my study suggests that states may find it appealing to leverage some investments as a means of coercion. Technology with the potential to level the playing field with stronger actors is likely to be quite appealing in this regard. As commercial actors drive forward innovation for peaceful purposes, governments may be able to spin off military weapons—or the capacity to produce such weapons—along the way (Alic et al. 1992; Horowitz 2010: 31). This trend could expand the menu of technical options for states to practice coercion with potential power. It remains to be seen whether new forms of latent power will provide the same bargaining benefits as nuclear technology. But the technical stage is set for coercion with latency to become a more central feature of the international landscape.

Policy Forecast

The main policy implication from this book is that nuclear latency will remain a potent means for states to put pressure on the United States and other great power nonproliferation sheriffs. This forecast is predicated on the assumption that Washington and other sheriffs will continue to oppose the spread of nuclear weapons in the years ahead.[12] I use the book's framework to tackle two more specific issues about the future proliferation landscape. First, I examine the factors that may lead US allies and partners to leverage latency again in the near future. Second, I make the case for the United States to proactively "buy out" the fissile material aspirations of partner nations with fledgling atomic energy programs.

Back to the Future: Why Allies and Partners Will Leverage Latency

Who is most likely to leverage latency in the years ahead? The tendency for US adversaries to pursue this strategy is on the wane. Iran is the only major adversary of the United States that remains a latent nuclear power. After President Donald Trump withdrew the United States from the JCPOA in April 2018, Tehran did launch a mobilization campaign with its enrichment program. But this effort was not designed to wrest fresh concessions from the West. Iran simply wanted to restore the status quo ante by pressuring the

Europeans to block new sanctions and the Americans to uphold the 2015 agreement (Brewer 2019). Diplomacy over Iran's nuclear program will no doubt remain a top priority for US officials. Beyond Iran, however, there is no other US adversary accumulating nuclear latency in lieu of the bomb.[13] Yet a handful of key American allies and partners are latent nuclear powers or aspire to attain such capabilities. I identify three trends that could drive these countries to bargain with nuclear programs built in plain sight.

First, the end of America's unipolar moment is creating another crisis of credibility in the US alliance system. The international distribution of power is shifting toward a bipolar division between the United States and China, with elements of multipolarity at the regional level in Europe and the Middle East. Under this new system, US allies and partners face greater incentives to counter concerns about American abandonment by developing and then leveraging nuclear hedge capabilities.[14] As the focal point of great power rivalry shifts toward Asia, long-standing US allies in the region are likely to push for stronger security guarantees and material assistance from Washington to offset Beijing's rise (Medeiros 2005). In Europe, key NATO members—notably France and Germany—are debating how best to insure themselves against the risk of US retrenchment (Meijer and Brooks 2021; Volpe and Kühn 2017). These fears about American reliability are most acute in the Middle East, where Gulf Arab nations lack formal US security commitments. Saudi Arabia has repeatedly pushed US officials for greater military support, even going so far as to request a formal defense treaty at a summit in Washington in May 2015 (Cooper 2015).

Second, growing competition between the United States, China, and Russia may enable states to play these nuclear suppliers off each other. During the Cold War, Washington and Moscow used civil nuclear exports to bolster alliance coalitions, court new partners, and gain influence over key countries (Colgan and Miller 2019; Fuhrmann 2012; Gibbons 2020). Yet the United States eventually ceded the nuclear marketplace to Russia and China— nineteen of the thirty-three commercial nuclear power plants exported from 2000 to 2020 came from these two authoritarian rivals (Miller and Volpe 2022). But US officials are taking steps to revitalize American nuclear exports as part of a larger effort to compete for influence with Russia and especially China.[15] One key reason is that Moscow and Beijing often target US allies and partners with valuable atomic assistance packages. Saudi Arabia, for instance, is considering bids to build nuclear power plants from the United States, China, Russia, and other suppliers.[16] If Washington, Moscow, and

Beijing continue to vie for dominance over civil nuclear exports, savvy states could exploit this dynamic to build up nuclear energy programs under generous and perhaps even permissive supply agreements.

Third, US allies and partners know they can accumulate latency in plain sight without breaking any international rules. The United States sharpened its coercive toolkit to deter many countries from pursuing secret nuclear weapon programs over the last four decades. Only the most determined nuclear aspirants—such as North Korea and Iran—were willing to suffer the economic costs of building hidden nuclear facilities outside of IAEA safeguards (Miller 2014b). Yet this track record highlights a gap in the US approach: the threat of punishment is far less credible against allies and partners who develop nuclear technologies in compliance with their nonproliferation obligations. There is little legal basis or political will to sanction an ally that decides to enrich uranium fuel for nuclear power plants, so long as all nuclear fuel cycle activities occur in the open under IAEA surveillance. The geopolitical consequences would also be severe. Unlike sanctions against Iran or North Korea, "Following through on punitive actions toward partners could have negative ramifications for important US interests," Eric Brewer (2021: 189) argues. In 2004, for example, Washington refused to allow South Korea to be censured at the UN Security Council for undeclared ENR experiments that violated the safeguard agreement with the IAEA (Acton 2009: 136–37). In addition, adherence to the NPT helps partners to take advantage of the aboveboard market for civil nuclear technology. Going forward, these countries will be in an ideal position to openly build hedge capabilities.

The trend lines point to a looming fourth wave of compellence with nuclear latency. In contrast to the most recent third wave (1991–2015), the next generation of challengers will be allies with atomic energy enterprises rather than adversaries with secret nuclear weapons programs. A number of US allies and partners—from Saudi Arabia and Turkey to South Korea—already face stronger incentives and better opportunities to flex their nuclear hedge options (Brewer 2020). Washington may well find itself confronting a situation similar to the first wave (1956–1974), when Japan and West Germany nurtured nuclear suspicions and wrested concessions from anxious US officials. The big difference is that US policy and the global nonproliferation regime have both evolved significantly since the 1960s (Dalton and Levite 2022). The key question then becomes whether the United States needs to retool its diplomatic strategy in anticipation of this next wave.

"Buyouts" and 123s: How to Manage Enrichment and Reprocessing Aspirations

How should the United States respond to its allies and partners leveraging latency again? The threat of punitive punishment and active counterproliferation measures should remain a central element of US strategy to inhibit proliferation. This toolkit has proven itself to be effective at keeping all but the most resolved nuclear aspirants from the bomb. However, a "pressure-centric" approach is neither credible nor prudent to employ against an ally or partner that accumulates latency as part of an atomic energy program in compliance with its nonproliferation obligations (Brewer 2021: 188). But the type of quid pro quo diplomacy embraced by US officials over the last seventy years will remain a viable option going forward. The book's framework recommends that the United States consider "buying out" the fissile material ambitions of allies and partners before they enter the sweet spot.[17]

An inducement strategy is a well-trodden policy prescription. As demonstrated in the book, US officials consistently made concessions and dangled offers of political, economic, and military assistance to latent nuclear challengers. In exchange, states sometimes agreed to trade away their weapons options. Cutting such deals was often the best way to keep countries with fissile material capabilities from building actual atomic weapons. The United States also baked additional nonproliferation commitments into nuclear cooperation agreements with its allies and partners. These pacts— referred to as "123 agreements" after the relevant section of the US Atomic Energy Act—set rules for how countries could use American nuclear equipment and materials in their civil energy programs.

Nuclear cooperation agreements are a critical tool for the United States to manage fissile material production in partner countries.[18] The relative strength of restrictions on ENR in these pacts varies along a spectrum. On the low end, there are just three agreements with Japan, EURATOM, and India that grant advance US consent to enrich uranium and reprocess nuclear fuel. On the high end, several "Gold Standard" 123 agreements completely forbid the development and operation of ENR technology. Although the United Arab Emirates and Taiwan accepted this restriction, US officials found it difficult to convince any other country to follow suit. Instead, most pacts in force utilize less onerous mechanisms to control—rather than outlaw—the development of ENR technology. Under these standard 123 agreements, the country accepts a long list of nonproliferation obligations, including a pledge to refrain from enriching or reprocessing US-origin nuclear material without prior consent from Washington. The upside is that countries tend to be more willing to accept such restrictions, especially in exchange for tangible inducements made at early stages of nuclear development (Kerr and Nikitin 2021; Varnum 2012).

The United States should double down on using standard nuclear cooperation agreements to limit the fissile material options of its allies and partners. These pacts offer significant nonproliferation benefits at marginal diplomatic cost. Nuclear cooperation under a standard 123 agreement gives the US government greater insight and influence over the evolution of an ally's nuclear energy program. The agreements provide the legal basis for the United States to condition atomic assistance on the recipient country accepting stringent safeguards and international inspections. This makes it easier to detect suspicious behavior and withhold valuable nuclear materials and services if the nonproliferation terms are breached (Gibbons 2020; Koch 2022; Miller 2017).

The prior consent clause also shields the United States from compellence with nuclear latency. Once the partner nation builds nuclear power plants with American assistance, this provision gives Washington a veto over enrichment or reprocessing with US-supplied nuclear fuel and equipment (Miller and Volpe 2018a: 31–33). Consider the nuclear cooperation framework between the United States and the Republic of Korea. Seoul signed a standard 123 agreement to build its civil nuclear reactor infrastructure around imported Westinghouse technology in the 1970s. Over the years, the South Koreans repeatedly requested prior US consent to enrich uranium and reprocess large amounts of spent reactor waste. Seoul offered justifications for developing the front and back end of the nuclear fuel cycle to meet commercial needs and conducted several diplomatic campaigns to make this case in Washington. Yet the requests were denied. South Korea therefore limited the development of ENR technology to small laboratory-scale experiments (McGoldrick et al. 2015; Pomper et al. 2016). As this example illustrates, prior consent provides the United States with a powerful lever to keep even its closest and most technically capable allies out of the fissile material sweet spot.

One key implication from this book is that Washington will be in the best position to secure such agreements when it engages with partners at low levels of latency. Nuclear energy programs are more vulnerable and open to policy change in the initial development phases, before large projects generate entrapment effects and path dependency barriers. American civil nuclear cooperation can be quite alluring to leaders looking to jump-start a fledgling atomic energy enterprise. Partner nations may be willing to accept prior consent constraints in exchange for other nonnuclear inducements, such as stronger defense commitments or greater access to US conventional weapons, military training, and intelligence support. The main downside with this approach is that it becomes far less feasible once a country builds nuclear energy infrastructure without signing a US 123 agreement. The prior consent clause loses its power, as the country may be able to enrich and re-process without using American-based nuclear fuel or technology.

An inducement strategy holds the best promise of neutralizing Saudi Arabia's ability to leverage latency against the United States. Over the last decade, Saudi Arabia threatened to match Iran's nuclear capabilities in several attempts to wrest concessions from the United States. The most explicit episode occurred over the summer of 2015, when proliferation threats from high-ranking Saudi officials seemed timed to coincide with demands for a defense treaty and advanced conventional weapons at a White House summit meeting (Obaid 2015). These threats rang hollow because Riyadh had no technical capacity to produce fissile material (Miller and Volpe 2018b). Going forward, however, the Saudis may find themselves in a far better position to develop nuclear latency under the guise of an atomic energy program. In the wake of the 2015 Iran nuclear deal, Riyadh outlined an ambitious plan to develop sixteen nuclear power plants, along with the human capital and support infrastructure necessary to operate such a large enterprise (Drollette 2016). In 2017, Saudi Arabia solicited bids for nuclear suppliers to build the first batch of nuclear reactors, including from the United States, Russia, China, France, and South Korea. Saudi officials also expressed interest in eventually mastering the front end of the nuclear fuel cycle to enrich uranium for peaceful purposes (Westall 2017). By building nuclear power plants to establish commercial demand for enriched fuel, Saudi Arabia appears to be positioning itself to move into the fissile material sweet spot without breaking any rules.

In late 2017, US officials began discussing the terms of a nuclear cooperation agreement with the Saudi leadership, which is required for US-based nuclear vendors such as Westinghouse to transfer nuclear power technology. The Trump administration demanded the Saudis forfeit ENR under a Gold Standard 123 agreement (El Gamal and Paul 2017; Mufson 2018). Yet the US position was at odds with past refusals by Saudi Arabia to sign an agreement depriving it of uranium enrichment. Moreover, no other foreign supplier made civil nuclear cooperation conditional on Riyadh giving up ENR technology. To no one's surprise, the talks stalled out, putting the potential 123 agreement on ice (Blanchard and Kerr 2020). The problem with sticking to the Gold Standard is that the United States may soon find itself watching from the sidelines as another supplier helps the Saudis build nuclear power plants. Without any legal mechanisms to influence the aboveboard development of enrichment technology, Washington would become susceptible to future bouts of compellence from Riyadh, this time with more concrete nuclear assets. US officials should therefore abandon the Gold Standard in favor of a standard 123 agreement with Saudi Arabia. The window to conclude such a pact will not remain open indefinitely. A package of inducements may still be needed to bring the Saudis on board, especially to secure Saudi adherence to the Additional Protocol as an enhanced check on secret nuclear activities. Convincing the Saudis to sign a standard 123 agreement with prior consent over ENR would align with decades of US nuclear diplomacy reviewed in this book. It would also put the United States in the best position to dampen the buildup of nuclear latency between Iran and Saudi Arabia in the years ahead.

Beyond the Saudi case, the power of prior consent in US nuclear cooperation agreements underscores the need for American nuclear firms to remain competitive on the global market. The United States ceded the marketplace for civil nuclear exports to Russia and China in part because Washington stopped supporting its domestic nuclear industry (Miller and Volpe 2022). Major US firms have so far failed to deliver new nuclear power plant build projects on schedule or budget—Westinghouse declared bankruptcy in 2017 after its premier AP1000 reactor projects in Georgia and South Carolina suffered serious setbacks (Cardwell and Soble 2017). By contrast, state-owned nuclear vendors in Russia and China have been quick to fill the vacuum left by the decline of the American nuclear industry. Moscow and Beijing can underwrite nuclear export deals with considerable sovereign capital under laxer legal frameworks (Levite and Dalton 2017). If US nuclear firms can no longer make viable offers to build nuclear power plants, there is little incentive for countries such as Saudi Arabia to conclude more stringent 123 agreements or depend on American technology (Brewer 2020). "It is hard to see why countries would allow America to set conditions on their civil nuclear energy programs," Matt Bowen (2020) argues about the demise of US nuclear exports, "if the United States is not able to offer nations anything of value in return." US officials seem to have embraced this logic, as both the Trump and Biden administrations took steps to revitalize the ailing US nuclear industry. It remains to be seen whether Washington will be able to regain its position as the pre-eminent supplier of civil nuclear technology. Unfortunately, failure to achieve this goal will leave the United States with few tools to manage the next wave of allies and partners leveraging latency in the years ahead.

Notes

Chapter 1

1. See, for example, US Department of State Cable 145139 to US Embassy India, "Nonproliferation in South [Asia]," June 6, 1979, *National Security Archive (NSA)*, https://www.documentcloud.org/documents/347012-doc-1-6-6-79.html.
2. Central Intelligence Agency, "Managing Nuclear Proliferation: The Politics of Limited Choice," Research Study, December 1975, https://www.cia.gov/library/readingroom/docs/CIA-RDP86T00608R000600170035-1.pdf.
3. Thomas Schelling (1966: 69–71) conceived the term "compellence" to denote coercive threats that are "intended to make an adversary do something." For an overview of the concept, see Biddle (2020).
4. For a similar treatment of this defining feature, see Sechser (2011).
5. Realist theories of international relations often define power in terms of a state's latent capacity build military forces; see Glaser (2010: 42); Mearsheimer (2001: 3).
6. This logic is often associated with the international relations theorist Kenneth Waltz (2002). But there is a vibrant debate about whether government leaders ascribe to a similar set of beliefs. See, for example, Gavin (2012b); Whitlark (2017).
7. I define great powers as states who possess the military capability to hold their own against any other powerful nation in the system. Secure second-strike nuclear arsenals and large conventional forces are essential requirements for modern great powers, see Mearsheimer (2001: 5) The global power projection requirement draws on Monteiro (2014: 44–45). As noted in Chapter 2, these characteristics narrow the scope to the United States, the Soviet Union, and perhaps China in the near future.
8. On the mixed incentives for smaller nations to act as "deputies" who also inhibit nuclear proliferation with great power sheriffs, see Gray (2012); Jabko and Weber (1998); O'Mahoney (2020).
9. Sheriffs can select from a wider range of specific policies and operations to support these three primary nonproliferation levers. For example, interdiction and other technology denial activities can help sheriffs manage the spread of latency. Sabotage can enable sheriffs to ramp up pressure during coercive diplomacy and delay technical progress.
10. On how power transitions create preventive motivations for war, see Fearon (1995: 406); Levy (1987: 87).
11. On the relative efficacy of coercive measure compared to assurances and inducements, see Debs and Monteiro (2016). For an extension to how sheriffs use these basic tools to bring countries in line with other goals beyond the nuclear realm, see Gortzak (2005).

12. This assumption holds the sheriff's level of concern about proliferation constant. However, sheriffs do vary in the strength of their opposition to the bomb. Chapter 2 considers how such variation shapes the threat-assurance trade-off that challengers face in making compellence work.

13. On the financial costs, see Horowitz (2010: 103); Kemp (2012). For overviews of the external consequences, see Beardsley and Asal (2013); Mehta and Whitlark (2017).

14. For a similar point in the context of North Korean proliferation, see Cha (2012: 300).

15. Itty Abraham (2006: 55–56) notes that the technical options in the nuclear development pool are almost always dual use in nature, which creates an ambivalence about civil or military applications as a "permanent feature of the nuclear condition." For a similar point about nuclear latency, see Harrington and Englert (2014); Roberts (2015: 218). On whether states pursue atomic energy programs as a deliberate hedge, see Fuhrmann (2012).

16. For a similar point about the blackmail utility of threatening proliferation against the United States, see Walt (2006: 159).

17. On alliance bargaining dynamics, see G. H. Snyder (2007: 6).

18. For an account of how abandonment concerns motivated nuclear choices during this era, see Goldstein (2000). On the link between alliances and hedging, see Lanoszka (2018b); Narang (2016).

19. On how supply-side controls shaped patterns of proliferation, see Gibbons (2020); Koch (2019). On the origins of the Nuclear Suppliers Group, see Anstey (2018); Burr (2014).

20. Chapter 2 checks for selection bias in a more systematic manner by comparing the state characteristics of challengers to the broader pool of nuclear aspirants. I find that both groups exhibit similar variation in regime type, relative power, and threat environment.

21. For the technical definition, see International Atomic Energy Agency (2002: 23).

22. See Braut-Hegghammer (2016); Fuhrmann (2019); Hymans (2012); Narang (2022); Kaplow (2022).

23. I review the contours of this debate to derive alternative explanations in Chapter 2.

24. On the credibility of assurances, see Knopf (2012); Kydd and McManus (2017); Pauly (2019).

Chapter 2

1. The theoretical framework in this chapter refines and extends the basic logic introduced in Volpe (2017).

2. As noted in Chapter 1, my theory assumes that nuclear aspirants target great powers that oppose proliferation to some degree. The goal is to better understand when compellence is likely to work against such sheriffs who opposed the bomb, as targeting a great power with sanguine views about proliferation is doomed to fail.

3. For a good overview, see Trager (2017). See also Bell and MacDonald (2019); Pape (1996).

4. For reviews of this extensive literature, see Bueno de Mesquita and Smith (2012); Hyde and Saunders (2020).

5. This signaling logic also helps international relations theorists explain broad patterns of cooperation and competition among nations; see Glaser (2010); Kydd (2007).

6. See Slantchev (2005). For an early articulation of this argument, see Jervis (1970: 38).

7. See Schelling (1966: 99, 102). For a skeptical view about the limits of brinkmanship in nuclear coercion, see Sechser and Fuhrmann (2017: 55).

8. To maintain this protective cloak, it behooves challengers to avoid taking unambiguous steps toward the bomb, which complicates the art of making proliferation threats credible.

9. For a similar point, see Narang (2016: 121). On the technical trade-offs, see Kemp (2014).

10. The idea of giving up hostages as a hand-tying mechanism comes from Schelling (1960: 43).

11. On the role public opposition groups play in tying hands of democratic leaders, see Schultz (2001). For a nuanced assessment of whether leaders suffer credibility consequences for irresolute action, see Lupton (2020).

12. Variation in the sheriff's level of opposition to proliferation can also shape the threat-assurance dilemma. When the sheriff is strongly opposed to proliferation, for example, the nuclear aspirant should find it somewhat easier to make credible proliferation threats but harder to offer assurances on the back end. But the core logic and hypotheses remain the same, as the sheriff is ultimately going to judge the credibility of threats and assurances in terms of actions associated with the challenger's capacity to build the bomb.

13. Fuhrmann (2012) makes a similar argument linking technical breakthroughs to the empowerment of nuclear bureaucracies, which in turn can become influential advocates for building the bomb. But he focuses on how importing civil nuclear technology from foreign suppliers can strengthen the domestic-political clout of nuclear enterprises "by enabling technological advances" (2012: 147).

14. The closest candidate comes from Muhammet Bas and Andrew Coe (2018), who advance an argument that appears to be the inverse of my sweet spot hypothesis. They argue that nonproliferation deals are most viable at "early" and "late" stages of nuclear development, but not in the "middle." This reads like a direct contrast to my central argument. But it is excluded as a competitor for several reasons.

First, Bas and Coe adopt different metrics for measuring nuclear development. They do not use a standard measure of latency or time to the bomb across the three stages of early, middle, and late. Instead, Bas and Coe (2018: 614) code a nuclear program as "early" if "it either has not yet started or has started but has not yet even begun to build the facilities necessary to actually produce fissile material." This metric bears some similarities to how I specify low levels of latency later in the chapter. But it is difficult to compare the results they find about the viability of deals over "early" nuclear programs because many do not appear to involve compellent demands from the potential proliferator. Other states are coded as "early" when they clearly possessed budding fissile material production capabilities in the sweet spot. West Germany in 1969 and Japan in 1970 are but the two most relevant examples of states that Bas and Coe code as having "early" nuclear programs.

Second, the deeper issue with comparing my argument to Bas and Coe emerges over how they measure the "middle" and "late" stages along the nuclear timeline. According to their research design (2018: 614), a state's nuclear program is "late" when a sheriff estimates it "to be within four years of acquiring nuclear weapons." Bas and Coe do not specify the precise boundaries of the "middle" stage. Instead, the "late" category captures states that I would code as possessing both "medium" and "high" levels of latency. This makes it difficult to draw clear comparisons between our respective empirical results. In addition, the large boundaries around the "late" stage of development seems to bias the results in favor of Bas and Coe's theory. Almost every state falls into either the early or late stages when deals happened; only Brazil and Argentina are coded as being in the "middle." The empirical results also only include cases where nonproliferation deals were successful, making it hard to compare with my claims about bargaining failure.

15. Spaniel's analysis focuses on military dispute reciprocation, so it is better suited to probing the utility of latent nuclear deterrence. He notes that the further research is needed to determine whether high levels of nuclear latency can coerce concessions in other bargaining situations. See Spaniel (2019: 15, 74).
16. Quoted in Schoff and Samuels (2013: 239–40, emphasis added).
17. See also Fuhrmann and Tkach (2015: 444).
18. On how the low-stakes issue plagues other forms of militarized compellence, see Sechser and Fuhrmann (2017: 50–51).
19. See, for example, Dalton et al. (2017); Harney et al. (2006); Jo and Gartzke (2007); Meyer (1986); Smith and Spaniel (2018); Wohlstetter (1979).
20. Recent efforts to define and measure latency in terms of ENR technology include Fuhrmann and Tkach (2015); Herzog (2020); Mehta and Whitlark (2017); Persbo (2019); Sagan (2010).
21. See US Department of Energy (2002).
22. See US Department of Energy (2002).
23. This metric extends the framework for measuring latency advanced in Persbo (2019: 2).
24. I exclude great powers such as the United States and Russia (Soviet Union) from this universe, even though each operated ENR plants prior to the acquisition of atomic weapons in 1945 and 1949, respectively. Data on ENR plant operation comes from Fuhrmann and Tkach (2015).
25. CINC scores come from the National Material Capabilities (v6.0) data set at the Correlates of War Project, https://correlatesofwar.org/data-sets/national-material-capab ilities. See also Singer, Bremer, and Stuckley (1972). Polity scores come from the Polity5 data set, see Polity Project, "Polity5: Political Regime Characteristics and Transitions, 1800–2018," Center for Systemic Peace, http://www.systemicpeace.org/inscrdata.html.
26. This proxy indicator comes from Narang (2014).

Chapter 3

1. But others contend that Japan's nuclear hedge options are inadvertent byproducts of Tokyo becoming entrapped in civil nuclear investments. See, for example, Acton (2015b); Hymans (2011). I bracket this debate about hedging because it focuses on the evolution of Japan's nuclear policy after the country signed the NPT.

2. See Buckley (1995); LaFeber (1998: 10); Welfield (1988).

3. For an overview, see LaFeber (1998: 289); Samuels (2008).

4. For a good example of how US officials perceived these "points of friction" between Japan and the United States, see Memorandum from the Deputy Assistant Secretary of State for Far Eastern Affairs (Sebald) to the Under Secretary of State (Hoover), Washington, February 1, 1957, *Foreign Relations of the United States* (*FRUS*), 1955–1957, Japan, vol. 23, pt. 1, doc. 115, https://history.state.gov/historicaldocuments/frus1955-57v23p1/d115.

5. Telegram from the Embassy in Japan to the Department of State Tokyo, May 8, 1957, *FRUS*, 1955–1957, Japan, vol. 23, pt. 1, doc. 132, https://history.state.gov/historicaldocuments/frus1955-57v23p1/d132.

6. Telegram from the Embassy in Japan, May 8, 1957.

7. Director of Central Intelligence, "Nuclear Weapons Production in Fourth Countries: Likelihood and Consequences," National Intelligence Estimate 100-6-57, June 18, 1957, *Digital National Security Archive* (*DNSA*), 6, https://nsarchive2.gwu.edu/NSAEBB/NSAEBB155/prolif-2.pdf.

8. National Intelligence Estimate 100-6-57, June 18, 1957, 6.

9. National Intelligence Estimate 100-6-57, June 18, 1957, 6.

10. National Intelligence Estimate 100-6-57, June 18, 1957, 3.

11. Memorandum from the Secretary of State to the President, Washington, June 12, 1957, *FRUS*, 1955–1957, Japan, vol. 23, pt. 1, doc. 173, https://history.state.gov/historicaldocuments/frus1955-57v23p1/d173.

12. The National Intelligence Estimate was ordered in early May 1967 by the State Department and delivered on June 18, 1957, merely one day before Kishi arrived in Washington for his meetings with Eisenhower and Dulles. It is not clear whether senior US officials had time to digest the rather alarming estimate about Japan. See Burr (2005).

13. Chapter 4 analyzes this point about Eisenhower in greater detail, as it enabled West German leaders to exploit Soviet fears of proliferation with tacit backing from Washington. See also Miller (2018: 40–44).

14. Memorandum of a Conversation, White House, Washington, June 19, 1957, 11:30 a.m., *FRUS*, 1955–1957, Japan, vol. 23, pt. 1, doc. 183, https://history.state.gov/historicaldocuments/frus1955-57v23p1/d183.

15. Memorandum of a Conversation, White House, June 19, 1957.

16. Memorandum of a Conversation between Secretary of State Dulles and Prime Minister Kishi, Department of State, Washington, June 20, 1957, 9:00 a.m., *FRUS*,

1955–1957, Japan, vol. 23, pt. 1, doc. 186, https://history.state.gov/historicaldocume nts/frus1955-57v23p1/d186.

17. Memorandum of a Conversation, Department of State, June 20, 1957.

18. As quoted in LaFeber (1998: 320).

19. For a superb account of Satō's tenure, see Hoey (2015).

20. Central Intelligence Agency, "Japanese Nuclear Energy Program," Scientific Intelligence Report, November 18, 1964, *NSA* #JU00365.

21. For a similar argument, see Solingen (2007).

22. US Department of State, "Background Paper on Factors Which Could Influence National Decisions Concerning Acquisition of Nuclear Weapons," December 12, 1964, *NSA* #JU00374, 9.

23. US Department of State, "Background Paper," December 12, 1964, 13.

24. US Department of State, "Background Paper," December 12, 1964, 13.

25. Robert S. Rochlin to Raymond L. Garthoff, "Comments on Non-proliferation Background Papers of December 12, 1964," US Arms Control and Disarmament Agency, December 31, 1964, *NSA* #CJU00402, 4.

26. Rochlin to Garthoff, "Comments," December 31, 1964, 4.

27. US Department of State, "Your Meeting with Prime Minister Satō," Memorandum for Secretary of State Dean Rusk, January 9, 1965, *NSA* #JU00430, 3.

28. US Department of State, "The Ryukyu and Bonin Islands," Appendix to Talking Paper, December 29, 1964, *NSA* #CJU00394.

29. US Department of State, "Current U.S.-Japanese and World Problems," Memorandum of Conversation, Office of the President, January 12, 1965, *NSA* #JU00436, 2.

30. US Department of State, "Current U.S.-Japanese and World Problems," Memorandum of Conversation, Cabinet Room, January 12, 1965, *NSA* #JU00437, 1–2.

31. Memorandum of Conversation, Cabinet Room, January 12, 1965, 2.

32. Memorandum of Conversation, Office of the President, January 12, 1965, 5.

33. US Department of State, "U.S.-Japan Security Ties," Memorandum of Conversation, January 12, 1965, *NSA* #CJU00446.

34. Memorandum of Conversation, Cabinet Room, January 12, 1965, 3.

35. Memorandum of Conversation, Cabinet Room, January 12, 1965, 3.

36. Memorandum of Conversation, Cabinet Room, January 12, 1965, 3.

37. Memorandum of Conversation, Cabinet Room, January 12, 1965, 4.

38. US Department of State, "Japan's Prospects in the Nuclear Weapons Field: Proposed U.S. Courses of Action," Annex A: Technological Factors, June 15, 1965, *NSA* #JU00485, A4.

39. Annex A: Technological Factors, June 15, 1965, A7.

40. Annex A: Technological Factors, June 15, 1965, A8.

41. Annex A: Technological Factors, June 15, 1965, A4.

42. US Department of State, "Japan's Prospects in the Nuclear Weapons Field: Proposed U.S. Courses of Action," Memorandum for the Committee on Nuclear Non-Proliferation, June 15, 1965, *NSA* #JU00485, 1.

43. Memorandum for the Committee, June 15, 1965, 1.

44. Memorandum for the Committee, June 15, 1965, 2.

45. Memorandum for the Committee, June 15, 1965, 10.

46. Memorandum for the Committee, June 15, 1965, 8.

47. Memorandum for the Committee, June 15, 1965, 3.

48. Memorandum for the Committee, June 15, 1965, 14.

49. US Department of State, "Position of Japan regarding Non-proliferation," Cable, February 24, 1966, *NSA* #JU00552, 2.

50. US Department of State, "U.S.-Japanese Relations," Memorandum of Conversation, December 2, 1966, *NSA* #JU00617.

51. Central Intelligence Agency, "Japan Rethinking Security Policy," Special Report, Office of Current Intelligence, April 29, 1966, *NSA* #JU00559, 1.

52. Office of Current Intelligence, April 29, 1966, 4.

53. Office of Current Intelligence, April 29, 1966, 4.

54. Office of Current Intelligence, April 29, 1966, 4.

55. American Embassy Tokyo to Department of State, "US Policy Assessment—Japan, 1966," Cable, April 17, 1967, *NSA* #JU00663, 7–8.

56. American Embassy Tokyo, April 17, 1967, 8–9.

57. US Department of Defense, "Reversion of Okinawa and the Bonins," Memorandum, August 7, 1967, *NSA* #JU00699, 1.

58. Memorandum, August 7, 1967, 1, 9.

59. US Department of State, "Sato Visit—Preparatory Meeting," Memorandum, October 13, 1967, *NSA* #JU00774, 2–3; US Department of State, "Talking Points for the NSC Discussion on the Ryukus and Bonins," Memorandum, August 29, 1967, *NSA* #JU00708, 3.

60. US Department of State, "President Johnson-Prime Minister Sato, Private Conversation," Memorandum of Conversation, The President's Office, November 14, 1967, *NSA* #JU00840, 9.

61. Memorandum of Conversation, The President's Office, November 14, 1967, 11.

62. US Department of Defense, "China and Japan's Security," Memorandum of Conversation, Blair House, November 14, 1967, *NSA* #JU00845, 4.

63. Memorandum of Conversation, Blair House, November 14, 1967, 4.

64. Memorandum of Conversation, Blair House, November 14, 1967, 4.

65. Memorandum of Conversation, Blair House, November 14, 1967, 5.

66. US Department of State, "Ryukyus and Bonins," Memorandum of Conversation, Part I of II, November 15, 1967, *NSA* #JU00843, 3.

67. US Department of State, "U.S.-Japanese Relations and Security Problems," Memorandum of Conversation, November 15, 1967, *NSA* #JU00842, 4.

68. As quoted and translated from Japanese in Hoey (2015: 43).

69. US Department of State, "Trip Report: Okinawa Reversion on the Front Burner," Memorandum, December 24, 1968, *NSA* #JU01028, 1–2.

70. American Embassy in Tokyo, "Ambassador Johnson's Farewell Call on Prime Minister Sato," Cable, January 14, 1969, *NSA* #JU01039.

71. US Department of Defense, "Response to NSSM 9: Review of the International Situation as of January 20, 1969, Volume V—Noncommunist Far East-Japan," Report, January 20, 1969, *NSA* #JA00036, II-15.

72. "Response to NSSM 9," January 20, 1969, II-3.

73. "Response to NSSM 9," January 20, 1969, II-15.

74. National Security Council, "Policy toward Japan," National Security Decision Memorandum 13, May 28, 1969, 2, https://www.nixonlibrary.gov/sites/default/files/virtuallibrary/documents/nsdm/nsdm_013.pdf.

75. National Security Decision Memorandum 13, 2.

76. US Department of State, "Okinawa Negotiating Strategy," Memorandum and Strategy Paper, July 3, 1969, *NSA* #JA01092, 4.

77. As quoted in Hoey (2016b: 170).

78. US Department of State, "Secretary's Private Talk with Fonmin Aichi," Cable, August 3, 1969, *NSA* #JU01109, 1.

79. "Secretary's Private Talk," August 3, 1969, 3.

80. Arms Control and Disarmament Agency, "NPT Signature and Disarmament," Background Paper, November 1969, *NSA* #JU01141, 1.

81. "NPT Signature and Disarmament," November 1969, 1.

82. US Department of State, "Your Meeting with Prime Minister Sato and Your Meeting with Foreign Minister Aichi, November 19," Briefing Memorandum, November 18, 1969, *NSA* #JU01168, 6.

83. National Security Council, "Prime Minister Eisaku Sato of Japan, The President," Memorandum of Conversation, The White House, November 19, 1969, *NSA* #JT00079, 8–9.

84. National Security Council, "Prime Minister Eisaku Sato of Japan, The President," Memorandum of Conversation, The White House, November 21, 1969, *NSA* #JT00079, 7.

85. Office of the White House, "Joint Communique between President Richard Nixon and His Excellency Prime Minister Sato," Unclassified Press Release, November 21, 1969, *NSA* #JU01174.

Chapter 4

1. The closest candidate is North Korea, who leveraged latency against the United States and China during the Six-Party Talks. But Washington remained the primary target throughout this compellence episode. Beijing acted as an outside intervener in the crisis and had yet to achieve great power status at the time.

2. See Western European Union, Brussels Treaty: As Amended by the Protocol Modifying and Completing the Brussels Treaty, signed at Paris, October 23, 1954, https://www.cvce.eu/content/publication/2003/11/26/7d182408-0ff6-432e-b793-0d1065ebe695/publishable_en.pdf.

3. Memorandum of Conversation (Memcon), "German Atomic Energy Program," October 27, 1954, *DNSA*, https://assets.documentcloud.org/documents/4364683/Document-01-Memorandum-of-Conversation-Memcon.pdf.

4. Director of Central Intelligence, "Development of Nuclear Capabilities by Fourth Countries: Likelihood and Consequences," National Intelligence Estimate 100-2-58, July 1, 1958, *DNSA*, https://nsarchive2.gwu.edu//NSAEBB/NSAEBB155/prolif-3a.pdf.

5. US Embassy Paris Telegram 3600 to Department of State, February 1, 1958, *DNSA*, https://assets.documentcloud.org/documents/4361058/Document-03B-U-S-Emba ssy-Paris-Telegram-3600-to.pdf.

6. For an English translation of the manifesto, see the digital copy hosted by the Georg-August-Universität Göttingen, https://www.uni-goettingen.de/en/the+manifesto/ 54320.html.

7. US Embassy Paris Telegram, February 1, 1958.

8. US Embassy Paris Telegram, February 1, 1958.

9. Memorandum of Conversation, John Foster Dulles and Chancellor Adenauer, Department of State, December 14, 1957, *DNSA*, https://assets.documentcloud.org/ documents/4361057/Document-03A-John-Foster-Dulles-Memorandum-of.pdf.

10. Memorandum of Discussion at the 415th Meeting of the National Security Council, Washington, July 30, 1959, *FRUS*, 1958–1960, National Security Policy, vol. 3, doc. 69, https://history.state.gov/historicaldocuments/frus1958-60v03/d69.

11. The formulation of the MLF was an important inducement offered to the West Germans at a low level of latency. However, it would be a stretch to consider the MLF as a coercive "concession" during this period. West Germany had not yet adopted a compellence strategy toward the United States when the Eisenhower administration formulated the plan. As this chapter documents, Eisenhower himself support the MLF in part because he wanted to use West Germany's nuclear status to counterbalance the Soviet Union.

12. Eisenhower believed that the Soviets were "really scared" of West Germany's growing economic and military power; see Memorandum of Discussion, "Nuclear Test Negotiations," Camp David, Maryland, March 28, 1960, *FRUS*, 1958–1960, vol. 3, doc. 251, https://history.state.gov/historicaldocuments/frus1958-60v03/d251. See also Trachtenberg (1999: 254).

13. On the validity of these claims in general, see Bell (2015).

14. For instance, Secretary of Defense McNamara and President Kennedy feared that the technological barriers to the bomb were eroding as states such as West Germany mastered civil nuclear energy technology; see Memorandum of Meeting with President Kennedy, "Disarmament Negotiations," July 30, 1962, *FRUS*, 1961–1963, vol. 7, doc. 206, https://history.state.gov/historicaldocuments/frus1961-63v07/d206. Kennedy and his top advisers were also influenced by prominent public articulations of the ally proliferation problem at the time. See, for example, Wohlstetter (1961). On Kennedy's nonproliferation policies and beliefs more broadly, see Maddock (2010: 159); Miller (2018: 45); Whitlark (2017).

15. Policy Directive, NATO and the Atlantic Nations, April 20, 1961, *FRUS*, 1961–1963, vol. 13, doc. 100, https://history.state.gov/historicaldocuments/frus1961-63v13/ d100. See also Miller (2018: 45–46); Trachtenberg (1999: 305).

16. Beyond the specter of ally proliferation in Europe, the Kennedy administration was also concerned about China building the bomb; see Burr and Richelson (2001); Miller (2014a).

17. Memorandum of Conversation, Ambassador Menshikov and Assistant Secretary Nitze, July 15, 1961, *FRUS*, 1961–1963, vol. 14, doc. 70, https://history.state.

gov/historicaldocuments/frus1961-63v14/d70. As referenced in Trachtenberg (1999: 254).

18. Telegram From the Department of State to the Embassy in France, October 2, 1961, *FRUS*, 1961–1963, vol. 14, doc. 164, https://history.state.gov/historicaldocuments/ frus1961-63v14/d164.

19. Memorandum of Conversation, "Germany and Berlin," Washington, October 6, 1961, *FRUS,* 1961–1963, vol. 14, doc. 170, https://history.state.gov/historicaldocume nts/frus1961-63v14/d170.

20. Memorandum of Conversation, Meeting between the President and Chairman Khrushchev in Vienna, June 4, 1961, *FRUS*, 1961–1963, vol. 5, doc. 87, https://history. state.gov/historicaldocuments/frus1961-63v05/d87.

21. Memorandum of Conversation, "Germany and Berlin," October 6, 1961.

22. Central Intelligence Agency, "Foreign Policy Aims of Strauss, Schroeder, and Some FDP Leaders," Information Report, November 20, 1961, *DNSA*, https://assets. documentcloud.org/documents/4364690/Document-06-Central-Intelligence-Age ncy.pdf.

23. "Foreign Policy Aims," November 20, 1961.

24. "Foreign Policy Aims," November 20, 1961.

25. "Foreign Policy Aims," November 20, 1961.

26. Director of Central Intelligence, "Likelihood and Consequences of the Development of Nuclear Capabilities by Additional Countries," National Intelligence Estimate 100-4-60, September 20, 1960, *DNSA*, https://nsarchive2.gwu.edu/NSAEBB/NSAEBB 155/prolif-5.pdf.

27. Director of Central Intelligence, "Nuclear Weapons and Delivery Capabilities of Free World Countries Other Than the US and UK," National Intelligence Estimate 4-3-61, September 21, 1961, *DNSA*, https://nsarchive2.gwu.edu/NSAEBB/NSAEBB155/pro lif-6b.pdf.

28. Hugh S. Cuming, Director, Office of Intelligence and Research, to Secretary of State, "Growing Revelation of West German Interest in Nuclear Striking Force in Europe," February 18, 1960, *DNSA*, https://assets.documentcloud.org/documents/4364688/ Document-04-Hugh-S-Cuming-Director-Office-of.pdf. The aforementioned 1961 NIE made the same point, noting that a German nuclear weapons program would "act as a provocation to the USSR."

29. National Intelligence Estimate 4-3-61, September 21, 1961.

30. As quoted in Radkau and Hahn (2013: 121). I am indebted to Ulrich Kühn for discovering and translating this quotation from the German source.

31. Telegram from the Department of State to the Embassy in Germany, June 17, 1961, *FRUS*, 1961–1963, vol. 14, doc. 43, https://history.state.gov/historicaldocuments/ frus1961-63v14/d43.

32. "Foreign Policy Aims," November 20, 1961.

33. Memorandum of Conversation, Private Conversations between the President and Chancellor Adenauer, "Germany," November 21, 1961, *DNSA*, https://assets.docume ntcloud.org/documents/4364691/Document-07-Memorandum-of-Conversation-Private.pdf.

34. Memorandum of Conversation, "Germany," November 21, 1961.
35. Memorandum of Conversation, "Germany," November 21, 1961.
36. This part of the discussion was deemed by the US government to be quite sensitive at the time. According to the memorandum of conversation, Kennedy requested approximately ten minutes of conversation be permanently stricken from the record at this point. In addition, the later lines of discussion where Adenauer insisted upon access to US nuclear weapons were only recently declassified. For the excised version, see Memorandum of Conversation, Private Conversations between the President and Chancellor Adenauer, Washington, November 21, 1961, *FRUS*, 1961–1963, vol. 14, doc. 219, https://history.state.gov/historicaldocuments/frus1961-63v14/d219.
37. Memorandum of Conversation, "Germany," November 21, 1961.
38. Memorandum of Conversation, "Germany," November 21, 1961.
39. Transcript of an Interview between President Kennedy and the Editor of Izvestia (Adzhubei), November 25, 1961, *FRUS*, 1961–1963, vol. 5, doc. 134, https://history.state.gov/historicaldocuments/frus1961-63v05/d134.
40. Transcript of an Interview, November 25, 1961.
41. Paper Prepared in the US Delegation, "Draft Principles," Geneva, undated, *FRUS*, 1961–1963, vol. 15, doc. 20, https://history.state.gov/historicaldocuments/frus1961-63v15/d20. On the meeting where Rusk gave Gromyko the working paper, see Memorandum of Conversation, "Germany and Berlin," March 22, 1962, *FRUS*, 1961–1963, vol. 15, doc. 19, https://history.state.gov/historicaldocuments/frus1961-63v15/d19. For more details about how the German nuclear issue was a central part of the package deal presented by Rusk, see Trachtenberg (1999: 344, 390).
42. Memorandum of Conversation, "Berlin and Disarmament," Department of State, March 11, 1962, *DNSA*, BC02736.
43. Memorandum of Conversation, "Berlin and Disarmament," March 11, 1962.
44. Memorandum of Conversation, "Berlin and Disarmament," March 11, 1962.
45. Memorandum of Conversation, "German Position on Rusk-Gromyko Talks," Department of State, March 11, 1962, *DNSA*, BC02735.
46. Memorandum of Conversation, Chancellor Adenauer and Mr. Nitze, Bonn, April 13, 1962, *FRUS*, 1961–1963, vol. 15, doc. 34, https://history.state.gov/historicaldocuments/frus1961-63v15/d34.
47. Memorandum of Conversation, Adenauer and Nitze, April 13, 1962.
48. Memorandum of Conversation, "NATO Nuclear Problems," Bonn, June 22, 1962, *FRUS*, 1961–1963, vol. 13, doc. 145, https://history.state.gov/historicaldocuments/frus1961-63v13/d145.
49. Memorandum of Conversation, "NATO Nuclear Problems," June 22, 1962.
50. Memorandum of Conversation, "NATO Nuclear Problems," June 22, 1962. *Rebus sic stantibus* is a clause in international agreements that allows a party to nullify or escape the treaty due to changed circumstances.
51. Telegram from Secretary of State Rusk to the Department of State, Rome, June 23, 1962, *FRUS*, 1961–1963, vol. 15, doc. 69, https://history.state.gov/historicaldocuments/frus1961-63v15/d69.
52. Telegram from Secretary of State, June 23, 1962.

53. Telegram from the Embassy in the United Kingdom to the Department of State, London, June 26, 1962, *FRUS*, 1961–1963, vol. 13, doc. 146, https://history.state.gov/historicaldocuments/frus1961-63v13/d146.

54. Telegram from the Embassy in the United Kingdom, June 26, 1962.

55. Memorandum of Conversation, "Non-diffusion of Nuclear Weapons," Washington, August 8, 1962, *FRUS*, 1961–1963, vol. 7, doc. 216, https://history.state.gov/historicaldocuments/frus1961-63v07/d216. See also Miller (2018: 47).

56. Central Intelligence Agency, "Likelihood and Consequences of a Proliferation of Nuclear Weapons Systems," National Intelligence Estimate 4-63, June 28, 1963, *History and Public Policy Program Digital Archive*, originally published in Burr (2005), https://digitalarchive.wilsoncenter.org/document/115992.

57. National Intelligence Estimate 4-63, June 28, 1963.

58. National Intelligence Estimate 4-63, June 28, 1963.

59. US Embassy Bonn, "Franco-German Cooperation in Atomic Energy Matters," December 28, 1962, *DNSA*, https://assets.documentcloud.org/documents/4361061/Document-11A-U-S-Embassy-West-Germany-Airgram-A.pdf.

60. Ministry of Defence, "Nuclear Problems in Europe," September 1962, *DNSA*, https://assets.documentcloud.org/documents/4364692/Document-08-Ministry-of-Defence-Notes-on-Talks.pdf. See also Gavin (2012: 42).

61. Ministry of Defence, "Nuclear Problems in Europe," September 1962.

62. US Embassy Bonn to Secretary of State, July 25, 1962, *DNSA*, https://assets.documentcloud.org/documents/4361059/Document-09A-U-S-Embassy-West-Germany-telegram.pdf; US Embassy Bonn to Secretary of State, December 10, 1962, *DNSA*, https://assets.documentcloud.org/documents/4361060/Document-09B-U-S-Embassy-West-Germany-telegram.pdf; US Atomic Energy Commission, "Reported Franco-German Cooperation in Development of French Gaseous Diffusion Efforts," Memorandum, June 11, 1963, *DNSA*, https://nsarchive.gwu.edu/sites/default/files/documents/4364706/Document-23-A-A-Wells-Director-of-Office-of.pdf.

63. Paper Prepared by the Secretary of State's Special Assistant (Bohlen), "Impressions In Regard to United States-European Relations," July 2, 1962, *FRUS*, 1961–1963, vol. 13, doc. 147, https://history.state.gov/historicaldocuments/frus1961-63v13/d147.

64. Memorandum of Conversation between Secretary of State Rusk and the Soviet Ambassador (Dobrynin), May 18, 1963, *FRUS*, 1961–1963, vol. 7, doc. 287, https://history.state.gov/historicaldocuments/frus1961-63v07/d287.

65. On the efficacy of nuclear test bans as a nonproliferation tool, see Altman and Miller (2017).

66. Discussion between Soviet Deputy Foreign Minister Vasilii Kuznetsov and the SED Politburo (Fragment), October 14, 1963, *History and Public Policy Program Digital Archive*, https://digitalarchive.wilsoncenter.org/document/113079.

67. US Embassy Bonn, "Secretary McNamara's Conversation with Chancellor Adenauer," Department of State, August 2, 1963, *DNSA*, https://nsarchive.gwu.edu/document/16432-document-01-u-s-embassy-bonn-airgram-250.

68. Johnson put the MLF on ice as an independent task force—the Gilpatric Committee—began a holistic review of US nonproliferation policy in November 1964. Chaired by

former deputy secretary of defense Roswell Gilpatric, the panel was charged with recommending a menu of options for Washington to manage the spread of nuclear weapons. The Johnson administration wanted the group to start with a clean slate, so the president issued several National Security Action Memoranda (NSAM 320 and NSAM 322) that paused US efforts to build the MLF. While these policy-decision papers and the Gilpatric Report remained classified, the director of the US Arms Control and Disarmament Agency (ACDA) penned a public version of the administration's new nuclear policies in a widely read journal; see Foster (1965). For detailed examinations of the Gilpatric Committee and demise of the MLF, see Brands (2006; 2007: 399–402); Miller (2018: 50–52); Schwartz (2003: 44).

69. Memorandum of Conversation, Tsarapkin and Foster, New York, May 19, 1965, *FRUS*, 1964–1968, vol. 11, doc. 78, https://history.state.gov/historicaldocuments/frus1964-68v11/d78; Telegram from the Embassy in the Soviet Union to the Department of State, Moscow, December 23, 1965, *FRUS*, 1964–1968, vol. 11, doc. 106, https://history.state.gov/historicaldocuments/frus1964-68v11/d106.

70. Memorandum of Conversation, "Nonproliferation," Department of State, July 9, 1965, *DNSA*, https://nsarchive.gwu.edu/sites/default/files/documents/4415099/Document-04-Memorandum-of-Conversation.pdf. See also Schwartz (2003: 58).

71. Memorandum of Conversation, "Nonproliferation," July 9, 1965.

72. Memorandum of Conversation, "Nonproliferation," July 9, 1965.

73. Memorandum of Conversation, "Nuclear Sharing," Washington, December 20, 1965, *FRUS*, 1964–1968, vol. 13, doc. 119, https://history.state.gov/historicaldocuments/frus1964-68v13/d119.

74. Memorandum of Conversation, "Nuclear Sharing," December 20, 1965.

75. US Department of State Policy Planning Council, "The Further Spread of Nuclear Weapons: Problems for the West," February 14, 1966, *DNSA*, https://nsarchive2.gwu.edu/nukevault/ebb253/doc01.pdf.

76. "The Further Spread of Nuclear Weapons," February 14, 1966.

77. Director of Central Intelligence, "West German Capabilities and Intentions to Produce and Deploy Nuclear Weapons," National Intelligence Estimate 23-66, April 28, 1966, *DNSA*, https://nsarchive.gwu.edu/sites/default/files/documents/4415112/Document-11-National-Intelligence-Estimate-23-66.pdf. On McNamara's role in ordering the NIE, see Burr (2018).

78. National Intelligence Estimate 23-66, April 28, 1966.

79. National Intelligence Estimate 23-66, April 28, 1966.

80. National Intelligence Estimate 23-66, April 28, 1966.

81. US Embassy Bonn to Department of State, "NIE-23-66," Airgram, April 12, 1966, *DNSA*, https://nsarchive2.gwu.edu/NSAEBB/NSAEBB155/prolif-13.pdf.

82. Memorandum, "German Attitudes on Nuclear Defense Questions," US Embassy Bonn, October 20, 1965, *DNSA*, https://nsarchive.gwu.edu/sites/default/files/documents/4415101/Document-06-U-S-Embassy-West-Germany-memorandum.pdf.

83. National Intelligence Estimate 23-66, April 28, 1966.

84. National Intelligence Estimate 23-66, April 28, 1966.

85. National Intelligence Estimate 23-66, April 28, 1966.

86. Memorandum of Conversation, "Offset and Troop Levels, Washington," September 26, 1966, *FRUS*, 1964–1968, vol. 13, doc. 207, https://history.state.gov/historicaldo cuments/frus1964-68v13/d207. On the genesis of the NPG from the NATO perspective, see Haftendorn (1996: 161–73).

87. On Erhard's problems at the summit, see Bark and Gress (1989b: 56). On the links between the troop offset issue, US extended deterrence, and Germany's nuclear status, see Gavin (2007: 142–52); Lanoszka (2018b: 68–69).

88. See Lutsch (2016b: 542, 554). On the contemporary benefits of NATO nuclear consultations, see Kühn (2018); Yost (2009).

89. Foreign Minister Brandt made a comment along these lines to US ambassador McGhee upon coming to government; see Telegram from the Embassy in Germany to the Department of State, Bonn, December 8, 1966, *FRUS*, 1964–1968, vol. 15, doc. 188, https://history.state.gov/historicaldocuments/frus1964-68v15/d188.

90. On West German exclusion from the UN disarmament talks, see Gray (2008: 247); Lutsch (2016a: 47). On the active collusion between the superpowers to birth the NPT, see Coe and Vaynman (2015).

91. As Foreign Minister Gromyko told Secretary Rusk in October 1966, "It is not prospect of a German 'voice' or other 'voices' in nuclear defense planning which bothers the Soviets." See Memorandum of Conversation, "Non-proliferation," October 10, 1966, *FRUS*, 1964–1968, vol. 11, doc. 158, https://history.state.gov/historicaldocuments/frus1 964-68v11/d158. On how US officials viewed the shift in the Soviet position at the time, see Memorandum from the Director of the Arms Control and Disarmament Agency (Foster) to Secretary of State Rusk, May 25, 1966, *FRUS*, 1964–1968, vol. 11, doc. 131, https://history.state.gov/historicaldocuments/frus1964-68v11/d131. For an extensive analysis of the superpower breakthrough in NPT negotiations, see Brands (2007: 407–8).

92. Telegram from the Department of State to the Embassy in Germany, December 21, 1966, *FRUS*, 1964–1968, vol. 15, doc. 194, https://history.state.gov/historicaldocume nts/frus1964-68v15/d194.

93. Memorandum of Conversation, "German Concern over Draft NPT Text," US Department of State, December 29, 1966, *DNSA*, https://nsarchive.gwu.edu/sites/ default/files/documents/4415119/Document-17-Memorandum-of-Conversation-German.pdf.

94. Telegram from the Embassy in Germany to the Department of State, Bonn, February 25, 1967, *FRUS*, 1964–1968, vol. 15, doc. 201, https://history.state.gov/historicaldo cuments/frus1964-68v15/d201.

95. On the broader diplomatic history of the NPT negotiations beyond the West German context, see Popp (2016); Shaker (1980).

96. Memorandum of Conversation, "Draft Articles of Non-proliferation Treaty," with draft treaty attached, US Department of State, January 13, 1967, *DNSA*, https://nsarch ive.gwu.edu/dc.html?doc=4415120-Document-18-Memorandum-of-Conversat ion-Draft. See also US Embassy Bonn, "Non-proliferation Treaty," January 18, 1967, *DNSA*, https://nsarchive2.gwu.edu//nukevault/ebb253/doc02.pdf.

97. Memorandum of Conversation, "Draft Articles of Non-proliferation Treaty," January 13, 1967.

98. Memorandum of Conversation, "Non-proliferation Treaty," Washington, February 8, 1967, *FRUS*, 1964–1968, vol. 11, doc. 180, https://history.state.gov/historicaldo cuments/frus1964-68v11/d180.

99. Memorandum of Conversation, "Non-proliferation Treaty," February 8, 1967.

100. Memorandum of Conversation, "Draft Articles of Non-proliferation Treaty," January 13, 1967.

101. On the genesis of EURATOM, see Krige (2016: 17–78); Winand (1996: 83–108).

102. Thomas L. Hughes to the Secretary, "Reasons for West German Opposition to the Non-proliferation Treaty," Research Memorandum REU-13, March 1, 1967, *DNSA*, https://nsarchive.gwu.edu/sites/default/files/documents/2830727/Document-24A-Thomas-L-Hughes-to-the-Secretary.pdf. See also Schrafstetter and Twigge (2004: 183).

103. Memorandum of Conversation, "Non-proliferation Treaty," February 8, 1967.

104. Memorandum of Conversation, "NPT," Vorontsov and Weiler, December 16, 1967, *DNSA*, https://nsarchive2.gwu.edu//nukevault/ebb253/doc08a.pdf.

105. Memorandum of Conversation, "Draft Articles of Non-proliferation Treaty," January 13, 1967; US Embassy Bonn, "Non-proliferation Treaty," January 18, 1967.

106. Memorandum of Conversation, "Non-proliferation Treaty," Washington, February 8, 1967.

107. Memorandum from the President's Special Assistant (Rostow) to President Johnson, November 7, 1967, *FRUS*, 1964–1968, vol. 11, doc. 215, https://history.state.gov/hist oricaldocuments/frus1964-68v11/d215.

108. Telegram from the Embassy in Germany, February 25, 1967.

109. US Department of State, "Interpretations regarding Draft Non-proliferation Treaty Formulations," Oral Note, February 22, 1967, *DNSA*, https://nsarchive.gwu.edu/sites/ default/files/documents/4415122/Document-20-U-S-Department-of-State.pdf.

110. Memorandum of Conversation, "NPT," December 16, 1967.

111. Memorandum of Conversation, Chancellor Kiesinger and President Johnson, Bonn, April 26, 1967, *FRUS*, 1964–1968, vol. 15, doc. 214, https://history.state.gov/historic aldocuments/frus1964-68v15/d214.

112. Memorandum of Conversation, Kiesinger and Johnson, April 26, 1967.

113. Memorandum of Conversation, Kiesinger and Johnson, April 26, 1967.

114. Memorandum of Conversation, Kiesinger and Johnson, April 26, 1967. See also Küntzel (1995: 100).

115. Memorandum from the President's Special Assistant (Rostow), November 7, 1967.

116. Memorandum of Conversation, "Non-proliferation Treaty," US Arms Control and Disarmament Agency, January 18, 1968, *DNSA*, https://nsarchive2.gwu.edu// nukevault/ebb253/doc09b.pdf.

117. US Mission NATO to State Department, "NAC January 18—Draft NPT," January 18, 1968, *DNSA*, https://nsarchive2.gwu.edu//nukevault/ebb253/doc09c.pdf.

118. US Embassy Bonn to Department of State, "FRG Defense Council Meeting on NPT," January 23, 1968, *DNSA*, https://nsarchive2.gwu.edu//nukevault/ebb253/doc10a.pdf.

119. "FRG Defense Council Meeting on NPT," January 23, 1968.

120. "FRG Defense Council Meeting on NPT," January 23, 1968.

121. US Embassy Bonn to Department of State, "Letter to the Secretary from Foreign Minister Brandt," February 10, 1968, *DNSA*, https://nsarchive2.gwu.edu//nukevault/ebb253/doc10c.pdf.

122. US Embassy Bonn to State Department, "Schnippenkoetter Comments on German Signature," April 10, 1968, *DNSA*, https://nsarchive2.gwu.edu//nukevault/ebb253/doc19.pdf.

123. Letter from Undersecretary of State Katzenbach to Secretary of Defense Clifford, with attachments (West German "non-paper," and proposed declaration), April 10, 1968, *DNSA*, https://nsarchive2.gwu.edu//nukevault/ebb253/doc18.pdf.

124. Memorandum for the President, "Reaffirmation of NATO at the Time of Nonproliferation Treaty Signing," The Secretary of State, June 11, 1968, *DNSA*, https://nsarchive2.gwu.edu//nukevault/ebb253/doc28.pdf.

125. Paper Prepared in the Department of State, "Germany in Perspective," May 5, 1968, *FRUS*, 1964–1968, vol. 15, doc. 262, https://history.state.gov/historicaldocuments/frus1964-68v15/d262.

126. Memorandum for the Record, "The President's Meeting with German Defense Minister Schroeder," The White House, July 25, 1968, *DNSA*, https://nsarchive2.gwu.edu//nukevault/ebb253/doc30c.pdf.

127. Memorandum of Conversation, "Non-proliferation," US Department of State, July 23, 1968, *DNSA*, https://nsarchive2.gwu.edu//nukevault/ebb253/doc30a.pdf.

128. See, for example, Memorandum of Conversation, "Part I—FRG Request for Consultations on NPT," Washington, February 3, 1969, *FRUS*, 1969–1976, vol. E-2, doc. 7, https://history.state.gov/historicaldocuments/frus1969-76ve02/d7.

129. See Memorandum from President's Special Assistant (Rostow), November 7, 1967.

130. For overviews of these issues, see Kühn and Volpe (2017); Volpe and Kühn (2017); Meier (2020); Kunz (2020); Bozo (2020); Egeland and Pelopidas (2021); Meijer and Brooks (2021).

Chapter 5

1. See Nuland (2012).

2. See also Panda (2016).

3. North Korea's total energy imports fell by 75% after Moscow cut off the patronage system in 1991. China was not eager to see the Kim regime implode but refused to make up this shortfall. For details, see Eberstadt (1999: 93–110); Eberstadt, Rubin, and Tretyakova (1995: 87–104); Noland (1997: 106); Oberdorfer (2002: 233).

4. According to US intelligence estimates at the time, North Korea reached out to Moscow because they needed help developing "advanced engineering techniques to

master the remote control operations that are necessary for handling highly radio-active materials." See Central Intelligence Agency, "North Korea: Nuclear Reactor under Construction," April 20, 1984, *DNSA*, https://nsarchive2.gwu.edu/NSAEBB/ NSAEBB87/nk04.pdf. See also Zhebin (1999).

5. See, for example, Director of Intelligence Assessment, Central Intelligence Agency, "North Korea: Potential for Nuclear Weapon Development," September 1986, *DNSA*, https://nsarchive2.gwu.edu/NSAEBB/NSAEBB87/nk07.pdf; Directorate of Intelligence, Central Intelligence Agency, "North Korea's Expanding Nuclear Efforts," May 3, 1988, *DNSA*, https://nsarchive2.gwu.edu/NSAEBB/NSAEBB87/ nk10.pdf.

6. Central Intelligence Agency, "Nuclear Proliferation Survey: The Next Generation," Director of Intelligence Reference Aid, November 1988, *DNSA*, https://nsarchive2. gwu.edu/NSAEBB/NSAEBB87/nk12.pdf.

7. Department of Defense, "US-ROK Basic Positions," Paper, August–September 1991, *DNSA*, https://nsarchive.gwu.edu/dc.html?doc=4176668-Document-03a-Paper-US-ROK-Basic-Positions-ca.

8. Memorandum for Under Secretary of Defense for Policy, "The Next Steps in the North Korea Nuclear Issue," Department of Defense, September 1991, *DNSA*, https://nsarch ive.gwu.edu/dc.html?doc=4176667-Document-02-Memorandum-for-Under-Secret ary-of. See also Oberdorfer (2002: 259–61).

9. Briefing Book, Deputies Committee Meeting, "Korea Nuclear Program," National Security Council, The White House, December 13, 1991, *DNSA*, https://nsarch ive.gwu.edu/dc.html?doc=4176673-Document-07-Briefing-Book-Deputies-Committee.

10. Memorandum for Undersecretary of Defense for Policy, "North Korean Nuclear Issue and DC Meeting," Department of Defense, February 7, 1992, *DNSA*, https:// nsarchive.gwu.edu/dc.html?doc=4176674-Document-08-Memorandum-for-Und ersecretary-of.

11. Memorandum for North Korea Deputies' Committee Meeting, National Security Council, March 12, 1992, *DNSA*, https://nsarchive.gwu.edu/dc.html?doc=4176675-Document-09-Memorandum-North-Korea-Deputies.

12. Memorandum for North Korea Deputies' Committee, March 12, 1992.

13. See also Gilinsky (1997); Lawrence (2020).

14. For details on the negotiations, see International Crisis Group (2006a: 5).

15. See "Joint Statement of the Fourth Round of the Six-Party Talks," Beijing, https:// 2001-2009.state.gov/r/pa/prs/ps/2005/53490.htm.

16. See "Joint Statement of the Fourth Round of the Six-Party Talks," September 19, 2005.

17. As quoted in Pritchard (2007: 122).

18. Six Scud and No Dong missiles, along with a Tapeo-Dong 2 SLV, were fired in rapid succession, with a final seventh test nine hours later.

19. Interview with senior US official, Washington, DC, July 2015.

20. Nicholas Eberstadt quoted in Gale and Lee (2016).

21. See also Panda (2020: 17).

Chapter 6

1. American Embassy Tehran to US Department of State, "The Atomic Energy Organization of Iran, AEOI," May 11, 1977, *DNSA*, Digital Document, https://nsarchi ve2.gwu.edu/nukevault/ebb268/doc14b.pdf.

2. In the early 1980s, the United States also launched a more comprehensive effort to cut off Iran from procuring military arms and advanced technology abroad; see Crist (2012: 101–2).

3. For an overview, see Crist (2012: 102); Patrikarakos (2012: 127). See also IAEA GOV/ 2007/58 (November 15, 2007), 2.

4. In particular, the IRGC created front companies, built purchase agent networks, mastered bribery and false documentation tradecraft, and learned to exploit export control laws. See Chubin (1994: 18); Salisbury (2020).

5. See Albright (2010: 70–81); MacCalman (2016).

6. See Albright (2010: 76); Patrikarakos (2012: 125); IAEA GOV/2007/58 (November 15, 2007), 3.

7. See Patrikarakos (2012: 132–36, 140–53); Greenhouse (1995); Richelson (2006: 508).

8. Reza Amrollahi had run the AEOI for almost two decades. Under his tenure, an unproductive array of research and develop efforts had sauntered along without making much tangible progress.

9. The organizational contours of the "AMAD Plan" were detailed by the IAEA in a notable 2011 report by the director general; see IAEA GOV/2011/63 (November 8, 2011), 5–7. On the Israeli operation, see Sanger and Bergman (2018).

10. See Director of Central Intelligence (2003).

11. The IAEA inspection team was barred from collecting evidence or visiting additional facilities to confirm this claim; see IAEA GOV/2003/40 (June 6, 2003), 2–8.

12. IAEA GOV/2003/63 (August 26, 2003), 2–7.

13. IAEA GOV/2003/69 (September 12, 2003), 3.

14. For a similar argument, see Bowen and Moran (2014). On hedging as a general proliferation strategy, see Narang (2016, 2022).

15. See National Intelligence Council, "National Intelligence Estimate—Iran: Nuclear Intentions and Capabilities," Unclassified Public Summary, November 2007, https:// www.dni.gov/files/documents/Newsroom/Reports%20and%20Pubs/20071203_rele ase.pdf.

16. Correspondence among Fereidoun, Majid, and Masoud, "Post-AMAD Activity," documents translated from Farsi in the Iran Archive, September 1–3, 2003.

17. Indeed, the IAEA soon reported that the Iranians were starting to pivot away from their previous "policy of concealment" to clear up inconsistencies, provide more information, and step toward implementing the Additional Protocol; see IAEA GOV/ 2003/75 (November 10, 2003), 10.

18. The production workshops produced around 120 centrifuges during this time, which was enough for a pilot cascade; see IAEA GOV/2004/11 (February 24, 2004), 11.

19. For more information on the technical estimates and details, see IAEA GOV/2004/11 (February 24, 2004) and IAEA GOV/2004/34 (June 1, 2004).

20. IAEA GOV/2004/34 (June 1, 2004), 9. Tehran denied inspectors access to the Parchin military complex and kept providing the IAEA with contradictory information about the enrichment program and suspicious weaponization activities; see IAEA GOV/ 2004/60 (September 1, 2004). In particular, the IAEA wanted to clarify issues about the history of Iran's efforts to import, manufacture, and use centrifuges of the P-1 and P-2 design, as well as the source of uranium contamination found at various sites. Iranian defense minister Ali Shamkhani acknowledged his country's military had built centrifuges, but claimed they were for civilian use. The exposure of the Khan network during the Libya nuclear deal in December 2003 further unmasked many of Iran's purchases. The Iranians also refused to clear up why they had razed buildings and scraped the earth at the Levizan-Shian site between August 2003 and March 2004. Regarding weaponization activities, as late as February 2004 the IAEA discovered experiments with exotic materials (polonium-210) used in neutron source initiators for atomic weapons; see IAEA GOV/2004/11 (February 24, 2004).

21. IAEA GOV/2004/49 (June 18, 2004).

22. IAEA GOV/2004/79 (September 18, 2004).

23. Hassan Rouhani as quoted in Kerr (2019: 58–59).

24. See Miller (2018: 231–32). For an alternative argument that the United States had maximum leverage vis-à-vis Iran during this period, see Litwak (2008: 101–4).

25. IAEA GOV/2006/64 (November 14, 2006), 1.

26. For the perspective within Tehran at the time, see International Crisis Group (2006b: 6–8).

27. Under Secretary Burns to Secretary Rice, "Meeting with the Iranians, July 19," US Department of State, July 19, 2008, Back Channel Archive, https://carnegieendowm ent.org/publications/interactive/back-channel/.

28. IAEA GOV/2009/74 (November 16, 2009), 2.

29. On the approximate amount of highly enriched uranium needed to manufacture a nuclear weapon, see International Atomic Energy Agency (2002: 23).

30. Reports from the IAEA board of governors during this time note the safeguards and surveillance measures in place for inspectors to monitor activities and verify Iran's physical inventory of nuclear material. For examples, see IAEA GOV/2009/35 (June 5, 2009); IAEA GOV/2009/74 (November 16, 2009).

31. Under Secretary Burns to Secretary Clinton, "A New Strategy toward Iran," US Department of State, January 24, 2009, Back Channel Archive, https://carnegieen dowment.org/publications/interactive/back-channel/. See also Crist (2012: 538–42); Parsi (2012: 114–15).

32. Author interview with former State Department official, Washington, DC, May 15, 2014.

33. Iran later informed the IAEA that it planned install around three thousand total centrifuges at Fordow; see IAEA GOV/2009/74 (November 16, 2009), 3.

34. Author interview with former White House official, Cambridge, MA, May 7, 2014.

35. Author interview with former State Department official, Washington, DC, May 15, 2014.

36. See Crist (2012: 548); Fitzpatrick (2010: 71).

37. Author interview with former State Department official, Washington, DC, May 15, 2014. In his memoir, Ambassador Burns notes that Jalili and Einhorn did produce a one-paragraph general summary of the agreement for public distribution; see Burns (2019: 352).

38. Author interview with former State Department official, Washington, DC, May 15, 2014. See also Slackman (2009).

39. Ahmadinejad told a jubilant crowd of supports, "I declare here that, with the grace of God, the Iranian nation will produce 20 percent fuel and anything it needs itself," as quoted in Broad (2009). See also Black (2009).

40. For an overview, see Fitzpatrick (2010); Parsi (2012: 10).

41. Author interview with former State Department official, Washington, DC, May 15, 2014.

42. For detailed studies of these alleged operations, see Crist (2012: 550–52); Lindsay (2013); Maher (2019).

43. For details, see IAEA GOV/2013/40 (August 28, 2013).

44. On the broader geopolitical incentives that made diplomacy attractive for both Iranian and American leaders during this time, see Saikal (2019: 211–15). For an overview from the perspective of the US secretary of state, see Clinton (2014: 347–48, 368–69).

45. See Burns (2019: 358). On the validity of this claim under international law, see Miller (2006).

46. Many other US officials shared this concern at the time; see Parsi (2017: 180–82).

47. US officials apparently began accepting this position in private once Iran started to enrich uranium in the final years of the Bush administration; see Kerry (2018: 493). In an internal 2008 memo to Secretary Rice, Burns himself made a similar point about the futility of the zero-enrichment standard: "I can think of no safer prediction today than that Iran will not agree to suspension of enrichment and reprocessing in response to the P5+1's refreshed incentives package. We have neither enough sticks nor enough carrots in play right now to fundamentally alter Iran's calculus." See Under Secretary Burns to Secretary Rice, "Regaining the Strategic Initiative on Iran," US Department of State, May 27, 2008, *Back Channel Archive,* https://carnegieendowment.org/publications/interactive/back-channel/.

48. See Burns (2019: 376–78); Kerry (2018: 497, 499–500).

49. For the original text, see International Atomic Energy Agency, "Communication Dated 27 November 2013 Received from the EU High Representative to the Agency concerning the Text of the Joint Plan of Action," INFCIRC/855, November 27, 2013, https://www.iaea.org/sites/default/files/publications/documents/infcircs/2013/infcirc855.pdf.

50. See also Kerry (2018: 18).

51. For an overview of these goals from a former US negotiator, see Einhorn (2014).

52. See, for example, Khamenei (2014). For assessments, see Hurst (2016: 552–53); Tabatabai (2015).

53. For an excellent assessment of the red lines, see Tabatabai (2017: 236–42).

54. The deadline for diplomacy had to be extended twice—first in July 2014 and then again in November 2014. The breakthrough on the final framework occurred in April 2015. But it took until July 2015 for diplomats to finalize the accord.

55. Specifically, Khamenei claimed that Iran needed 190,000 separative work units (SWUs) of enrichment capacity. At the time of his announcement, Iran had approximately 24,000 SWU in total from centrifuges at Natanz and Fordow. For an overview, see Hibbs (2014).

56. For additional evidence in support of this argument, see Karami (2014).

57. Khamenei voiced his doubts that the United States would honor its promises to phase out sanctions against Iran. See Erdbrink (2015).

58. UNSC, Security Council Resolution 2231 (2015) [on Joint Comprehensive Plan of Action on the Islamic Republic of Iran's nuclear program], July 20, 2015, https://www.refworld.org/docid/55b9e2084.html.

59. Anonymous American official quoted in International Crisis Group (2014: 29).

60. Mohammad Ali Jafari quoted in Erdbrink (2013).

61. On this point in the Iran context, see Hurst (2016); Tabatabai (2017). For the classic articulation, see Putnam (1988).

62. Ayatollah Ali Khamenei quoted in Bozorgmehr (2013).

63. Some military organizations, for instance, benefited from the harsh sanctions. For an overview of Iran's political economy, see Maloney (2015); Thaler et al. (2010).

64. For an earlier study that reached similar conclusions, see Vaez and Sadjadpour (2013).

Chapter 7

1. For counterarguments on the utility of compellence with strategic nuclear forces, see Betts (1987); Kroenig (2013). See also Anderson, Debs, and Monteiro (2019); Bell and MacDonald (2019). On coercion with conventional weapons, see Pape (1996).

2. On proliferation strategies in general, see Narang (2016, 2022).

3. See, for example, Bowers and Hiim (2021); Early (2014); Moltz (2014); Nolan (1991).

4. For overviews, see Kemp (2014); Snyder (2016); Zimmerman (1994).

5. For useful overviews, see Einhorn (2006); McGoldrick (2011).

6. For an extension to the coercive campaign against Russia over Ukraine, see Vaynman and Volpe (2022).

7. For an overview of these studies, see Downes (2018).

8. See Pilat (2019); Sagan (2010); Saunders (2019).

9. On empirical measures of nuclear latency, see Fuhrmann and Tkach (2015); Herzog (2020); Smith and Spaniel (2018). On how nuclear latency shapes outcomes in international relations, see Bas and Coe (2016); Beardsley and Asal (2013); Mehta and Whitlark (2017); Narang (2016).

10. See Fuhrmann (2019). So far, the empirical scholarship on the deterrent effects of nuclear latency points to a wide range of preliminary results. On the one hand, some studies find that countries with nuclear power programs or ENR capabilities

are somewhat less likely to end up in military disputes. See, for example, Fuhrmann and Tkach (2015); Horowitz (2013); Spaniel (2019). However, scholars also find that countries with enrichment or reprocessing capabilities are no less likely to be the targets of militarized disputes; see Mehta and Whitlark (2017).

11. On the dual-use nature of cyberweapons and information technology, see Lin (2016); Lindsay (2020); Valeriano, Jensen, and Maness (2018). For broader assessments of dual-use technology issues, see Lupovici (2021); Nacht and Davis (2014); Reppy (2006).

12. However, it is possible that the United States could weaken or abandon entrenched nonproliferation policies, perhaps as part of an isolationist foreign policy or radical change in national security leadership. This would likely usher in a more dangerous nuclear age, albeit one wherein states find it difficult to leverage latency as a coercive instrument against Washington. For a similar assessment, see Lanoszka (2018a).

13. There is little prospect of even North Korea trading away its atomic weapons or production complex. For overviews, see Panda (2020); Warden (2017).

14. For detailed overviews of US efforts to assure allies amid this structural shift, see Rapp-Hooper (2020); Roberts (2015).

15. See, for example, US Department of Energy (2020).

16. See Miller and Volpe (2018a, 2018b).

17. For an early articulation of this argument, see Volpe (2016).

18. This argument heavily draws from the nonproliferation assessment of civil nuclear cooperation deals in Miller and Volpe (2018a).

References

Abbott, Kenneth W. 1993. "Trust but Verify: The Production of Information in Arms Control Treaties and Other International Agreements." *Cornell International Law Journal* 26(1): 1–58.

Abraham, Itty. 2006. "The Ambivalence of Nuclear Histories." *Osiris* 21(1): 49–65. https://doi.org/10.1086/507135.

Abulof, Uriel. 2013. "Nuclear Diversion Theory and Legitimacy Crisis: The Case of Iran." *Politics & Policy* 41(5): 690–722. https://doi.org/10.1111/polp.12035.

Acheson-Lilienthal. 1946. *The Acheson-Lilienthal Report on the International Control of Atomic Energy.* Washington, DC: Prepared for the Secretary of State's Committee on Atomic Energy.

Acton, James M. 2009. "The Problem with Nuclear Mind Reading." *Survival* 51(1): 119–42. https://doi.org/10.1080/00396330902749756.

Acton, James M. 2015a. "Virtual Nuclear Deterrence and Strategic Stability." Pp. 61–74 in *Global Nuclear Disarmament: Strategic, Political, and Regional Perspectives*, edited by N. Hynek and M. Smetana. London: Routledge.

Acton, James M. 2015b. *Wagging the Plutonium Dog: Japanese Domestic Politics and Its International Security Implications.* Washington, DC: Carnegie Endowment for International Peace.

Acton, James M. 2016. "On the Regulation of Dual-Use Nuclear Technology." Pp. 8–59 in *Governance of Dual-Use Technologies: Theory and Practice*, edited by E. Harris. Cambridge, MA: American Academy of Arts and Sciences.

Ahonen, Pertti. 1995. "Franz-Josef Strauss and the German Nuclear Question, 1956–1962." *Journal of Strategic Studies* 18(2): 25–51. https://doi.org/10.1080/01402399508437593.

Albright, David. 2010. *Peddling Peril: How the Secret Nuclear Trade Arms America's Enemies.* New York: Free Press.

Albright, David, and Corey Hinderstein. 2002. *Iran Building Nuclear Fuel Cycle Facilities: International Transparency Needed. ISIS Issue Brief.* Washington, DC: Institute for Science and International Security.

Albright, David, and Corey Hinderstein. 2004. "The Centrifuge Connection." *Bulletin of the Atomic Scientists* 60(2): 61–66. https://doi.org/10.2968/060002017.

Alic, John A., Lewis M. Branscomb, Harvey Brooks, Ashton B. Carter, and Gerald L. Epstein. 1992. *Beyond Spinoff: Military and Commercial Technologies in a Changing World.* Boston: Harvard Business Review Press.

Altman, Dan. 2018. "Advancing without Attacking: The Strategic Game around the Use of Force." *Security Studies* 27(1): 58–88. https://doi.org/10.1080/09636412.2017.1360074.

Altman, Dan, and Nicholas L. Miller. 2017. "Red Lines in Nuclear Nonproliferation." *Nonproliferation Review* 24(3–4): 315–42. https://doi.org/10.1080/10736700.2018.1433575.

Anderson, Nicholas D., Alexandre Debs, and Nuno P. Monteiro. 2019. "General Nuclear Compellence: The State, Allies, and Adversaries." *Strategic Studies Quarterly* 13(3): 93–121.

Ansari, Ali M. 2010. *Crisis of Authority: Iran's 2009 Presidential Election*. London: Chatham House.

Anstey, Isabelle. 2018. "Negotiating Nuclear Control: The Zangger Committee and the Nuclear Suppliers' Group in the 1970s." *International History Review* 40(5): 975–95. https://doi.org/10.1080/07075332.2018.1449764.

Arjomand, Said Amir. 2009. *After Khomeini: Iran under His Successors*. Oxford: Oxford University Press.

Arnold, Aaron, Matthew Bunn, Caitlin Chase, Steven E. Miller, Rolf Mowatt-Larssen, and William H. Tobey. 2019. *The Iran Nuclear Archive: Impressions and Implications*. Cambridge, MA: Harvard Belfer Center for Science and International Affairs.

Arreguín-Toft, Ivan. 2005. *How the Weak Win Wars: A Theory of Asymmetric Conflict*. New York: Cambridge University Press.

Arrow, Kenneth J. 1963. "Uncertainty and the Welfare Economics of Medical Care." *American Economic Review* 53(5): 941–73.

Art, Robert J. 1980. "To What Ends Military Power?" *International Security* 4(4): 3–35. https://doi.org/10.2307/2626666.

Art, Robert J., and Kelly M. Greenhill. 2018a. "Coercion: An Analytic Overview." Pp. 3–32 in *Coercion: The Power to Hurt in International Politics*, edited by Kelly M. Greenhill and Peter Krause. New York: Oxford University Press.

Art, Robert J., and Kelly M. Greenhill. 2018b. "The Power and Limits of Compellence: A Research Note." *Political Science Quarterly* 133(1): 77–97. https://doi.org/10.1002/polq.12738.

Arthur, W. Brian. 1994. *Increasing Returns and Path Dependence in the Economy*. Ann Arbor: University of Michigan Press.

Bark, Dennis L., and David R. Gress. 1989a. *A History of West Germany*. Vol. 1: *From Shadow to Substance, 1945–1963*. Oxford: Basil Blackwell.

Bark, Dennis L., and David R. Gress. 1989b. *A History of West Germany*. Vol. 2: *Democracy and Its Discontents, 1963–1988*. Oxford: Basil Blackwell.

Bas, Muhammet A., and Andrew J. Coe. 2016. "A Dynamic Theory of Nuclear Proliferation and Preventive War." *International Organization* 70(4): 655–85. https://doi.org/10.1017/S0020818316000230.

Bas, Muhammet A., and Andrew J. Coe. 2018. "Give Peace a (Second) Chance: A Theory of Nonproliferation Deals." *International Studies Quarterly* 62(3): 606–17. https://doi.org/10.1093/isq/sqy015.

Beardsley, Kyle, and Victor Asal. 2009. "Winning with the Bomb." *Journal of Conflict Resolution* 53(2): 278–301. https://doi.org/10.1177/0022002708330386.

Beardsley, Kyle, and Victor Asal. 2013. "Nuclear Weapons Programs and the Security Dilemma." Pp. 265–87 in *The Nuclear Renaissance and International Security*, edited by M. Fuhrmann and A. Stulberg. Stanford, CA: Stanford University Press.

Bechtol, Bruce E. 2010. *Defiant Failed State: The North Korean Threat to International Security*. Washington, DC: Potomac Books.

Bell, Mark S. 2015. "Beyond Emboldenment: How Acquiring Nuclear Weapons Can Change Foreign Policy." *International Security* 40(1): 87–119. https://doi.org/10.1162/ISEC_a_00204.

Bell, Mark S. 2019. "Nuclear Opportunism: A Theory of How States Use Nuclear Weapons in International Politics." *Journal of Strategic Studies* 42(1): 3–28. https://doi.org/10.1080/01402390.2017.1389722.

Bell, Mark S., and Julia MacDonald. 2019. "How to Think about Nuclear Crises." *Texas National Security Review* 2(2): 40–64. http://dx.doi.org/10.26153/tsw/1944.

Benson, Brett V., and Quan Wen. 2011. "A Bargaining Model of Nuclear Weapons Development and Disarmament." Pp. 111–37 in *Causes and Consequences of Nuclear Proliferation*, edited by R. Rauchhaus, M. Kroenig, and E. Gartzke. New York: Routledge.

Bergman, Ronen. 2018a. "Iran's Great Nuclear Deception." *YNetNews*. Retrieved July 31, 2019 (https://www.ynetnews.com/articles/0,7340,L-5412157,00.html).

Bergman, Ronen. 2018b. *Rise and Kill First: The Secret History of Israel's Targeted Assassinations*. New York: Random House.

Bermudez, Joseph, Jr. 2006. "North Korea Claims Nuclear Test." *Jane's Defence Weekly*, October 18.

Betts, Richard K. 1987. *Nuclear Blackmail and Nuclear Balance*. Washington, DC: Brookings Institution Press.

Biddle, Tami Davis. 2020. "Coercion Theory: A Basic Introduction for Practitioners." *Texas National Security Review* 3(2): 94–109.

Black, Ian. 2009. "Iran Defies United Nations with Plans for 10 New Nuclear Plants." *The Guardian*, November 29.

Blanchard, Christopher M., and Paul K. Kerr. 2020. *Prospects for Enhanced U.S.-Saudi Nuclear Energy Cooperation*. Washington, DC: Congressional Research Service.

Bluth, Christoph. 1995. *Britain, Germany, and Western Nuclear Strategy*. Oxford: Oxford University Press.

Bollfrass, Alexander K. 2017. "The Half-Lives of Others: The Democratic Advantage in Nuclear Intelligence Assessment." PhD dissertation, Princeton University.

Bowen, Matt. 2020. *Why the United States Should Remain Engaged on Nuclear Power: Geopolitical and National Security Considerations*. New York: Columbia University; SIPA: Center on Global Energy Policy.

Bowen, Wyn, Jeffrey W. Knopf, and Matthew Moran. 2020. "The Obama Administration and Syrian Chemical Weapons: Deterrence, Compellence, and the Limits of the 'Resolve Plus Bombs' Formula." *Security Studies* 29(5): 797–831. https://doi.org/10.1080/09636412.2020.1859130.

Bowen, Wyn, and Matthew Moran. 2014. "Iran's Nuclear Programme: A Case Study in Hedging?" *Contemporary Security Policy* 35(1): 26–52. https://doi.org/10.1080/13523260.2014.884338.

Bowers, Ian, and Henrik Stålhane Hiim. 2021. "Conventional Counterforce Dilemmas: South Korea's Deterrence Strategy and Stability on the Korean Peninsula." *International Security* 45(3): 7–39. https://doi.org/10.1162/isec_a_00399.

Bozo, Frédéric. 2016. *French Foreign Policy since 1945: An Introduction*. New York: Berghahn Books.

Bozo, Frédéric. 2020. "The Sanctuary and the Glacis: France, the Federal Republic of Germany, and Nuclear Weapons in the 1980s (Part 1)." *Journal of Cold War Studies* 22(3): 119–79. https://doi.org/10.1162/jcws_a_00929.

Bozorgmehr, Najmeh. 2013. "Iran's Supreme Leader Pushes for Flexibility in Nuclear Talks." *Financial Times*, September 17.

Brands, Hal. 2006. "Rethinking Nonproliferation: LBJ, the Gilpatric Committee, and U.S. National Security Policy." *Journal of Cold War Studies* 8(2): 83–113.

Brands, Hal. 2007. "Non-proliferation and the Dynamics of the Middle Cold War: The Superpowers, the MLF, and the NPT." *Cold War History* 7(3): 389–423. https://doi.org/10.1080/14682740701474857.

Braut-Hegghammer, Målfrid. 2016. *Unclear Physics: Why Iraq and Libya Failed to Build Nuclear Weapons*. Ithaca, NY: Cornell University Press.

Brewer, Eric. 2019. "Iran's Latest Nuclear Provocation: What It Means, What Comes Next." *Center for Strategic and International Studies*. July 1. https://www.csis.org/analysis/irans-latest-nuclear-provocation-what-it-means-what-comes-next.

Brewer, Eric. 2020. *Toward a More Proliferated World? The Geopolitical Forces That Will Shape the Spread of Nuclear Weapons*. Washington, DC: Center for New American Security; Center for Strategic and International Studies.

Brewer, Eric. 2021. "The Nuclear Proliferation Landscape: Is Past Prologue?" *Washington Quarterly* 44(2): 181–97. https://doi.org/10.1080/0163660X.2021.1934250.

Broad, William J. 2009. "Iran President Says Nuclear Enrichment Will Grow." *New York Times*, December 2.

Brokaw, Tom. 2003. "Full Text of Brokaw's Interview with Bush." *New York Times*, April 25.

Buckley, Roger. 1995. *US-Japan Alliance Diplomacy, 1945–1990*. Cambridge: Cambridge University Press.

Bueno de Mesquita, Bruce, and Alastair Smith. 2012. "Domestic Explanations of International Relations." *Annual Review of Political Science* 15(1): 161–81. https://doi.org/10.1146/annurev-polisci-070209-174835.

Burns, William J. 2019. *The Back Channel: A Memoir of American Diplomacy and the Case for Its Renewal*. New York: Random House.

Burr, William. 2005. "National Intelligence Estimates of the Nuclear Proliferation Problem: The First Ten Years, 1957–1967." National Security Archive Briefing Book #155. June 5. https://nsarchive2.gwu.edu/NSAEBB/NSAEBB155/.

Burr, William. 2014. "A Scheme of 'Control': The United States and the Origins of the Nuclear Suppliers' Group, 1974–1976." *International History Review* 36(2): 252–76. https://doi.org/10.1080/07075332.2013.864690.

Burr, William. 2018a. "Preoccupations with West Germany's Nuclear Weapons Potential Shaped Kennedy-Era Diplomacy." National Security Archive Briefing Book #617. February 2. https://nsarchive.gwu.edu/briefing-book/nuclear-vault/2018-02-02/german-nuclear-question-nonproliferation-treaty.

Burr, William. 2018b. "The Nuclear Nonproliferation Treaty and the German Nuclear Question Part II, 1965–1969." National Security Archive Electronic Briefing Book #622. March 21. https://nsarchive.gwu.edu/briefing-book/nuclear-vault/2018-03-21/nuclear-nonproliferation-treaty-german-nuclear-question-part-ii-1965-1969.

Burr, William, and Jeffrey T. Richelson. 2001. "Whether to 'Strangle the Baby in the Cradle': The United States and the Chinese Nuclear Program, 1960–64." *International Security* 25(3): 54–99. https://doi.org/10.1162/016228800560525.

Bush, George W. 2011. *Decision Points*. New York: Crown.

Byman, Daniel, and Jennifer Lind. 2010. "Pyongyang's Survival Strategy." *International Security* 35(1): 44–74.

Cardwell, Diane, and Jonathan Soble. 2017. "Westinghouse Files for Bankruptcy, in Blow to Nuclear Power." *New York Times*, March 29.

Carson, Austin. 2018. *Secret Wars: Covert Conflict in International Politics*. Princeton, NJ: Princeton University Press.

Carson, Cathryn. 2010. *Heisenberg in the Atomic Age: Science and the Public Sphere*. New York: Cambridge University Press.

Carter, Ashton B., and William J. Perry. 2000. *Preventive Defense: A New Security Strategy for America*. Washington, DC: Brookings Institution Press.

Castillo, Jasen J., and Alexander B. Downes. 2020. "Loyalty, Hedging, or Exit: How Weaker Alliance Partners Respond to the Rise of New Threats." *Journal of Strategic Studies* 1–42. https://doi.org/10.1080/01402390.2020.1797690.

Cha, Victor D. 2002. "North Korea's Weapons of Mass Destruction: Badges, Shields, or Swords?" *Political Science Quarterly* 117(2): 209–30. https://doi.org/10.2307/798181.

Cha, Victor D. 2012. *The Impossible State: North Korea, Past and Future*. New York: Ecco.

Chamberlain, Dianne Pfundstein. 2016. *Cheap Threats: Why the United States Struggles to Coerce Weak States*. Washington, DC: Georgetown University Press.

Chinoy, Mike. 2009. *Meltdown: The Inside Story of the North Korean Nuclear Crisis*. New York: St. Martin's Griffin.

Christopher, William. 1995. *North Korea Nuclear Agreement*. Hearings before the Committee on Foreign Relations, United States Senate, January 24 and 25. Washington, DC: Government Printing Office.

Chubin, Shahram. 1994. *Iran's National Security Policy: Intentions, Capabilities, and Impact*. Washington, DC: Carnegie Endowment for International Peace.

Chubin, Shahram. 2002. *Whither Iran? Reform, Domestic Politics and National Security*. Oxford: International Institute of Strategic Studies.

Chyba, Christopher F. 2020. "New Technologies and Strategic Stability." *Daedalus* 149(2): 150–70. https://doi.org/10.1162/daed_a_01795.

Cioc, Mark. 1988. *Pax Atomica: The Nuclear Defense Debate in West Germany during the Adenauer Era*. New York: Columbia University Press.

Clinton, Hillary Rodham. 2014. *Hard Choices*. New York: Simon and Schuster.

Coe, Andrew J., and Jane Vaynman. 2015. "Collusion and the Nuclear Nonproliferation Regime." *Journal of Politics* 77(4): 983–97. https://doi.org/10.1086/682080.

Coe, Andrew J., and Jane Vaynman. 2020. "Why Arms Control Is So Rare." *American Political Science Review* 114(2): 342–55. https://doi.org/10.1017/S000305541900073X.

Colgan, Jeff D., and Nicholas L. Miller. 2019. "Rival Hierarchies and the Origins of Nuclear Technology Sharing." *International Studies Quarterly* 63(2): 310–21. https://doi.org/10.1093/isq/sqz002.

Cooper, Helene. 2015. "Saudi Arabia Says King Won't Attend Meetings in U.S." *New York Times*, May 10.

Coughlin, Con. 2010. *Khomeini's Ghost: The Iranian Revolution and the Rise of Militant Islam*. New York: Ecco.

Crist, David. 2012. *The Twilight War: The Secret History of America's Thirty-Year Conflict with Iran*. New York: Penguin Press.

Dalton, Toby. 2019. "Policy Implications of Nuclear Hedging: Observations on East Asia." Pp. 247–74 in *Nuclear Latency and Hedging: Concepts, History, and Issues, Nuclear Proliferation International History Program*, edited by J. F. Pilat. Washington, DC: Woodrow Wilson Center Press.

Dalton, Toby, Wyatt Hoffman, Ariel E. Levite, Li Bin, George Perkovich, and Tong Zhao. 2017. *Toward a Nuclear Firewall: Bridging the NPT's Three Pillars*. Washington, DC: Carnegie Endowment for International Peace.

Dalton, Toby, and Ariel Levite. 2022. "The Nonproliferation Regime Is Breaking." *Foreign Affairs*, February 16.

Davenport, Kelsey. 2020. "The Joint Comprehensive Plan of Action (JCPOA) at a Glance." *Arms Control Association*. Retrieved December 14, 2020 (https://www.armscontrol.org/factsheets/JCPOA-at-a-glance).

Davies, Graeme A. M. 2012. "Coercive Diplomacy Meets Diversionary Incentives: The Impact of US and Iranian Domestic Politics during the Bush and Obama Presidencies." *Foreign Policy Analysis* 8(3): 313–31.

De Bellaigue, Christopher. 2007. *The Struggle for Iran*. New York: New York Review Books.

Debs, Alexandre, and Nuno P. Monteiro. 2014. "Known Unknowns: Power Shifts, Uncertainty, and War." *International Organization* 68(1): 1–31.

Debs, Alexandre, and Nuno P. Monteiro. 2016. *Nuclear Politics: The Strategic Causes of Proliferation*. New York: Cambridge University Press.

Director of Central Intelligence. 2003. *The Worldwide Threat in 2003: Evolving Dangers in a Complex World*. Washington, DC: Central Intelligence Agency.

Downes, Alexander B. 2018. "Step Aside or Face the Consequences: Explaining the Success and Failure of Compellent Threats to Remove Foreign Leaders." Pp. 93–116 in *Coercion: The Power to Hurt in International Politics*, edited by R. J. Art and K. M. Greenhill. New York: Oxford University Press.

Drennan, William M. 2003. "Nuclear Weapons and North Korea: Who's Coercing Whom?" Pp. 157–224 in *The United States and Coercive Diplomacy*, edited by R. J. Art and P. M. Cronin. Washington, DC: United States Institute of Peace.

Drollette, Dan, Jr. 2016. "View from the Inside: Prince Turki al-Faisal on Saudi Arabia, Nuclear Energy and Weapons, and Middle East Politics." *Bulletin of the Atomic Scientists* 72(1): 16–24. https://doi.org/10.1080/00963402.2016.1124655.

Early, Bryan R. 2014. "Exploring the Final Frontier: An Empirical Analysis of Global Civil Space Proliferation." *International Studies Quarterly* 58(1): 55–67. https://doi.org/10.1111/isqu.12102.

Eberstadt, Nicholas. 1999. *The End of North Korea*. Washington, DC: AEI Press.

Eberstadt, Nicholas, Mark Rubin, and Albina Tretyakova. 1995. "The Collapse of Soviet and Russian Trade with the DPRK, 1989–1993." *Korean Journal of National Unification* 4: 87–104.

Eckert, Michael. 1990. "Primacy Doomed to Failure: Heisenberg's Role as Scientific Adviser for Nuclear Policy in the FRG." *Historical Studies in the Physical and Biological Sciences* 21(1): 29–58. https://doi.org/10.2307/27757654.

Egeland, Kjølv, and Benoît Pelopidas. 2021. "European Nuclear Weapons? Zombie Debates and Nuclear Realities." *European Security* 30(2): 237–58. https://doi.org/10.1080/09662839.2020.1855147.

Einhorn, Robert J. 2006. "Identifying Nuclear Aspirants and Their Pathways to the Bomb." *Nonproliferation Review* 13(3): 491–99. https://doi.org/10.1080/1073670060 1071546.

Einhorn, Robert J. 2014. *Preventing a Nuclear-Armed Iran: Requirements for a Comprehensive Nuclear Agreement*. Washington, DC: Brookings.

El Gamal, Rania, and Katie Paul. 2017. "Saudi Arabia Hopes to Start Nuclear Pact Talks with U.S. in Weeks." Reuters, December 20.

ElBaradei, Mohamed. 2011. *The Age of Deception: Nuclear Diplomacy in Treacherous Times*. New York: Metropolitan Books.

Ellis, Jason D. 2003. "The Best Defense: Counterproliferation and U.S. National Security." *Washington Quarterly* 26(2): 115–33. https://doi.org/10.1162/01636600360569739.

Ellsberg, Daniel. 1968. *The Theory and Practice of Blackmail*. P-3883. Santa Monica, CA: RAND Corporation.

Erdbrink, Thomas. 2013. "Military Chief in Iran Scolds a Top Official." *New York Times*, December 11.

Erdbrink, Thomas. 2015. "Iran's Supreme Leader Is Skeptical of Nuclear Talks with U.S." *New York Times*, January 7.

Fathi, Nazila, and David E. Sanger. 2006. "Iran Says It Is Making Nuclear Fuel, Defying U.N." *New York Times*, April 12.

Fearon, James D. 1992. "Threats to Use Force: Costly Signals and Bargaining in International Crises." PhD dissertation, University of California, Berkeley.

Fearon, James D. 1994. "Domestic Political Audiences and the Escalation of International Disputes." *American Political Science Review* 88(3): 577–92.

Fearon, James D. 1995. "Rationalist Explanations for War." *International Organization* 49(3): 379–414.

Fearon, James D. 1997. "Signaling Foreign Policy Interests: Tying Hands versus Sinking Costs." *Journal of Conflict Resolution* 41(1): 68–90.

Feng, Zhu. 2006. "Shifting Tides: China and North Korea." *China Security* 35–51.

Filkins, Dexter. 2013. "The Shadow Commander." *New Yorker*, September 30.

Fitzpatrick, Mark. 2010. "Iran: The Fragile Promise of the Fuel-Swap Plan." *Survival* 52(3): 67–94. https://doi.org/10.1080/00396338.2010.494878.

Fitzpatrick, Mark. 2016. *Asia's Latent Nuclear Powers: Japan, South Korea and Taiwan.* London: Routledge.

Ford, Christopher A. 2011. "Nuclear Weapons Reconstitution and Its Discontents: Challenges of 'Weaponless Deterrence.'" Pp. 131–201 in *Deterrence: Its Past and Future*, edited by G. P. Shultz, S. D. Drell, and J. E. Goodby. Stanford, CA: Hoover Institution Press.

Foster, William C. 1965. "New Directions in Arms Control and Disarmament." *Foreign Affairs* 43(4): 587–601. https://doi.org/10.2307/20039124.

Freedman, Lawrence. 1998. "Strategic Coercion." Pp. 1–28 in *Strategic Coercion: Concepts and Cases*, edited by L. Freedman. New York: Oxford University Press.

Freedman, Lawrence. 2003. *The Evolution of Nuclear Strategy.* New York: Palgrave Macmillan.

Fuhrmann, Matthew. 2012. *Atomic Assistance: How Atoms for Peace Programs Cause Nuclear Insecurity.* Ithaca, NY: Cornell University Press.

Fuhrmann, Matthew. 2012. "Splitting Atoms: Why Do Countries Build Nuclear Power Plants?" *International Interactions* 38(1): 29–57. https://doi.org/10.1080/03050 629.2012.640209.

Fuhrmann, Matthew. 2019. "Explaining the Proliferation of Latent Nuclear Capabilities." Pp. 289–314 in *Nuclear Latency and Hedging: Concepts, History, and Issues*, edited by J. F. Pilat. Washington, DC: Woodrow Wilson Center Press.

Fuhrmann, Matthew, and Benjamin Tkach. 2015. "Almost Nuclear: Introducing the Nuclear Latency Dataset." *Conflict Management and Peace Science* 32(4): 443–61. https://doi.org/10.1177/0738894214559672.

Gale, Alastair, and Carol E. Lee. 2016. "U.S. Agreed to North Korea Peace Talks before Latest Nuclear Test." *Wall Street Journal*, February 22.

Gallucci, Robert L. 1994. *Implications of the U.S.-North Korea Nuclear Agreement.* Washington, DC: US Government Printing Office.

Gavin, Francis J. 2002. "The Gold Battles within the Cold War: American Monetary Policy and the Defense of Europe, 1960–1963." *Diplomatic History* 26(1): 61–94. https://doi.org/10.1111/1467-7709.00300.

Gavin, Francis J. 2007. *Gold, Dollars, and Power: The Politics of International Monetary Relations, 1958–1971.* Chapel Hill: University of North Carolina Press.

Gavin, Francis J. 2012a. *Nuclear Statecraft: History and Strategy in America's Atomic Age.* Ithaca, NY: Cornell University Press.

Gavin, Francis J. 2012b. "Politics, History and the Ivory Tower-Policy Gap in the Nuclear Proliferation Debate." *Journal of Strategic Studies* 35(4): 573–600. https://doi.org/10.1080/01402390.2012.715736.

Gavin, Francis J. 2015. "Strategies of Inhibition: U.S. Grand Strategy, the Nuclear Revolution, and Nonproliferation." *International Security* 40(1): 9–46. https://doi.org/10.1162/ISEC_a_00205.

Gelman, Harry, and Norman Levin. 1984. *The Future of Soviet-North Korean Relations.* R-3159-AF. Santa Monica, CA: Rand Corporation.

George, Alexander L., and Andrew Bennett. 2005. *Case Studies and Theory Development in the Social Sciences.* Cambridge, MA: MIT Press.

Gerring, John. 2004. "What Is a Case Study and What Is It Good For?" *American Political Science Review* 98(2): 341–54.

Gerzhoy, Gene. 2015. "Alliance Coercion and Nuclear Restraint: How the United States Thwarted West Germany's Nuclear Ambitions." *International Security* 39(4): 91–129.

Gibbons, Rebecca Davis. 2020. "Supply to Deny: The Benefits of Nuclear Assistance for Nuclear Nonproliferation." *Journal of Global Security Studies* 5(2): 282–98. https://doi.org/10.1093/jogss/ogz059.

Gibbons, Rebecca Davis. 2022. *The Hegemon's Tool Kit: US Leadership and the Politics of the Nuclear Nonproliferation Regime.* Ithaca, NY: Cornell University Press.

Gilinsky, Victor. 1997. "Nuclear Blackmail: The 1994 US-DPRK Agreed Framework on North Korea's Nuclear Program." *Essays in Public Policy* (76).

Gilinsky, Victor, and Paul Fritz Langer. 1967. *The Japanese Civilian Nuclear Program.* Santa Monica, CA: Rand Corporation.

Glaser, Charles L. 2010. *Rational Theory of International Politics: The Logic of Competition and Cooperation.* Princeton, NJ: Princeton University Press.

Goemans, H. E. 2000. *War and Punishment: The Causes of War Termination and the First World War.* Princeton, NJ: Princeton University Press.

Goldstein, Avery. 2000. *Deterrence and Security in the 21st Century: China, Britain, France, and the Enduring Legacy of the Nuclear Revolution.* Stanford, CA: Stanford University Press.

Gordon, Michael R. 1993. "North Korea Rebuffs Nuclear Inspectors, Reviving U.S. Nervousness." *New York Times*, February 1.

Gordon, Michael R. 1994. "Korea Speeds Nuclear Fuel Removal, Impeding Inspection." *New York Times*, May 28.

Gortzak, Yoav. 2005. "How Great Powers Rule: Coercion and Positive Inducements in International Order Enforcement." *Security Studies* 14(4): 663–97. https://doi.org/10.1080/09636410500468826.

Gray, William Glenn. 2008. "Abstinence and Ostpolitik: Brandt's Government and the Nuclear Question." Pp. 244–68 in *Ostpolitik, 1969–1974: European and Global Responses*, edited by C. Fink and B. Schaefer. Cambridge: Cambridge University Press.

Gray, William Glenn. 2012. "Commercial Liberties and Nuclear Anxieties: The US-German Feud over Brazil, 1975–7." *International History Review* 34(3): 449–74.

Green, Michael J., and Katsuhisa Furukawa. 2008. "Japan: New Nuclear Realism." Pp. 347–72 in *The Long Shadow: Nuclear Weapons and Security in 21st Century Asia*, edited by M. Alagappa. Stanford, CA: Stanford University Press.

Greenhill, Kelly M. 2010. *Weapons of Mass Migration: Forced Displacement, Coercion, and Foreign Policy*. Ithaca, NY: Cornell University Press.

Greenhouse, Steven. 1995. "U.S. Gives Russia Secret Data on Iran to Discourage Atom Deal." *New York Times*, April 3.

Haftendorn, Helga. 1996. *NATO and the Nuclear Revolution: A Crisis of Credibility, 1966–1967*. Oxford: Clarendon Press.

Haggard, Stephan, and Marcus Noland. 2017. *Hard Target: Sanctions, Inducements, and the Case of North Korea*. Stanford, CA: Stanford University Press.

Harney, Robert, Gerald Brown, Matthew Carlyle, Eric Skroch, and Kevin Wood. 2006. "Anatomy of a Project to Produce a First Nuclear Weapon." *Science & Global Security* 14(2–3): 163–82.

Harrington, Anne, and Matthias Englert. 2014. "How Much Is Enough? The Politics of Technology and Weaponless Nuclear Deterrence." Pp. 287–302 in *The Global Politics of Science and Technology*, edited by M. Mayer, M. Carpes, and R. Knoblich. Berlin: Springer-Verlag.

Harris, Kevin. 2013. "Iran, the Twenty-First-Century Island of Stability." *Middle East Report Online*. Retrieved April 27, 2022 (https://merip.org/2013/09/iran-the-twenty-first-century-island-of-stability/).

Harrison, Michael M. 1981. *The Reluctant Ally: France and Atlantic Security*. Baltimore: Johns Hopkins University Press.

Haun, Phil. 2015. *Coercion, Survival, and War: Why Weak States Resist the United States*. Stanford, CA: Stanford Security Studies.

Hecker, Siegfried S. 2004. *Visit to the Yongbyon Nuclear Scientific Research Center in North Korea*. Hearings before the Committee on Foreign Relations, United States Senate, January 21. Washington, DC: Government Printing Office.

Hecker, Siegfried S. 2005. "Technical Summary of DPRK Nuclear Program." Presented at the 2005 Carnegie International Non-proliferation Conference, November 8, Washington, DC.

Herzog, Stephen. 2020. "The Nuclear Fuel Cycle and the Proliferation 'Danger Zone.'" *Journal for Peace and Nuclear Disarmament* 3(1): 60–86. https://doi.org/10.1080/25751654.2020.1766164.

Heuser, Beatrice. 1997. *NATO, Britain, France and the FRG: Nuclear Strategies and Forces for Europe, 1949–2000*. London: Macmillan.

Hibbs, Mark. 2014. "Revisiting Enrichment for Bushehr." *Arms Control Wonk*. Retrieved December 14, 2020 (https://www.armscontrolwonk.com/archive/1102830/revisiting-enrichment-for-bushehr/).

Hiim, Henrik Stålhane. 2022. "Revisiting Nuclear Hedging: Ballistic Missiles and the Iranian Example." *International Affairs* 98(4): 1367–84. https://doi.org/10.1093/ia/iiac103.

Hoey, Fintan. 2015. *Satō, America and the Cold War: US-Japanese Relations, 1964–72*. New York: Palgrave Macmillan.

Hoey, Fintan. 2016a. "Japan and Extended Nuclear Deterrence: Security and Non-proliferation." *Journal of Strategic Studies* 39(4): 484–501. https://doi.org/10.1080/01402390.2016.1168010.

Hoey, Fintan. 2016b. "Non-nuclear Japan? Satō, the NPT, and the US Nuclear Umbrella." Pp. 161–77 in *Negotiating the Nuclear Non-proliferation Treaty: Origins of the Nuclear Order*, edited by R. Popp, L. Horovitz, and A. Wenger. London: Routledge.

Horowitz, Michael C. 2010. *The Diffusion of Military Power: Causes and Consequences for International Politics*. Princeton, NJ: Princeton University Press.

Horowitz, Michael C. 2013. "Nuclear Power and Militarized Conflict: Is There a Link?" Pp. 288–312 in *The Nuclear Renaissance and International Security*, edited by A. N. Stulberg and M. Fuhrmann. Palo Alto, CA: Stanford University Press.

Horowitz, Michael C. 2020. "Do Emerging Military Technologies Matter for International Politics?" *Annual Review of Political Science* 23(1): 385–400. https://doi.org/10.1146/annurev-polisci-050718-032725.

Hurst, Steven. 2016. "The Iranian Nuclear Negotiations as a Two-Level Game: The Importance of Domestic Politics." *Diplomacy & Statecraft* 27(3): 545–67. https://doi.org/10.1080/09592296.2016.1196075.

Hyde, Susan D., and Elizabeth N. Saunders. 2020. "Recapturing Regime Type in International Relations: Leaders, Institutions, and Agency Space." *International Organization* 1–33. https://doi.org/10.1017/S0020818319000365.

Hymans, Jacques E. C. 2010. "When Does a State Become a 'Nuclear Weapon State'? An Exercise in Measurement Validation." *Nonproliferation Review* 17(1): 162–80.

Hymans, Jacques E. C. 2011. "Veto Players, Nuclear Energy, and Nonproliferation: Domestic Institutional Barriers to a Japanese Bomb." *International Security* 36(2): 154–89.

Hymans, Jacques E. C. 2012. *Achieving Nuclear Ambitions: Scientists, Politicians, and Proliferation*. Cambridge: Cambridge University Press.

International Atomic Energy Agency. 2002. *IAEA Safeguards Glossary 2001 Edition*. Vienna.

International Crisis Group. 2006a. *China and North Korea: Comrades Forever?* Asia Report No. 112. Seoul/Brussels.

International Crisis Group. 2006b. *Iran: Is There a Way Out of the Nuclear Impasse? Middle East Report No. 51*. Brussels.

International Crisis Group. 2014. *Iran and the P5+1: Solving the Nuclear Rubik's Cube*. Middle East Report No. 152. Brussels.

Irish, E. R., and W. H. Reas. 1957. *The PUREX Process: A Solvent Extraction Reprocessing Method for Irradiated Uranium*. HW-49483 A, 4341712. Richland, WA: Hanford Atomic Products Operation. https://doi.org/10.2172/4341712.

Jabko, Nicolas, and Steven Weber. 1998. "A Certain Idea of Nuclear Weapons: France's Nuclear Nonproliferation Policy in Theoretical Perspective." *Security Studies* 8(1): 108–50. https://doi.org/10.1080/09636419808429367.

Jackson, Van. 2017. *Rival Reputations: Coercion and Credibility in US-North Korea Relations*. New York: Cambridge University Press.

Jackson, Van. 2018. *On the Brink: Trump, Kim, and the Threat of Nuclear War*. New York: Cambridge University Press.

Jervis, Robert L. 1970. *The Logic of Images in International Relations*. New York: Columbia University Press.

Jo, Dong-Joon, and Erik Gartzke. 2007. "Determinants of Nuclear Weapons Proliferation." *Journal of Conflict Resolution* 51(1): 167–94. https://doi.org/10.1177/0022002706296158.

Juneau, Thomas. 2015. *Squandered Opportunity: Neoclassical Realism and Iranian Foreign Policy*. Stanford, CA: Stanford University Press.

Juneau, Thomas, and Sam Razavi. 2018. "Costly Gains: A Cost-Benefit Assessment of Iran's Nuclear Program." *Nonproliferation Review* 25(1–2): 69–86. https://doi.org/10.1080/10736700.2018.1477456.

Kahn, Joseph. 2006a. "China May Be Using Oil to Press North Korea." *New York Times*, October 31.

Kahn, Joseph. 2006b. "China May Press North Koreans." *New York Times*, October 20.

Kaplan, Lawrence. 1999. *The Long Entanglement: NATO's First Fifty Years*. Westport, CT: Praeger.

Kaplow, Jeffrey M. 2022. "State Compliance and the Track Record of International Security Institutions: Evidence from the Nuclear Nonproliferation Regime." *Journal of Global Security Studies* 7(1): ogab027. https://doi.org/10.1093/jogss/ogab027.

Karami, Arash. 2014. "Chief of Iran's Atomic Energy Organization Clarifies Nuclear Needs." *Al-Monitor*. Retrieved December 14, 2020 (https://www.al-monitor.com/pulse/originals/2014/07/iran-nuclear-chief-clarifies-nuclear-needs.html).

Karl, Jonathan. 2009. "Is the U.S. Preparing to Bomb Iran?" *ABC News*, October 6.

Kase, Yuri. 2001. "The Costs and Benefits of Japan's Nuclearization: An Insight into the 1968/70 Internal Report." *Nonproliferation Review* 8(2): 55–68.

Katzman, Kenneth. 2014. *Iran Sanctions*. Washington, DC: Congressional Research Service.

Kaussler, Bernd. 2014. *Iran's Nuclear Diplomacy: Power Politics and Conflict Resolution*. New York: Routledge.

KCNA. 2003. "'Detailed Report' Explains NPT Withdrawal." *Korean Central News Agency*. Retrieved April 27, 2022 (https://nuke.fas.org/guide/dprk/nuke/dprk012203.html).

KCNA. 2005. "DPRK FM on Its Stand to Suspend Its Participation in Six-Party Talks for Indefinite Period." *Korean Central News Agency*. Retrieved April 27, 2022 (https://kcnawatch.org/newstream/1452005410-802594470/dprk-fm-on-its-stand-to-suspend-its-participation-in-six-party-talks-for-indefinite-period/?t=1600606977533).

KCNA. 2006a. "DPRK Foreign Ministry Spokesman on Its Missile Launches." *Korean Central News Agency*. Retrieved April 27, 2022 (http://www.kcna.co.jp/item/2006/200607/news07/07.htm#1).

KCNA. 2006b. "DPRK Foreign Ministry Spokesman on U.S. Moves Concerning Its Nuclear Test." *Korean Central News Agency*.

KCNA. 2006c. "DPRK's Readiness to Boost Ties of Cooperation with International Community Reiterated." *Korean Central News Agency*.

Kelleher, Catherine McArdle. 1975. *Germany and the Politics of Nuclear Weapons*. New York: Columbia University Press.

Kemp, R. Scott. 2012. "The End of Manhattan: How the Gas Centrifuge Changed the Quest for Nuclear Weapons." *Technology and Culture* 53(2): 272–305. https://doi.org/10.1353/tech.2012.0046.

Kemp, R. Scott. 2014. "The Nonproliferation Emperor Has No Clothes." *International Security* 38(4): 39–78.

Kerr, Paul K. 2019. *Iran's Nuclear Program: Status*. RL34544. Washington, DC: Congressional Research Service.

Kerr, Paul K., and Mary Beth D. Nikitin. 2021. *Nuclear Cooperation with Other Countries: A Primer*. RS22937. Washington, DC: Congressional Research Service.

Kerry, John. 2018. *Every Day Is Extra*. New York: Simon and Schuster.

Khamenei, Ayatollah Ali. 2014. "Khamenei's Red Lines on Nuclear Talks." *United States Institute of Peace: The Iran Primer*. Retrieved December 15, 2020 (https://iranprimer.usip.org/blog/2014/apr/16/khamenei%E2%80%99s-red-lines-nuclear-talks).

Kissinger, Henry A. 2012. "Henry Kissinger: Iran Must Be President Obama's Immediate Priority." *Washington Post*, November 16.

Knopf, Jeffrey W. 2012. "Varieties of Assurance." *Journal of Strategic Studies* 35(3): 375–99. https://doi.org/10.1080/01402390.2011.643567.

Knorr, Klaus. 1956. *The War Potential of Nations.* Princeton, NJ: Princeton University Press.

Koch, Lisa Langdon. 2019. "Frustration and Delay: The Secondary Effects of Supply-Side Proliferation Controls." *Security Studies* 28(4): 773–806. https://doi.org/10.1080/09636 412.2019.1631383.

Koch, Lisa Langdon. 2022. "Holding All the Cards: Nuclear Suppliers and Nuclear Reversal." *Journal of Global Security Studies* 7(1): 1–20. https://doi.org/10.1093/jogss/ ogab034.

Kreps, Sarah E., and Matthew Fuhrmann. 2011. "Attacking the Atom: Does Bombing Nuclear Facilities Affect Proliferation?" *Journal of Strategic Studies* 34(2): 161–87. https://doi.org/10.1080/01402390.2011.559021.

Krige, John. 2006. "Atoms for Peace, Scientific Internationalism, and Scientific Intelligence." *Osiris* 21(1): 161–81. https://doi.org/10.1086/507140.

Krige, John. 2016. *Sharing Knowledge, Shaping Europe: US Technological Collaboration and Nonproliferation.* Cambridge, MA: MIT Press.

Kroenig, Matthew. 2009. "Exporting the Bomb: Why States Provide Sensitive Nuclear Assistance." *American Political Science Review* 103(1): 113–33. https://doi.org/10.1017/ S0003055409090017.

Kroenig, Matthew. 2013. "Nuclear Superiority and the Balance of Resolve: Explaining Nuclear Crisis Outcomes." *International Organization* 67(1): 141–71.

Kroenig, Matthew. 2014. *A Time to Attack: The Looming Iranian Nuclear Threat.* New York: St. Martin's Press.

Kühn, Ulrich. 2018. *Preventing Escalation in the Baltics: A NATO Playbook.* Washington, DC: Carnegie Endowment for International Peace.

Kühn, Ulrich, and Tristan Volpe. 2017. "Why Germany Should Not Go Nuclear." *Foreign Affairs* 96(4): 103–12.

Küntzel, Matthias. 1995. *Bonn and the Bomb: German Politics and the Nuclear Option.* London: Pluto Press.

Kunz, Barbara. 2020. "Switching Umbrellas in Berlin? The Implications of Franco-German Nuclear Cooperation." *Washington Quarterly* 43(3): 63–77. https://doi.org/ 10.1080/0163660X.2020.1814007.

Kurosaki, Akira. 2017. "Nuclear Energy and Nuclear-Weapon Potential: A Historical Analysis of Japan in the 1960s." *Nonproliferation Review* 24(1–2): 47–65. https://doi. org/10.1080/10736700.2017.1367536.

Kurosaki, Akira. 2020. "Public Opinion, Party Politics and Alliance: The Influence of Domestic Politics on Japan's Reliance on the U. S. Nuclear Umbrella, 1964–8." *International History Review* 42(4): 774–93. https://doi.org/10.1080/07075 332.2019.1650794.

Kusunoki, Ayako. 2008. "The Sato Cabinet and the Making of Japan's Non-nuclear Policy." *Journal of American-East Asian Relations* 15(1–2): 25–50. https://doi.org/10.1163/187 656108793645806.

Kydd, Andrew H. 2007. *Trust and Mistrust in International Relations.* Princeton, NJ: Princeton University Press.

Kydd, Andrew H., and Roseanne W. McManus. 2017. "Threats and Assurances in Crisis Bargaining." *Journal of Conflict Resolution* 61(2): 325–48. https://doi.org/10.1177/ 0022002715576571.

LaFeber, Walter. 1998. *The Clash: U.S.-Japanese Relations throughout History.* New York: Norton.

Lakshmanan, Indira A. R. 2015. "'If You Can't Do This Deal . . . Go Back to Tehran': The Inside Story of the Obama Administration's Iran Diplomacy." *Politico Magazine.* Retrieved November 9, 2020 (https://www.politico.com/magazine/story/2015/09/iran-deal-inside-story-213187).

Lanoszka, Alexander. 2015. "Do Allies Really Free Ride?" *Survival* 57(3): 133–52. https://doi.org/10.1080/00396338.2015.1046229.

Lanoszka, Alexander. 2018a. "Alliances and Nuclear Proliferation in the Trump Era." *Washington Quarterly* 41(4): 85–101. https://doi.org/10.1080/0163660X.2018.1557976.

Lanoszka, Alexander. 2018b. *Atomic Assurance: The Alliance Politics of Nuclear Proliferation.* Ithaca, NY: Cornell University Press.

Lawrence, Christopher. 2020. "Normalization by Other Means—Technological Infrastructure and Political Commitment in the North Korean Nuclear Crisis." *International Security* 45(1): 9–50. https://doi.org/10.1162/isec_a_00385.

Lee, Julia Joo-A. 2009. "To Fuel or Not to Fuel: China's Energy Assistance to North Korea." *Asian Security* 5(1): 45–72. https://doi.org/10.1080/14799850802689749.

Levite, Ariel E. 2003. "Never Say Never Again: Nuclear Reversal Revisited." *International Security* 27(3): 59–88.

Levite, Ariel E. 2019. "Nuclear Hedging and Latency: History, Concepts, and Issues." Pp. 21–42 in *Nuclear Latency and Hedging: Concepts, History, and Issues,* edited by J. F. Pilat. Washington, DC: Woodrow Wilson Center Press.

Levite, Ariel E., and Toby Dalton. 2017. "Leveling Up the Nuclear Trade Playing Field." *Carnegie Endowment for International Peace.* Retrieved January 22, 2018 (http://carnegieendowment.org/2017/09/07/leveling-up-nuclear-trade-playing-field-pub-73038).

Levy, Jack S. 1987. "Declining Power and the Preventive Motivation for War." *World Politics* 40(1): 82–107.

Lin, Herbert. 2016. "Governance of Information Technology and Cyber Weapons." Pp. 112–57 in *Governance of Dual-Use Technologies: Theory and Practice,* edited by E. Harris. Cambridge, MA: American Academy of Arts and Sciences.

Lindsay, Jon R. 2013. "Stuxnet and the Limits of Cyber Warfare." *Security Studies* 22(3): 365–404. https://doi.org/10.1080/09636412.2013.816122.

Lindsay, Jon R. 2020. *Information Technology and Military Power.* Ithaca, NY: Cornell University Press.

Lindsay, Jon R., and Erik Gartzke. 2019. "Introduction: Cross-Domain Deterrence, from Practice to Theory." Pp. 1–26 in *Cross-Domain Deterrence: Strategy in an Era of Complexity,* edited by Erik Gartzke and Jon R. Lindsay. New York: Oxford University Press.

Lissner, Rebecca Friedman. 2017. "Nuclear Legacies of the First Gulf War." *Survival* 59(5): 143–56. https://doi.org/10.1080/00396338.2017.1375265.

Litwak, Robert S. 2008. "Living with Ambiguity: Nuclear Deals with Iran and North Korea." *Survival* 50(1): 91–118. https://doi.org/10.1080/00396330801899496.

Long, Austin. 2015. "If You Really Want to Bomb Iran, Take the Deal." *Washington Post,* April 3.

Long, Tom. 2017. *Latin America Confronts the United States: Asymmetry and Influence.* New York: Cambridge University Press.

Lupovici, Amir. 2021. "The Dual-Use Security Dilemma and the Social Construction of Insecurity." *Contemporary Security Policy* 42(3): 257–85. https://doi.org/10.1080/13523260.2020.1866845.

Lupton, Danielle L. 2020. *Reputation for Resolve: How Leaders Signal Determination in International Politics*. Ithaca, NY: Cornell University Press.

Lutsch, Andreas. 2016a. "In Favor of 'Effective' and 'Non-discriminatory' Non-dissemination Policy: The FRG and the NPT Negotiation Process (1962–1966)." Pp. 36–57 in *Negotiating the Nuclear Non-proliferation Treaty: Origins of the Nuclear Order*, edited by R. Popp, L. Horovitz, and A. Wenger. New York: Routledge.

Lutsch, Andreas. 2016b. "Merely 'Docile Self-Deception'? German Experiences with Nuclear Consultation in NATO." *Journal of Strategic Studies* 39(4): 535–58. https://doi.org/10.1080/01402390.2016.1168014.

Lutsch, Andreas. 2019. *Alignment with the West or Balancing? West German Nuclear Security Policy between the Nuclear Non-proliferation Treaty and the NATO Double-Track Decision (1961–1979)*. Berlin: De Gruyter Oldenbourg.

MacCalman, Molly. 2016. "A.Q. Khan Nuclear Smuggling Network." *Journal of Strategic Security* 9(1): 104–18. https://doi.org/10.5038/1944-0472.9.1.1506.

Maddock, Shane J. 2010. *Nuclear Apartheid: The Quest for American Atomic Supremacy from World War II to the Present*. Chapel Hill: University of North Carolina Press.

Maher, Richard. 2019. "The Covert Campaign against Iran's Nuclear Program: Implications for the Theory and Practice of Counterproliferation." *Journal of Strategic Studies* 44(7): 1014–40. https://doi.org/10.1080/01402390.2019.1662401.

Mahncke, Dieter. 1972. *Nukleare Mitwirkung: Die Bundesrepublik Deutschland in der Atlantischen Allianz, 1954–1970*. Berlin: de Gruyter.

Maloney, Suzanne. 2015. *Iran's Political Economy since the Revolution*. New York: Cambridge University Press.

Mansourov, Alexandre Y. 1995. "The Origins, Evolution, and Current Politics of the North Korean Nuclear Program." *Nonproliferation Review* 2(3): 25–38. https://doi.org/10.1080/10736709508436590.

Mazarr, Michael J. 1995. *North Korea and the Bomb: A Case Study in Nonproliferation*. New York: St. Martin's Press.

McGoldrick, Fred. 2011. *Limiting Transfers of Enrichment and Reprocessing Technology: Issues, Constraints, Options*. Cambridge, MA: Project on Managing the Atom, Harvard University.

McGoldrick, Fred, Robert J. Einhorn, Duyeon Kim, and James L. Tyson. 2015. *ROK-U.S. Civil Nuclear and Nonproliferation Collaboration in Third Countries*. Washington, DC: Brookings Institution.

Mearsheimer, John J. 2001. *The Tragedy of Great Power Politics*. New York: Norton.

Medeiros, Evan S. 2005. "Strategic Hedging and the Future of Asia-pacific Stability." *Washington Quarterly* 29(1): 145–67. https://doi.org/10.1162/016366005774859724.

Medeiros, Evan S. 2007. *Reluctant Restraint: The Evolution of China's Nonproliferation Policies and Practices, 1980–2004*. Stanford, CA: Stanford University Press.

Mehta, Rupal N. 2020. *Delaying Doomsday: The Politics of Nuclear Reversal*. New York: Oxford University Press.

Mehta, Rupal N., and Rachel Elizabeth Whitlark. 2017. "The Benefits and Burdens of Nuclear Latency." *International Studies Quarterly* 61(3): 517–28. https://doi.org/10.1093/isq/sqx028.

Meier, Oliver. 2020. "Why Germany Won't Build Its Own Nuclear Weapons and Remains Skeptical of a Eurodeterrent." *Bulletin of the Atomic Scientists* 76(2): 76–84. https://doi.org/10.1080/00963402.2020.1728967.

Meijer, Hugo, and Stephen G. Brooks. 2021. "Illusions of Autonomy: Why Europe Cannot Provide for Its Security If the United States Pulls Back." *International Security* 45(4): 7–43. https://doi.org/10.1162/isec_a_00405.

Meyer, Stephen M. 1986. *The Dynamics of Nuclear Proliferation*. Chicago: University of Chicago Press.

Michishita, Narushige. 2009. *North Korea's Military-Diplomatic Campaigns, 1966–2008*. London: Routledge.

Miller, Nicholas L. 2014a. "Nuclear Dominoes: A Self-Defeating Prophecy?" *Security Studies* 23(1): 33–73. https://doi.org/10.1080/09636412.2014.874189.

Miller, Nicholas L. 2014b. "The Secret Success of Nonproliferation Sanctions." *International Organization* 68(4): 913–44. https://doi.org/10.1017/S0020818314000216.

Miller, Nicholas L. 2017. "Why Nuclear Energy Programs Rarely Lead to Proliferation." *International Security* 42(2): 40–77. https://doi.org/10.1162/ISEC_a_00293.

Miller, Nicholas L. 2018. *Stopping the Bomb: The Sources and Effectiveness of US Nonproliferation Policy*. Ithaca, NY: Cornell University Press.

Miller, Nicholas L., and Tristan A. Volpe. 2018a. "Abstinence or Tolerance: Managing Nuclear Ambitions in Saudi Arabia." *Washington Quarterly* 41(2): 27–46. https://doi.org/10.1080/0163660X.2018.1484224.

Miller, Nicholas L., and Tristan A. Volpe. 2018b. "Geostrategic Nuclear Exports: The Competition for Influence in Saudi Arabia." *War on the Rocks*. Retrieved February 7, 2018 (https://warontherocks.com/2018/02/geostrategic-nuclear-exports-competition-influence-saudi-arabia/).

Miller, Nicholas L., and Tristan A. Volpe. 2022. "The Rise of the Autocratic Nuclear Marketplace." *Journal of Strategic Studies* 1–39. https://doi.org/10.1080/01402390.2022.2052725.

Miller, Steven E. 2006. "Proliferation Gamesmanship: Iran and the Politics of Nuclear Confrontation." *Syracuse Law Review* 57(3): 551–600.

Mochizuki, Mike M. 2007. "Japan Tests the Nuclear Taboo." *Nonproliferation Review* 14(2): 303. https://doi.org/10.1080/10736700701379393.

Moltz, James Clay. 2014. *Crowded Orbits: Conflict and Cooperation in Space*. New York: Columbia University Press.

Monteiro, Nuno P. 2014. *Theory of Unipolar Politics*. New York: Cambridge University Press.

Montgomery, Alexander H. 2013. "Stop Helping Me: When Nuclear Assistance Impedes Nuclear Programs." Pp. 177–202 in *The Nuclear Renaissance and International Security*, edited by A. N. Stulberg and M. Fuhrmann. Stanford, CA: Stanford University Press.

Morrow, James D. 1999. "The Strategic Setting of Choices: Signaling, Commitment, and Negotiation in International Politics." Pp. 77–114 in *Strategic Choice and International Relations*, edited by D. A. Lake and R. Powell. Princeton, NJ: Princeton University Press.

Mousavian, Seyyed Hossein. 2012. *The Iranian Nuclear Crisis: A Memoir*. Washington, DC: Carnegie Endowment for International Peace.

Mufson, Steven. 2018. "Pompeo: Saudis Must Not Enrich Uranium If It Seeks Civilian Nuclear Cooperation." *Washington Post*, May 24.

Musgrave, Paul. 2019. "Asymmetry, Hierarchy, and the Ecclesiastes Trap." *International Studies Review* 21(2): 284–300. https://doi.org/10.1093/isr/viz002.

Nacht, Michael, and Zachary S. Davis. 2014. "Exploring Latency and Power." Pp. 1–3 in *Strategic Latency and World Power: How Technology Is Changing Our Concepts of*

Security, edited by Z. S. Davis, M. Nacht, and R. Lehman. Livermore, CA: Lawrence Livermore National Laboratory.

Narang, Vipin. 2014. *Nuclear Strategy in the Modern Era: Regional Powers and International Conflict*. Princeton, NJ: Princeton University Press.

Narang, Vipin. 2016. "Strategies of Nuclear Proliferation: How States Pursue the Bomb." *International Security* 41(3): 110–50. https://doi.org/10.1162/ISEC_a_00268.

Narang, Vipin. 2022. *Seeking the Bomb: Strategies of Nuclear Proliferation*. Princeton, NJ: Princeton University Press.

Nephew, Richard. 2015. "How the Iran Deal Prevents a Covert Nuclear Weapons Program." *Arms Control Association*. Retrieved December 14, 2020 (https://www.armscontrol.org/act/2015-09/features/iran-deal-prevents-covert-nuclear-weapons-program).

Nephew, Richard. 2017. *The Art of Sanctions: A View from the Field*. New York: Columbia University Press.

Nolan, Janne E. 1991. *Trappings of Power: Ballistic Missiles in the Third World*. Washington, DC: Brookings Institution Press.

Noland, Marcus. 1997. "Why North Korea Will Muddle Through." *Foreign Affairs* 76(4): 105–18.

Nuland, Victoria. 2012. "U.S.-DPRK Bilateral Discussions: Department Spokesperson, Office of the Spokesperson." *U.S. Department of State*. Retrieved April 27, 2022 (https://2009-2017.state.gov/r/pa/prs/ps/2012/02/184869.htm).

O'Mahoney, Joseph. 2020. "The Smiling Buddha Effect: Canadian and US Policy after India's 1974 Nuclear Test." *Nonproliferation Review* 27(1–3): 161–79. https://doi.org/10.1080/10736700.2020.1803561.

Obaid, Nawaf. 2015. "Saudi Arabia Is Preparing Itself in Case Iran Develops Nuclear Weapons." June 29. https://www.telegraph.co.uk/news/general-election-2015/politics-blog/11705381/Nawaf-Obaid-Saudi-Arabia-is-preparing-itself-in-case-Iran-develops-nuclear-weapons.html.

Obama, Barack H. 2013. "Saban Forum, Washington, DC." https://obamawhitehouse.archives.gov/the-press-office/2013/12/07/remarks-president-conversation-saban-forum.

Oberdorfer, Don. 2002. *The Two Koreas: A Contemporary History*. New York: Basic Books.

Panda, Ankit. 2016. "A Great Leap to Nowhere: Remembering the US-North Korea 'Leap Day' Deal." *The Diplomat*, February 29. https://thediplomat.com/2016/02/a-great-leap-to-nowhere-remembering-the-us-north-korea-leap-day-deal/.

Panda, Ankit. 2020. *Kim Jong Un and the Bomb: Survival and Deterrence in North Korea*. New York: Oxford University Press.

Pape, Robert A. 1996. *Bombing to Win: Air Power and Coercion in War*. Ithaca, NY: Cornell University Press.

Parsi, Trita. 2012. *A Single Roll of the Dice: Obama's Diplomacy with Iran*. New Haven, CT: Yale University Press.

Parsi, Trita. 2017. *Losing an Enemy: Obama, Iran, and the Triumph of Diplomacy*. New Haven, CT: Yale University Press.

Patrikarakos, David. 2012. *Nuclear Iran: The Birth of an Atomic State*. New York: I. B. Tauris.

Pauly, Reid B. C. 2019. "Stop or I'll Shoot, Comply and I Won't: Coercive Assurance in International Politics." PhD dissertation, MIT.

Pauly, Reid B. C. 2021. "Deniability in the Nuclear Nonproliferation Regime: The Upside of the Dual-Use Dilemma." *International Studies Quarterly* 66(1): 1–13. https://doi.org/10.1093/isq/sqab036.

Perkovich, George. 1993. "A Nuclear Third Way in South Asia." *Foreign Policy* 91: 85–104. https://doi.org/10.2307/1149061.

Persbo, Andreas. 2019. "Latent Nuclear Power, Hedging, and Irreversibility." Pp. 43–72 in *Nuclear Latency and Hedging: Concepts, History, and Issues*, edited by J. F. Pilat. Washington, DC: Woodrow Wilson Center Press.

Peterson, Scott. 2013. "Stalled Nuclear Talks Fuel Sharp Exchange at Iran's Final Presidential Debate." *Christian Science Monitor*, June 8.

Pierson, Paul. 2004. *Politics in Time: History, Institutions, and Social Analysis*. Princeton, NJ: Princeton University Press.

Pilat, Joseph F., ed. 2019. *Nuclear Latency and Hedging: Concepts, History, and Issues*. Washington, DC: Woodrow Wilson Center Press.

Pollack, Jonathan D. 2011. *No Exit: North Korea, Nuclear Weapons and International Security*. Abingdon, UK: Routledge.

Pomper, Miles, Toby Dalton, Scott Snyder, and Ferenc Dalnoki-Veress. 2016. *Strengthening the ROK-US Nuclear Partnership*. Monterey, CA: Center for Nonproliferation Studies.

Popp, Roland. 2016. "The Long Road to the NPT: From Superpower Collusion to Global Compromise." Pp. 11–35 in *Negotiating the Nuclear Non-proliferation Treaty: Origins of the Nuclear Order*, edited by R. Popp, L. Horovitz, and A. Wenger. New York: Routledge.

Pritchard, Charles L. 2007. *Failed Diplomacy: The Tragic Story of How North Korea Got the Bomb*. Washington, DC: Brookings Institution Press.

Program on Science and Global Security. 2015. *Plutonium Separation in Nuclear Power Programs*. Princeton, NJ: Princeton University Press.

Putnam, Robert D. 1988. "Diplomacy and Domestic Politics: The Logic of Two-Level Games." *International Organization* 42(3): 427–60.

Quester, George H. 1970. "Japan and the Nuclear Non-proliferation Treaty." *Asian Survey* 10(9): 765–78.

Quester, George H. 1972. "Some Conceptual Problems in Nuclear Proliferation." *American Political Science Review* 66(2): 490–97. https://doi.org/10.2307/1957793.

Quinn, Andrew. 2012. "Insight: Obama's North Korean Leap of Faith Falls Short." *Reuters*, March 30.

Radkau, Joachim, and Lothar Hahn. 2013. *Aufstieg und Fall der Deutschen Atomwirtschaft*. Munich: Oekom.

Rapp-Hooper, Mira. 2020. *Shields of the Republic: The Triumph and Peril of America's Alliances*. Cambridge, MA: Harvard University Press.

Reiss, Mitchell. 1988. *Without the Bomb: The Politics of Nuclear Nonproliferation*. New York: Columbia University Press.

Reppy, Judith. 2006. "Managing Dual-Use Technology in an Age of Uncertainty." *The Forum* 4(1). https://doi.org/10.2202/1540-8884.1116.

Rezaian, Jason. 2013. "Iran's Presidential Debate Gets Personal." *Washington Post*, June 7.

Richelson, Jeffrey T. 2006. *Spying on the Bomb: American Nuclear Intelligence from Nazi Germany to Iran and North Korea*. New York: Norton.

Roberts, Brad. 2015. *The Case for U.S. Nuclear Weapons in the 21st Century*. Stanford, CA: Stanford Security Studies.

Rouhani, Hassan. 2005. "Nuclear Case from Beginning to End (Part 1: We Are Testing Europe)." *Tehran Keyhan*. Interviewed by Mehdi Mohammadi. Translated from the

Persian. July 26. http://lewis.armscontrolwonk.com/files/2012/08/Rowhani_Interv iew.pdf.

Rozen, Laura. 2013. "Exclusive: Burns Led Secret US Back Channel to Iran." *Al-Monitor*, November 24.

Rozen, Laura. 2014. "Three Days in March: New Details on How US, Iran Opened Direct Talks." *Al-Monitor*, January 8.

Russell, James A. 2012. "Nuclear Proliferation and the Middle East's Security Dilemma: The Case of Saudi Arabia." Pp. 47–67 in *Over the Horizon Proliferation Threats*, edited by J. J. Wirtz and P. R. Lavoy. Palo Alto, CA: Stanford University Press.

Sagan, Scott D. 2002. "More Will Be Worse." Pp. 46–87 in *The Spread of Nuclear Weapons: A Debate Renewed*, 2nd ed., edited by S. D. Sagan and K. N. Waltz. Norton.

Sagan, Scott D. 2010. "Nuclear Latency and Nuclear Proliferation." Pp. 80–101 in *Forecasting Nuclear Proliferation in the 21st Century: Volume 1 The Role of Theory*, edited by W. Potter and G. Mukhatzhanova. Stanford Security Studies.

Sagan, Scott D. 2011. "The Causes of Nuclear Weapons Proliferation." *Annual Review of Political Science* 14(1): 225–44.

Saikal, Amin. 2019. *Iran Rising: The Survival and Future of the Islamic Republic*. Princeton, NJ: Princeton University Press.

Salisbury, Daniel. 2020. "Arming Iran from the Heart of Westminster? The Iranian Military Procurement Offices, Rumours and Intelligence, 1981–1987." *Intelligence and National Security* 35(7): 1042–58. https://doi.org/10.1080/02684527.2020.1778380.

Samore, Gary S. 2004. *North Korea's Weapons Programmes: A Net Assessment*. London: International Institute for Strategic Studies.

Samore, Gary S. 2017. *The Iran Nuclear Deal: A Definitive Guide*. Cambridge, MA: Harvard Belfer Center for Science and International Affairs.

Samuels, Richard J. 2008. *Securing Japan: Tokyo's Grand Strategy and the Future of East Asia*. Ithaca, NY: Cornell University Press.

Sanger, David E. 1993. "U.S. Revising North Korea Strategy." *New York Times*, November 22.

Sanger, David E. 2002. "Threats and Responses: Weapons Programs; U.S. Says Russia Helped Iran in Nuclear Arms Effort, Adding to Concerns about Allies." *New York Times*, December 16.

Sanger, David E. 2005. "Steps at Reactor in North Korea Worry the U.S." *New York Times*, April 18.

Sanger, David E. 2006. "North Koreans Say They Tested Nuclear Device." *New York Times*, October 9.

Sanger, David E., and Ronen Bergman. 2018. "How Israel, in Dark of Night, Torched Its Way to Iran's Nuclear Secrets." *New York Times*, July 15.

Sanger, David E., and William J. Broad. 2009. "U.S. and Allies Warn Iran over Nuclear 'Deception.'" *New York Times*, September 26.

Saunders, Elizabeth N. 2019. "The Domestic Politics of Nuclear Choices—A Review Essay." *International Security* 44(2): 146–84. https://doi.org/10.1162/isec_a_00361.

Schaller, Michael. 1997. *Altered States the United States and Japan since the Occupation*. New York: Oxford University Press.

Schell, Jonathan. 1984. *The Abolition*. New York: Knopf.

Schelling, Thomas C. 1960. *Strategy of Conflict*. Cambridge, MA: Harvard University Press.

Schelling, Thomas C. 1966. *Arms and Influence*. New Haven, CT: Yale University Press.

Schneider, Jacquelyn. 2019. "The Capability/Vulnerability Paradox and Military Revolutions: Implications for Computing, Cyber, and the Onset of War." *Journal of Strategic Studies* 42(6): 841–63. https://doi.org/10.1080/01402390.2019.1627209.

Schoff, James L., and Richard J. Samuels. 2013. "Japan's Nuclear Hedge: Beyond 'Allergy' and Breakout." Pp. 233–66 in *Strategic Asia 2013–14: Asia in the Second Nuclear Age*, edited by A. J. Tellis, A. M. Denmark, and T. Tanner. Washington, DC: National Bureau of Asian Research.

Schrafstetter, Susanna. 2004. "The Long Shadow of the Past." *History and Memory* 16(1): 118–45.

Schrafstetter, Susanna, and Stephen Twigge. 2004. *Avoiding Armageddon: Europe, the United States, and the Struggle for Nuclear Non-proliferation, 1945–1970*. Westport, CT: Praeger.

Schultz, Kenneth A. 2001. *Democracy and Coercive Diplomacy*. Cambridge: Cambridge University Press.

Schwartz, Thomas Alan. 2003. *Lyndon Johnson and Europe: In the Shadow of Vietnam*. Cambridge, MA: Harvard University Press.

Sechser, Todd S. 2010. "Goliath's Curse: Coercive Threats and Asymmetric Power." *International Organization* 64(04): 627–60.

Sechser, Todd S. 2011. "Militarized Compellent Threats, 1918–2001." *Conflict Management and Peace Science* 28(4): 377–401. https://doi.org/10.1177/073889421 1413066.

Sechser, Todd S., and Matthew Fuhrmann. 2013. "Crisis Bargaining and Nuclear Blackmail." *International Organization* 67(1): 173–95.

Sechser, Todd S., and Matthew Fuhrmann. 2017. *Nuclear Weapons and Coercive Diplomacy*. Cambridge: Cambridge University Press.

Shaker, Mohamed Ibrahim. 1980. *The Nuclear Non-proliferation Treaty: Origin and Implementation, 1959–1979*. London: Oceana Publications.

Sherman, Ambassador Wendy R. 2018. *Not for the Faint of Heart: Lessons in Courage, Power, and Persistence*. New York: Public Affairs.

Sigal, Leon V. 1999. *Disarming Strangers: Nuclear Diplomacy with North Korea*. Princeton, NJ: Princeton University Press.

Singer, J. David, Stuart Bremer, and John Stuckley. 1972. "Capability Distribution, Uncertainty, and Major Power War, 1820–1965." Pp. 19–48 in *Peace, War, and Numbers*, edited by B. Russett. Beverly Hills, CA: Sage.

Slackman, Michael. 2009. "Iran's Politics Stand in the Way of a Nuclear Deal." *New York Times*, November 2.

Slantchev, Branislav L. 2005. "Military Coercion in Interstate Crises." *American Political Science Review* 99(4): 533–47. https://doi.org/10.1017/S0003055405051865.

Slantchev, Branislav L. 2011. *Military Threats: The Costs of Coercion and the Price of Peace*. New York: Cambridge University Press.

Smith, Bradley C., and William Spaniel. 2018. "Introducing v-CLEAR: A Latent Variable Approach to Measuring Nuclear Proficiency." *Conflict Management and Peace Science* 37(2): 232–56. https://doi.org/10.1177/0738894217741619.

Snyder, Glenn H. 2007. *Alliance Politics*. Ithaca, NY: Cornell University Press.

Snyder, Ryan. 2016. "A Proliferation Assessment of Third Generation Laser Uranium Enrichment Technology." *Science & Global Security* 24(2): 68–91. https://doi.org/ 10.1080/08929882.2016.1184528.

Snyder, Scott. 1999. *Negotiating on the Edge: North Korean Negotiating Behavior.* Washington, DC: United States Institute of Peace Press.

Snyder, Scott. 2003. "China-Korea Relations: Regime Change and Another Nuclear Crisis." *Comparative Connections* 5(1).

Snyder, Scott. 2007. *China-Korea Relations: Political Fallout from North Korea's Nuclear Test.* Washington, DC: Center for Strategic and International Studies.

Solingen, Etel. 2007. *Nuclear Logics: Contrasting Paths in East Asia and the Middle East.* Princeton, NJ: Princeton University Press.

Solomon, Jay. 2016. *The Iran Wars: Spy Games, Bank Battles, and the Secret Deals That Reshaped the Middle East.* New York: Random House.

Spaniel, William. 2019. *Bargaining over the Bomb: The Successes and Failures of Nuclear Negotiations.* Cambridge: Cambridge University Press.

Stent, Angela. 2014. *The Limits of Partnership: U.S.-Russian Relations in the Twenty-First Century.* Princeton, NJ: Princeton University Press.

Stone, Richard. 2015. "Iran Nuclear Deal Opens Door to Scientific Collaborations." *Science.* Retrieved December 14, 2020 (https://www.sciencemag.org/news/2015/07/iran-nuclear-deal-opens-door-scientific-collaborations).

Szalontai, Balazs, and Sergey Radchenko. 2006. *North Korea's Efforts to Acquire Nuclear Technology and Nuclear Weapons: Evidence from Russian and Hungarian Archives.* Washington, DC: Woodrow Wilson International Center for Scholars.

Tabatabai, Ariane M. 2014. *Iran's Evolving Nuclear Narrative.* Cambridge, MA: Harvard Belfer Center for Science and International Affairs.

Tabatabai, Ariane M. 2015. "Reading the Nuclear Politics in Tehran." *Arms Control Today.* Retrieved December 14, 2020 (https://www.armscontrol.org/act/2015-09/features/reading-nuclear-politics-tehran).

Tabatabai, Ariane M. 2017. "Negotiating the 'Iran Talks' in Tehran: The Iranian Drivers That Shaped the Joint Comprehensive Plan of Action." *Nonproliferation Review* 24(3–4): 225–42. https://doi.org/10.1080/10736700.2018.1426180.

Tabatabai, Ariane M. 2019. *Iran's National Security Debate: Implications for Future U.S.-Iran Negotiations.* Rand Corporation. https://doi.org/10.7249/PE344.

Takeyh, Ray. 2003. "Iran's Nuclear Calculations." *World Policy Journal* 20(2): 21–28.

Takeyh, Ray. 2007. *Hidden Iran: Paradox and Power in the Islamic Republic.* New York: Council on Foreign Relations Press.

Takeyh, Ray. 2009. *Guardians of the Revolution: Iran and the World in the Age of the Ayatollahs.* New York: Oxford University Press.

Tertrais, Bruno. 2004. "'Destruction Assurée': The Origins and Development of French Nuclear Strategy, 1945–1981." Pp. 51–122 in *Getting MAD: Nuclear Mutual Assured Destruction, Its Origins and Practice,* edited by H. D. Sokolski. Carlisle, PA: Strategic Studies Institute, US Army War College.

Thaler, David E., Alireza Nader, Shahram Chubin, Jerrold D. Green, Charlotte Lynch, and Frederic Wehrey. 2010. *Mullahs, Guards, and Bonyads.* Santa Monica, CA: Rand Corporation.

Trachtenberg, Marc. 1999. *A Constructed Peace: The Making of the European Settlement, 1945–1963.* Princeton, NJ: Princeton University Press.

Trager, Robert F. 2017. *Diplomacy: Communication and the Origins of International Order.* New York: Cambridge University Press.

Twomey, Christopher. 2008. "Explaining Chinese Foreign Policy toward North Korea: Navigating between the Scylla and Charybdis of Proliferation and Instability."

Journal of Contemporary China 17(56): 401–23. https://doi.org/10.1080/1067056080
2000167.

US Department of Energy. 2002. "Fission Weapons." Pp. in *Restricted Data Declassification Decisions, 1946 to the Present*. RDD-7. Washington, DC: US Department of Energy, Office of Declassification. https://sgp.fas.org/othergov/doe/rdd-7.html.

US Department of Energy. 2020. *Restoring America's Competitive Nuclear Advantage: A Strategy to Assure U.S. National Security*. Washington, DC: US Department of Energy.

Vaez, Ali, and Karim Sadjadpour. 2013. *Iran's Nuclear Odyssey: Costs and Risks*. Washington, DC: Carnegie Endowment for International Peace.

Valeriano, Brandon, Benjamin Jensen, and Ryan C. Maness. 2018. *Cyber Strategy: The Evolving Character of Power and Coercion*. New York: Oxford University Press.

Varnum, Jessica C. 2012. "U.S. Nuclear Cooperation as Nonproliferation: Reforms, or the Devil You Know?" *Nuclear Threat Initiative*. Retrieved July 29, 2021 (https://www.nti. org/analysis/articles/us-nuclear-cooperation-nonproliferation-reforms-or-devil-you-know/).

Vaynman, Jane. 2014. "Enemies in Agreement: Domestic Politics, Uncertainty, and Cooperation between Adversaries." PhD dissertation, Harvard University.

Vaynman, Jane, and Tristan Volpe. 2022. "Making Coercion Work against Russia." *War on the Rocks*. Retrieved April 27, 2022 (https://warontherocks.com/2022/03/making-coercion-work-against-russia/).

Volpe, Tristan A. 2016. "Atomic Inducements: The Case for 'Buying out' Nuclear Latency." *Nonproliferation Review* 23(3–4): 481–93. https://doi.org/10.1080/10736 700.2016.1246103.

Volpe, Tristan A. 2017. "Atomic Leverage: Compellence with Nuclear Latency." *Security Studies* 26(3): 517–44. https://doi.org/10.1080/09636412.2017.1306398.

Volpe, Tristan, and Ulrich Kühn. 2017. "Germany's Nuclear Education: Why a Few Elites Are Testing a Taboo." *Washington Quarterly* 40(3): 7–27. https://doi.org/10.1080/0163660X.2017.1370317.

Walker, William. 1999. *Nuclear Entrapment: THORP and the Politics of Commitment*. London: Institute for Public Policy Research.

Walker, William. 2000. "Entrapment in Large Technology Systems: Institutional Commitment and Power Relations." *Research Policy* 29(7–8): 833–46. https://doi.org/10.1016/S0048-7333(00)00108-6.

Walt, Stephen M. 2006. *Taming American Power: The Global Response to U.S. Primacy*. New York: Norton.

Waltz, Kenneth N. 1997. "Thoughts about Virtual Nuclear Arsenals." *Washington Quarterly* 20(3): 153–61. https://doi.org/10.1080/01636609709550267.

Waltz, Kenneth N. 2002. "More May Be Better." Pp. 3–45 in *The Spread of Nuclear Weapons: A Debate Renewed*, 2nd ed., edited by S. D. Sagan and K. N. Waltz. Norton.

Waltz, Kenneth N. 2012. "Why Iran Should Get the Bomb." *Foreign Affairs* 91(4): 2–5.

Warden, John K. 2017. *North Korea's Nuclear Posture: An Evolving Challenge for U.S. Deterrence*. Proliferation Papers. Paris: Institut français des relations internationales (Ifri).

Watts, Jonathan. 2003. "China Cuts Oil Supply to North Korea." *The Guardian*, April 1.

Weeks, Jessica L. P. 2014. *Dictators at War and Peace*. Ithaca, NY: Cornell University Press.

Welfield, John. 1988. *An Empire in Eclipse: Japan in the Postwar American Alliance System*. Atlantic Highlands, NJ: Athlone Press.

Westall, Sylvia. 2017. "Saudi Arabia to Extract Uranium for 'Self-Sufficient' Nuclear Program." *Reuters*, October 30.

Whitlark, Rachel Elizabeth. 2017. "Nuclear Beliefs: A Leader-Focused Theory of Counter-proliferation." *Security Studies* 26(4): 545–74. https://doi.org/10.1080/09636 412.2017.1331628.

Winand, Pascaline. 1996. *Eisenhower, Kennedy, and the United States of Europe*. New York: Palgrave Macmillan.

Wit, Joel S., Daniel B. Poneman, and Robert L. Gallucci. 2005. *Going Critical: The First North Korean Nuclear Crisis*. Washington, DC: Brookings Institution Press.

Wohlstetter, Albert J. 1961. "Nuclear Sharing: NATO and the N+1 Country." *Foreign Affairs*. March. https://www.foreignaffairs.com/articles/1961-04-01/nuclear-sharing-nato-and-n1-country.

Wohlstetter, Albert J. 1979. *Swords from Plowshares: The Military Potential of Civilian Nuclear Energy*. Chicago: University of Chicago Press.

Womack, Brantly. 2016. *Asymmetry and International Relationships*. New York: Cambridge University Press.

Wood, Houston G., Alexander Glaser, and R. Scott Kemp. 2008. "The Gas Centrifuge and Nuclear Weapons Proliferation." *Physics Today* 61(9): 40–45. https://doi.org/10.1063/1.2982121.

Worth, Robert F., and Nazila Fathi. 2009. "Protests Flare in Tehran as Opposition Disputes Vote." *New York Times*, June 13.

Wright, Robin. 2014. "The Adversary: Is Iran's Foreign Minister for Real?" *New Yorker*, May 26, n/a.

Yost, David S. 2009. "Assurance and US Extended Deterrence in NATO." *International Affairs* 85(4): 755–80.

Zhebin, Alexander. 1999. "A Political History of Soviet-North Korean Nuclear Cooperation." Pp. 27–41 in *The North Korean Nuclear Program: Security, Strategy and New Perspectives from Russia*, edited by J. C. Moltz and A. Y. Mansourov. London: Routledge.

Zimmerman, Peter D. 1994. "Proliferation: Bronze Medal Technology Is Enough." *Orbis* 38(1): 67–82. https://doi.org/10.1016/0030-4387(94)90106-6.

Zubok, Vladislav M. 1993. *Khrushchev and the Berlin Crisis, 1958–1962*. Washington, DC: Woodrow Wilson International Center for Scholars.

Index

For the benefit of digital users, indexed terms that span two pages (e.g., 52–53) may, on occasion, appear on only one of those pages.

Tables are indicated by *t* following the page number